Thirsting for God

Thirsting
for
GOD

**A Devotional Study of the
PSALMS,
in Light of their
Historical
Background**

C. Donald Cole

CROSSWAY BOOKS • WESTCHESTER, IL
A DIVISION OF GOOD NEWS PUBLISHERS

Thirsting for God. Copyright © 1986 by C. Donald Cole. Published by Crossway Books, a division of Good News Publishers, Westchester, Illinois 60153.

First printing, 1986.

Printed in the United States of America.

Library of Congress Catalog Card Number 85-72918

ISBN 0-89107-376-0

Your statutes are wonderful;
therefore I obey them.
The entrance of your words gives
light;
it gives understanding to the
simple.
I open my mouth and pant,
longing for your commands.
Turn to me and have mercy on me,
as you always do to those who love
your name.
Direct my footsteps according to
your word;
let no sin rule over me.
Redeem me from the oppression of
men,
that I may obey your precepts.
Make your face shine upon your
servant
and teach me your decrees.
Streams of tears flow from my eyes,
for your law is not obeyed.

Psalm 119:129-135

CONTENTS

INTRODUCTION TO THE PSALMS

Welcome to a study in the Psalms.

The Book of Psalms is the third of three divisions of the Old Testament, or what the Jews might call the "Hebrew Bible." The *law,* primarily the Pentateuch, begins with Genesis 1:1. Joshua 1:1 opens the great section called the *prophets,* which continues on through to Malachi. The third division is the *psalms* (see Luke 24:44).

The Book of Psalms is a superb collection of some of the most splendid pieces of literature ever written. Thoroughly under the control of the Holy Spirit of God, the authors of the Psalms recorded the full gamut of emotions experienced by those who know and follow God: from ecstatic praise to oppressive despair; from full confidence in the Lord to blind terror; from boundless rejoicing to deep sorrow.

The Book of Psalms is a multifaceted gem. It is exquisite poetry, desperately honest prayer, and a joyful hymnal all in one.

FIVE COMPILATIONS, FIVE HISTORICAL PERIODS

Five books actually comprise what we today call the Book of Psalms. Many Bibles and Bible study aids divide those five books like this:

Book One Psalms 1—41
Book Two Psalms 42—72
Book Three Psalms 73—89
Book Four Psalms 90—106
Book Five Psalms 107—150

You can see that each of these smaller books is a smaller collection of psalms, just as the whole Book of Psalms is a larger one.

Why are there five different books, or collections, in the Psalms? I believe it's because each of these books corresponds to a different period of ancient Israel's history.

The first and second books were both used at the same time—David's era. Note the last verse of the last psalm of the second book (Psalm 72): "this concludes the prayers of David son of Jesse."

Book 3, which begins with Psalm 73, is a collection put together for use by godly people during Rehoboam's disruptive rebellion. Rehoboam, son of Solomon, began a tragic civil war that ripped the once united kingdom in two (see 1 Kings). It was a split that never healed—until both halves of the kingdom were carried away into captivity. During the time of the Divided Kingdom, apparently godly people on both sides of the divide used this hymnbook, the third book of Psalms.

The fourth book is the book of the captivities. The Israelites living in captivity probably had the first three books also, but they added this fourth book, a collection of psalms wonderfully appropriate to the difficult circumstances of their day. Psalm 90, for instance, begins, "Lord, you have been our dwelling place throughout all generations." The captives, severed from their homeland and from Zion, where God had placed His name, took great comfort in knowing that they still dwelt in God.

The fifth book deals with the Israelites' return from captivity. Their return was a miracle, brought about by God through a pagan emperor named Cyrus, who decreed that the people could return to their homeland. Ezra and Nehemiah led the returning captives, who expressed their exultant happiness through psalms in this collection. Consider the first three verses of the first psalm in this collection, Psalm 107: "Give thanks to the Lord, for he is good; his love endures forever. Let the redeemed of the Lord say this—those he redeemed from the hand of the foe, those he gathered from the lands, from east and west, from north and south" (Psalm 107:1-3). This ringing praise is in direct thanksgiving for the answer to the prayer made at the close of the fourth book: "Save us, O Lord our

God, and gather us from the nations, that we may give thanks to your holy name and glory in your praise" (Psalm 106:42).

Not until the Jews came back from captivity was the compilation of the Book of Psalms completed, thus completing their Old Testament Scriptures.

So these five collections were put together purposefully. The psalms they contain are not just a hodge-podge. If we bear this purpose in mind when we read a psalm, we will find insights into its meaning that we might otherwise miss.

Seeing the historical divisions of the psalms alerts us to another fact: we must know something of Bible history in order to understand this book. Other books of the Bible can be read and studied simply for themselves—Joshua or Judges, for instance. But Bible history from Genesis on passes through the Book of Psalms. We must know something of what went before—and what comes after—in order to appreciate this fascinating and challenging book. Much in Psalms is prophetic as well as historical.

DATE OF WRITING, DATE OF USAGE

The psalms each book contains are *appropriate* to the period in which that book was compiled, no matter when those psalms were written. Psalm 90, for example, was composed by Moses and is probably the earliest psalm to be written. Yet it was not used publicly until the time of the captivities, when the feelings it expresses seemed appropriate to the captives' situation. So some psalms by earlier authors do appear in later books.

But we cannot take a psalm that appears in an earlier book and ascribe it to a later author. Although some scholars do this, using a method of literary criticism called "higher criticism," such views have no basis. For example, Psalm 45, ascribed to "the Sons of Korah," appears in the second book, which means it was being sung during David's day. Scholars of higher criticism, however, ascribe the authorship of this psalm to King Jehoshaphat, who came much later. This simply isn't possible.

Likewise, Psalm 46 is ascribed by some critics to King Asa. Again, King Asa wasn't even alive in the days when this book was being sung.

Or consider Psalm 50. Not only was this psalm being sung or

played in David's day, but the authorship is ascribed to Asaph, who was a choir director at that very time. How, then, could anyone say that this was written by Hezekiah? To do that is to reveal an appalling ignorance. I'm convinced of the accurate structure as well as of the spirit of the Book of Psalms.

AUTHORSHIP

About 101 of the psalms identify their authors—in seventy-three cases, David. But a few more were also authored by Israel's premier king. We know, for instance, that Psalm 2 is David's because Peter said so (Acts 4). We can then conclude that Psalm 1 is also David's because of certain affinities between the two.

Psalms 9 and 10 present a parallel situation. I feel, from what may be called internal evidence, that a number of other psalms are David's as well. They seem to echo events in his life, or are very similar to other psalms that do have David's name. I think it's safe to say we could find eighty psalms written by David, so that David's authorship accounts for more than half of the Book of Psalms.

INTRODUCTION TO BOOKS ONE AND TWO

Books one and two of the Psalms are called "the prayers of David" at their conclusion in Psalm 72:20. These were obviously David's hymnbooks, used also by Solomon later on in the Temple.

We know from 1 Chronicles 16:25 that David worked hard at organizing choirs. He set up a system of worship, and it included music.

Central to this system of worship was the ark of God, a box in which various holy things were placed, holy in the sense that they were set aside for the Lord's service. The ark was a very significant symbol of God's presence among His people.

David brought this ark to the tent which became the Tabernacle in Zion, and Zion became one of two places where worship was conducted. First Chronicles 16:37 tells us that "David left Asaph and his associates before the ark of the covenant of the Lord, to minister there regularly, according to each day's requirements." Asaph was the choir director.

But then in 1 Chronicles 16:39, 40 we read:

> David left Zadok the priest and his fellow priests before the tabernacle of the Lord at the high place in Gibeon to present burnt offerings to the Lord on the altar of burnt offering regularly, morning and evening.

Evidently Gibeon was the second of the two places of worship. At Gibeon was a second choir. Note the reference in verses 41 and 42 to "sacred song":

> With them were Heman and Jeduthun and the rest of those chosen and designated by name to give thanks to the Lord, "for his love endures forever." Heman and Jeduthun were responsible for the sounding of the trumpets and cymbals and for the playing of the other instruments for sacred song.

The hymnbook used by the first choir, in Zion, was the first book of psalms; the hymnbook used by the choir in Gibeon was the second book of psalms.

These two hymnbooks were in use simultaneously in the days of David's reign. It's conceivable that some psalms were also added to these two books in the days of Solomon.

PSALM 1

I'm sure you know that the psalms are lyrical. That is, they are lyrics—words that were set to music. The word *lyrics* is closely related to the word *lyre,* or harp.

We sometimes call the Book of Psalms the "hymnbook of the people of Israel." But technically a hymn is a poem set to music, whereas a psalm is music that inspires the writing of words. The very word *psalming* means sweeping the strings of a harp or a lyre. As the psalmist swept his hands over the strings, he produced the words to go with the music.

Psalm 1 is a wonderful example of Hebrew poetry, and illustrates some of its features, ones that we will be noticing repeatedly in our study of the Psalms.

Hebrew poetry is very different from rhyming poetry or today's contemporary poetic forms, yet it is almost unmatched in beauty. Hebrew poetry operates on a structure called *parallelism,* meaning it has parallel ideas that follow each other.

We can see this parallelism easily in Psalm 1. "Blessed is the man who does not walk in the counsel of the wicked," begins verse 1. The thought is repeated in the next line, but in slightly different language: he does not "stand in the way of sinners," and again, he does not "sit in the seat of mockers." All these are different ways of expressing the same parallel idea: the blessed person is the one who has no association with evil.

Furthermore, there is parallelism between verses 1 and 2. Verse 1 tells us what the blessed person does not do. Verse 2 tells us what the blessed person *does* do: "His delight is in the law of the Lord," and (parallelism again) "in his law he meditates day and night."

So, you see, Hebrew poetry is determined by words and content, not by jingles or rhymes.

Before we go on to further examine the content of Psalm 1

let's look a bit at its historical background and authorship. In some ancient manuscripts, Psalm 1 is not even counted as one of the Psalms, but as a preface. However, we take it to be the first of the actual psalms because of the New Testament reference to "the second Psalm," which is the second psalm in our Bibles, too. "What God promised our fathers he has fulfilled for us, their children, by raising up Jesus. As it is written in the second Psalm: 'You are my Son; today I have become your Father'" (Acts 13:33).

In the New Testament, the second psalm is ascribed to David, and the connection between the first and second psalms is fairly clear. Certain basic words are repeated, so we may conclude that both Psalms 1 and 2 were written by David, even though they don't have his name as part of the title. In fact, they don't have titles at all.

Now let's look in more detail at the psalm itself. As you could begin to see from our discussion of its parallelism, Psalm 1 is a fascinating contrast between the blessed person and the one who is under the curse, described in verse 6 as one whose way will perish.

The first three verses of the psalm refer to the blessed person. This person is righteous, and as we've seen, his character is described in both negative and positive terms. The negative triad is that he doesn't walk, doesn't stand, and doesn't sit anywhere near the wicked. "Walking" seems to indicate active participation in evil; "standing" seems to be acquiescence or silence in the presence of sin; while to "sit in the seat of mockers" may mean association with the scoffer. These are three grades of sin. It may be that a person progresses from one to the other, but the scoffer seems to be the worst type.

Proverbs 21:24 presents a fuller picture of the scoffer: "The proud and arrogant man—'Mocker' is his name; he behaves with overweening pride."

Psalm 1 has been aptly compared with Proverbs, especially Proverbs 1 and 4. This is not surprising; much of the early chapters of Proverbs is a record of Solomon instructing his son in the things his father, David, had taught him (Prov. 4:3, 4). We can see in comparing Psalm 1 with the first few chapters of Proverbs how this teaching about avoiding the paths of the wicked and choosing instead the paths of life was passed along from father to son to grandson.

The word used in Psalm 1 verses 1 and 4 for the "wicked" or "ungodly" whom the righteous person avoids is a very strong word in the original language. It is not generally applied to sinning believers. Job tells us, for instance, even in the midst of his wild charges against God, "I stand aloof from the counsel of the wicked" (Job 21:16).

The blessed, or righteous, person is described also in positive terms in verses 2 and 3 of Psalm 1. The blessed person has an inner allegiance to and love of God's law. He not only delights in it, he meditates on it day and night.

We can compare this with other psalms, such as Psalm 19, which again refers to delighting in the law of the Lord. Also, in Romans 7, the Apostle Paul talks about his own delight in the law of God. It's possible that Paul was thinking of this very psalm when he said in verse 22, "For in my inner being I delight in God's law."

There's also a strong resemblance between Psalm 1 and Joshua 1. Psalm 1 describes the person whose delight is in the law of the Lord and who meditates in it day and night; Joshua was the first person who was told to meditate on the Book of the Law day and night (Josh. 1:8). So Joshua 1:8 and Psalm 1:1-3 are parallel passages that tell us of the importance of paying attention to the written Word of God. Again in the New Testament, Paul congratulated Timothy because Timothy had known the Scriptures from the days of his youth (2 Tim. 3:15). Would you like to be an adequate person? Then I encourage you to study God's Word. Take the time to look up these parallel passages as you study each psalm. And not only study God's Word, but do it.

As a consequence of his love of God's law, the blessed person will be like a tree firmly planted by streams of water. This is a kind of figure of speech used often in the psalms. It's a *simile*, saying something is *like* something else. The godly person is *like* a tree. Trees that are near water sources grow and flourish. So will the godly person.

Furthermore, the "leaf" of the godly "does not wither." Whatever this man or woman of God does, prospers.

Ezekiel uses this very same simile in Ezekiel 17: 5, 8, 9:

"He took some of the seed of your land and put it in fertile soil. He planted it like a willow by abundant water. . . . It had been planted in good soil by abundant water so that it would produce branches, bear fruit and become a splendid vine." Say to them, "This is what the Sovereign Lord says: Will it thrive? Will it not be uprooted and stripped of its fruit so that it withers?"

Verses 4-6, by contrast, describe the wicked. In verse 4, the wicked are described not as a tree firmly planted, but as chaff. Chaff is rootless and useless, and the wind easily drives it away. In the Bible the wind is a symbol of judgment as well as a symbol of the Holy Spirit of God.

The last verse tells us, "The Lord watches over the way of the righteous." God approves of the way of the righteous. The way of the righteous is one of prosperity—but the way of the wicked will perish. Two roads; two destinies. God forbid that any of us should fail to know God and walk in a path He approves.

SOME FIGURES OF SPEECH

We noticed in verse 3 one figure of speech, the *simile* ("He is like a tree . . . "). As a helpful sideline, let's consider some of the other figures of speech used in the Psalms—indeed, throughout the Bible.

A *metaphor* is a comparison by representation. For example, the Lord says, "I am the way," "I am the door," "I am the bread of life." When the Lord said, "I am the door," He didn't mean He was a hollow wood door or a solid oak door. He was using the door as the representation of something much more important: He Himself is the way into Heaven. We often see metaphor in the Psalms, as for example, in Psalm 3:3: "But you are a shield around me, O Lord."

Hyperbole is a figure of speech that uses exaggeration. In the last verse of the Gospel According to John we read, "Jesus did many other things as well. If every one of them were written down, I suppose that even the whole world would not have room for the books that would be written." This is hyperbole. John didn't intend us to take him literally, to measure the area of the earth and calculate the number of books that would fit into it.

Psalm 6:6, 7 is another interesting example of hyperbole. "I am weary with my groaning; all the night make I my bed to swim; I water my couch with my tears. Mine eye is consumed because of grief; it waxeth old because of all mine enemies" (KJV). Who ever heard of a bed swimming? Did the psalmist mean that literally? Of course not. In this day of waterbeds, it may not be quite as big an exaggeration as in David's day, but beds still don't swim. Nor did the writer wear out his eye with his tears. He's exaggerating for the sake of emphasis. This is the language of imagination.

We find yet another example of hyperbole in Psalm 3:7. "Arise, O Lord! Deliver me, O my God! For you have struck all my enemies on the jaw; you have broken the teeth of the wicked." Is the psalmist saying that God had struck the whole army in the face? Probably not. It's simply an emphatic expression of the defeat of that army.

Metonymy is very similar to metaphor. In metonymy, one word or phrase is used in place of another, and there's a relationship between the two. Psalm 128:2 is a perfect example of metonymy. "Thou shalt eat the labor of thine hands" (KJV). This means, of course, that the people are going to eat the food they've grown. Their hands labor, and because their hands labor, they produce food. "The labor of thine hands" is the expression used in place of the less poetic word "food."

We will learn more about figures of speech used in the Bible as we progress in our understanding of the Book of Psalms.

PSALM 2

Psalm 2 is called a *messianic* psalm, that is, a psalm in which we find the Messiah.

Some would say we find the Messiah, meaning Christ, in all the psalms. Certainly if we strained our imaginations we might find something seeming to suggest an aspect of our Lord's life and ministry. But strictly speaking, a messianic psalm is one in which the reference to the Messiah is obvious—and obviously reinforced in the New Testament. This is certainly true of the second psalm.

Many psalms also contain a strong *prophetic* element, and this second psalm is one of those, too. When I say *prophetic,* I mean the psalm looks forward. It doesn't look back to the history of the nation of Israel, it looks ahead. A prophetic psalm predicts something that has never happened before, something future. Sometimes this prophecy has to do with the future of the nation of Israel, sometimes with the future of the Gentiles.

A messianic psalm is prophetic of the Messiah. The Messiah, according to the Old Testament, is the hope of the world. The Messiah was the Anointed One who would come from the nation of Israel. The Apostle Paul referred to this in Romans 9:

> . . . my kinsmen according to the flesh; who are Israelites; to whom pertaineth the adoption, and the glory, and the covenants, and the giving of the law, and the service of God, and the promises; whose are the fathers, and of whom as concerning the flesh Christ came, who is over all, God blessed for ever. (vv. 3-5, KJV)

Throughout the Psalms we find reference to the Messiah and various aspects of the Messiah's ministry. In fact, the entire Old Testament points to Christ. After our Lord was raised from the dead, He met two disciples on the road to Emmaus (Luke 24). Jesus rebuked them for not realizing that all the Old Testament had spoken about Him. He repeated that message to the apostles, who were hiding from the Jews. Jesus told them that all things had to be fulfilled which were written in the law and the prophets and the psalms concerning Him (Luke 24:44).

The Gospels tell how the Lord took various psalms and applied them to Himself. For example, in Matthew 21:42 He used a direct quotation from Psalm 18 concerning Himself. Matthew 22:42-45 contains a reference to Psalm 110, which refers to the Messiah, to Christ.

Psalm 2 makes two references to Christ. First, regarding His Sonship: "You are my Son." Second, a reference to His resurrection, a reference corroborated in Acts 13:32, 33.

Psalm 2 is a beautiful psalm. Its conclusion, "Blessed are all who take refuge in him," reminds me of the first psalm, which begins with the blessedness of the person who does not walk in the counsel of the wicked. In Psalm 2 we see the blessedness of the person who, instead of walking in the counsel of rebels against God, takes refuge in the Son, in the Lord.

Psalm 2 divides quite easily into four different sections. The obvious theme of the first three verses is worldwide rebellion against God. The nations are in an uproar and the peoples (meaning the Gentile nations) are devising a vain plot.

Generally speaking, the world has been in rebellion against God from the days of Cain. First John 5:19 tells us that the whole world lies in the power of the evil one; 2 Corinthians 4:3 speaks of the god of this age—that is, the prince of this world. Before conversion to our Lord Jesus Christ, everyone lives according to the course of this world.

> As for you, you were dead in your transgressions and sins, in which you used to live when you followed the ways of this world and of the ruler of the kingdom of the air, the spirit who is now at work in those who are disobedient. (Ephesians 2:1, 2)

Verse 2 gives a striking picture of this worldwide rebellion. It refers to the kings of the earth taking their stand and the rulers taking counsel together against the Lord and against His

Anointed, meaning against Jehovah and against the Messiah. There has always been a rebellion against God, but it will come to a terrible climax near the end of a future period called the Tribulation. I think many Bible scholars are right to interpret this psalm in terms of that final rebellion, a rebellion that will culminate in the battle of Armageddon. There will be at that time a rejection of God, and a determination to surround the Holy City and to destroy the Lord Himself if at all possible. Verse 3 tells of the language of these rebels: "Let us break their chains, and throw off their fetters."

But verses 4-6 proclaim God's wrath against this rebellion, a theme that runs throughout the Old Testament and climaxes in the Book of Revelation. These verses describe God in *anthropomorphic* terms, meaning He is spoken of as doing things a human being would do. "The One enthroned in heaven laughs." I don't think the writer neccesarily wants us to picture God on His throne laughing. Rather, the word "laughs" expresses God's assurance that the rebellion against Him will be utterly futile. God will have His way. The sooner all of us realize that, the better off we will be. God will speak in His anger and terrify rebels with His fury. The Book of Revelation tells us that people in a coming day will call upon the rocks and the hills to fall upon them to hide them from the fury of the wrath of the Lamb. It will be a terrible day when God speaks in His anger.

Today, however, God speaks to us all in great compassion, inviting, yes, beseeching people to come and be saved. But someday His merciful call will end.

Verse 6 makes a lovely proclamation: "I have installed my King on Zion, my holy hill." This has not yet been done; the King has not yet returned to take His throne on Zion, the holy hill (Jerusalem).

Notice how God can use the past tense to speak of something that is future. Romans 8:28-30 does the same thing.

And we know that in all things God works for the good of those who love him, who have been called according to his purpose. For those God foreknew he also predestined to be conformed to the likeness of his Son, that he might be the firstborn among many brothers. And those he predestined, he also called; those he called, he also justified; those he justified, he also glorified.

Actually, we have not yet been glorified. But since this glorification (meaning the exaltation of God's people to the eternal state) is all part of a plan God devised before the foundations of the earth were laid, He can speak of it in the past tense as if it were already accomplished. Anything God plans is as good as done; nothing can frustrate His purposes.

In effect God is saying in these verses in Psalm 2, "You kings of the earth think you can divide the world among yourselves and get rid of God. But the King of kings is the Messiah, and I have installed Him on Zion, My holy hill."

In John 1:49, Nathanael answered Jesus, "Rabbi, you are the Son of God; you are the King of Israel." That seems to be an allusion to the second psalm, though it could have in mind a verse in Isaiah 44. John 6:69 may also echo it: "the Holy One of God."

Let's move on to verse 7, where the messianic nature of this psalm is quite clear. Verse 7 is quoted in Acts 13:32, 33, which records the preaching of Paul to a literate group of people in a town called Antioch.

> We tell you the good news: What God promised to our fathers he has fulfilled for us, their children, by raising up Jesus. As it is written in the second Psalm: "You are my Son; today I have become your Father." The fact that God raised him from the dead, never to decay, is stated in these words: "I will give you the holy and sure blessings promised to David." So it is stated elsewhere: "You will not let your Holy One see decay." (Acts 13:32-35)

Here Paul's preaching confirms that the resurrection of our Lord Jesus fulfilled verse 7: "You are my Son; today I have become your Father."

The first chapter of Hebrews also uses Psalm 2:7 to present another aspect of the Messiah's life. Hebrews 1:4, 5 tells us: "So he [Christ] became as much superior to the angels as the name he has inherited is superior to theirs. For to which of the angels did God ever say, 'You are my Son; today I have become your Father'?" Here Psalm 2:7 is quoted to display the Sonship of our Lord.

Later in the Book of Hebrews (5:5, 6) we read: "So Christ also did not take upon himself the glory of becoming a high priest. But God said to him, 'You are my Son; today I have become your Father.' And he says in another place, 'You are a priest forever, in the order of Melchizedek.'" Hebrews 5:8 also speaks of Christ as a Son: "Although he was a son, he learned obedience from what he suffered."

The point is, Psalm 2 is a messianic psalm. We know this because the New Testament quotes it at least three times with reference to our Lord Jesus, twice in reference to His incarnation as God the Son, and once (Acts 13) in reference to His resurrection.

Verse 8 of Psalm 2 says that the nations are our Lord's inheritance—not only by His right as Creator, but also by His right as the Redeemer, the One who died in order to take possession of the earth.

In verse 9, the breaking of Messiah's enemies with a rod of iron, or "an iron sceptre," is a work of judgment.

Ruling with "an iron sceptre" is, of course, a figure of speech, as is the comparison of the nations to pottery. The King comes with His iron sceptre and smashes the pottery to pieces. David chose this image to tell us something about the thoroughness of divine judgment of rebel kings and rebel nations. During the future thousand-year reign of the Messiah, all the nations will be subject to Him, and He will indeed reign.

The idea of Messiah ruling with "an iron sceptre" is certainly very different from our concept of Him as the "meek and gentle" Jesus. In the New Testament, Jesus corrects this misconception of Himself as being only "meek and mild." No one spoke more vigorously about hell than did Jesus. For example:

> But suppose that servant is wicked and says to himself, "My master is staying away a long time," and he then begins to beat his fellow servants and to eat and drink with drunkards. The master of that servant will come on a day when he does not expect him and at an hour he is not aware of. He will cut

him to pieces and assign him a place with the hypocrites, where there will be weeping and gnashing of teeth. (Matthew 24:48-51)

The following chapter, Matthew 25:31 to the end, speaks of the judgment of the nations. "But when the Son of Man comes in His glory, and all the angels with him, he will sit on his throne in heavenly glory. All the nations will be gathered before him, and he will separate the people one from another as a shepherd separates the sheep from the goats" (Matthew 25:31, 32). Referring to those who failed to pass the test, Jesus says, "Then they will go away to eternal punishment, but the righteous to eternal life" (Matthew 25:46). Eternal punishment is there pronounced by this One who will break the nations with His iron sceptre.

The "iron sceptre," or "rod of iron," is used as a symbol of great power in Revelation in at least three places: 2:27; 12:5; and 19:15. This is what is written about the One who is described as the Word of God: "Out of his mouth comes a sharp sword with which to strike down the nations. 'He will rule them with an iron scepter.' He treads the winepress of the fury of the wrath of God Almighty" (Revelation 19:15). These verses echo Psalm 2.

In view of all this, verse 10 to the end of Psalm 2 exhorts:

Therefore, you kings, be wise; be warned, you rulers of the earth. Serve the Lord with fear and rejoice with trembling. Kiss the Son, lest he be angry and you be destroyed in your way, for his wrath can flare up in a moment. Blessed are all who take refuge in him.

The "Son," of course, is an anticipation of God's Son, Jesus Christ. John 5:23 tells us that if anyone does not honor the Son, he does not honor the Father who sent Him. The second psalm anticipates that truth. "Serve the Lord," "Kiss [or, do homage to] the Son." If you do not do homage to the Son, you are certainly not worshiping the Lord.

We read in verse 12 that God's wrath may soon be kindled. There we have the double imagery of the Book of Revelation:

27

the Lamb who becomes the Lion; the wrath of the Lamb. That's an appalling concept, but it's absolutely Biblical. But the end of Psalm 2 again gives us comfort and hope: "Blessed are all who take refuge in him." How blessed indeed.

PSALM 3

Psalm 3 is titled, "a psalm of David. When he fled from Absalom his son." This beautiful psalm is the first in the collection to have a title. *The King James Version* adds the additional title, "A Morning Prayer of Trust in God." It's called a morning prayer because the fifth verse says, "I lie down and sleep; I wake again, because the Lord sustains me." The fourth psalm is called "An Evening Prayer of Trust in God" because it says, "When you are on your beds, search your hearts and be silent" (verse 4).

Phrases like "A Morning Prayer of Trust in God," or "A Prayer for Protection" are not actual titles to the psalms. These "titles" were added by rabbis who conceivably edited the earliest editions of the psalms. The titles are very helpful, though, because they tell us something about the psalms and their content.

Another thing to note in this psalm is the word "selah," a word the origin of which is locked in mystery. Many believe it's a musical term that means pause or interlude. Remember, the words of the psalms grew out of music. Perhaps the psalmist strummed away on his lyre for a while and then proceeded with the words.

Years ago, when I was only a boy, I heard a preacher say that the meaning of "selah" is, "stop and think about it." He may not have been technically correct, but certainly this musical pause was designed not only for musical effect, but in order to give listeners an opportunity to reflect on the significance of what they were hearing.

The first three and the last two verses of Psalm 3 are prayer. In between, the psalmist tells what happened to evoke his prayer. History is echoed in this psalm. If we simply read David's history in the books of Samuel, we see it from a historian's point of view. But in this psalm and others, we get vivid insights into David's soul. We see things from his point of view, and discover how he felt when these historical events were happening to him.

We know from the title of this psalm that David wrote it when he fled from his son Absalom. Absalom was an evil person, and absolutely treacherous. He would stop people as they were coming into the city and say, in effect, "Your claims are good and right, but nobody listens to you because David the king is getting old. He's passé, and we ought to get rid of him" (see 2 Samuel 15). Absalom wanted to be king, and he stole the hearts of Israel. He corrupted them with glittering political promises. Then, when he thought he had a large enough backing to overthrow David and stage a successful coup d'etat, he took action.

As Absalom's following gained strength, David and the few who remained loyal to him had to flee Jerusalem. Second Samuel 15:30 describes intense grief, including covering the head, a symbol for deep mourning. This is a very poignant scene, and in a few words, the historian depicts it. David gives full expression to it in this psalm.

Verses 1 and 2 may also refer to another tragic event in David's life—David's murder of Uriah the Hittite, with whose wife David had committed adultery. If we look at David's history very carefully (especially Psalms 32 and 51), we find that Absalom's rebellion was part of the aftermath of David's terrible sin when he murdered Uriah.

Because of this terrible sin, many people were telling David that God would not deliver him (verse 2)—i.e., from Absalom. One person, named Shimei, actually cursed David (2 Sam. 16:5-8).

But David says in verse 3 that God is a "shield" around him. Genesis 15:1 is the first place that expression is used in the Bible, when God spoke to Abraham to reassure him of His protection. Abraham had just rescued his nephew, Lot, from five kings. But the thought of those five kings whose ire he had aroused returning to raid was probably giving Abraham chills. So God spoke to him in a vision, saying, "Do not be afraid, Abram. I am your shield, your very great reward." The shield was a decisive weapon that soldiers in those times held in front of them to fend off the spears and swords of their opponents.

God was telling Abraham He was his protection—his troops, his tanks, his combat planes.

So David uses this image. He says the Lord is a shield around him, as if the shield were a tube and David was inside. God's protection surrounded him on all sides. Not only that, but David knew he had forgiveness: David says God "lifts up" his head.

This psalm was written after the series of penitential psalms, in which David confessed his terrible sin. Those psalms are probably climaxed with Psalm 32, in which David said, "Blessed is he whose transgressions are forgiven." In other words, he had then gained assurance of forgiveness.

"To the Lord I cry aloud, and he answers me from his holy hill" (verse 4). "Holy hill" is a figure for heaven. David then says, "I lie down and sleep."

If we go back to 2 Samuel 17, we find that Absalom's armies pursued David and camped very near where David himself was camped. There they prepared for battle. They were a vast number, and David had only a very small group. Yet he said he would not be afraid. Why? Because the Lord was his shield. God had said He would look after David.

In verse 7 David prays, "Arise, O Lord!" He is celebrating the victory of the Lord. That expression was used whenever the ark was carried (Num. 10:35). David knew his Old Testament, and his psalms echo it.

The psalm concludes with a wonderful word of praise: "From the Lord comes deliverance. May your blessing be on your people."

PSALM 4

Psalms 3 and 4 both reflect a single period in David's history—his flight from Absalom. Certain links between the two psalms suggest that they are closely connected. For instance, the last word of Psalm 3 is "selah." This may have been only a musical instruction telling the choir leader what to do, but its placement seems to suggest that there is more to come, as if Psalms 3 and 4 were to be played together. The one is a morning prayer of trust in God, and the other is an evening prayer of trust in God.

The history behind this psalm, as with the preceding one, is found in 2 Samuel 15—19. Absalom's rebellion was a very painful experience for David, since it was in all likelihood part of the aftermath of his great sin. David went through a horrible period of deep remorse and repentance, and as a result wrote a number of psalms reflecting his growing sense of forgiveness. This psalm is one of several I put in that class. Many commentators list only six or seven penitential psalms, but I include many others. I personally consider both Psalms 3 and 4 to be penitential, and link Psalm 23 with them, too, as psalms written when David was being pursued by Absalom.

Psalm 4 consists of four short paragraphs of two verses each, the same structure as Psalm 3. Verse 1 is a call to God; verse 2 is reproof of David's companions, those on his side. Verses 4 and 5 are an exhortation to David's friends. Verses 6-8 are a contrast between their despondency and David's personal gladness and peace of mind. The final verse shows that because of God, David could lie down and sleep, even though many who did not know God and lacked any assurance of God's salvation and forgiveness would have spent the night pacing or tossing and turning on their beds.

Let's look at Psalm 4 in more detail now. The expression in verse 1, "God of my righteousness" (KJV), is beautiful. It doesn't mean, "my righteous God," though God of course is righteous. It means, "answer me when I call, O God from whom my righteousness comes." In other words, David is talking about imputed righteousness. He has confessed his sin and found assurance of forgiveness in Psalms 51 and 32, and he now prays to God without any inhibitions at all because he knows he is talking to the God who imparts righteousness to those who call on Him.

Romans 4, speaking of righteousness apart from works, quotes Psalm 32: "Blessed are they whose transgressions are forgiven, whose sins are covered. Blessed is the man whose sin the Lord will never count against him." David learned that God reckons righteousness to a person. He treats me, He treats you, He treats as many as trust Him as if we were righteous. The righteousness He sees is His own, which was transferred to our account.

We are sinners, but it's not good to dwell on our sin continually. David did not do that. After his confession to God (Psalm 51), he was able to come to the point where he enjoyed the peace of mind, the blessedness, as he said, of someone who knows that God is not imputing sin to his account.

David begins his prayer in verse 1 of Psalm 4 by saying, "Answer me." I think we can assume that God hears us when we pray, but it's very natural to begin a prayer as David did here. Some theologians might say we are wasting time if we do—that we can assume God always does listen to our prayer when we come in Christ's name. After all, Christ told us that if we ask for anything in His name—that is, in the authority He gives us, based on His righteousness—God hears us. But sometimes those of us who study theology can become marvelous splitters of hairs, ignoring the fact that it's very natural to ask God to listen.

Verse 2 is David's admonition to those who were with him in exile. These people were loyal subjects of David their king, but not all of them were good people. Joab, for example, was always loyal to David; yet when David was dying, he gave orders to his son Solomon to kill Joab. Joab had been a murderous man in his lifetime. Some of David's protectors were harsh, fierce people.

I'm inclined to think that verse 2 also includes Absalom and his cohorts. David asks them, "How long will you turn my glory into shame?" I think he really means, How long are you going to use my sin with Bathsheba and Uriah as an excuse to do your dirty work? Absalom had stolen the hearts of the people by poisoning them against David (2 Sam. 15).

In verse 3, is David calling himself a godly person? Yes, he is; but this is not arrogance. The "godly" is the Old Testament equivalent of the New Testament idea of "saints." Even though he had experienced a sad failure in his personal moral life, David never linked himself with godless people—those who did not acknowledge God. We do well to remember that life is complex. It's quite possible for a truly godly person to experience a serious fall, just as David did. But David's fall—adultery followed by murder—is not characteristic of his life. He was at the point of that fall acting out of character. Overall, his life was marked by godliness. This is why he can protest to his enemies in verse 3 that he is godly, and speak with assurance that God will hear him.

David addresses his own companions again in verse 4. "Stand in awe and sin not" (KJV) seems to be a warning against the ferocity that characterized people like Joab. David warns them not to let their burning anger against Absalom and his followers cause them to sin. The Apostle Paul quotes this verse in Ephesians 4:26: "Be ye angry and sin not" (KJV).

Was David's exhortation heeded? We know that Joab murdered Absalom, and that was doubless one of the reasons David left orders for Joab's death with Solomon when he handed over the reins of government.

Psalm 77 resembles the last part of verse 4. "When you are on your beds, search your hearts and be silent." A wonderful exercise for Christian people today is to meditate in their hearts and be still.

"Offer right sacrifices and trust in the Lord," says verse 5. One activity of worship is to offer the sacrifices of righteousness. This is a contrast to the sacrifices Absalom was offering. Second Samuel 15 tells us that Absalom wanted to make a vow, a sacrifice, so David let him go. But Absalom actually used that as an occasion to organize the rebellion. Absalom's "sacrifice" was a sham.

God doesn't need our ritual. He doesn't need observance of

the outer forms of religion if it isn't accompanied with the genuineness of heart that seeks and worships Him. He already owns "the cattle on a thousand hills" (Psalm 50). We can't really "give" Him anything material that He doesn't already own. What He wants is our genuine sacrifices of praise, as betokened by our material offerings.

Verse 6 indicates that many of David's own group were despairing. They thought Absalom's forces were too strong. David responds by reminding them that God was still with them. Verse 6 is an echo of the high priestly blessing recorded in Numbers 6. "Let the light of your face shine upon us, O Lord," David prays. He follows this with, "You have filled my heart with greater joy than when their grain and new wine abound." He is saying, I have something better than those who are sending us fleeing into the wilderness.

In verse 8 we see David's confidence that he will sleep peacefully, echoing Deuteronomy 33:28 and 12. Psalms abounds with references to the Pentateuch, especially to the Book of Deuteronomy. The authors of many of these psalms knew their Bible. Their minds were steeped in the Scriptures available at that time. God's own Word was the inspiration for the Psalms, themselves part of Holy Writ.

PSALM 5

Notice the title of Psalm 5: "For the director of music. For flutes. A psalm of David." Your Bible may include the word *mehiloth,* a Hebrew word scholars think should be translated "for flute accompaniment."

Psalm 5 was written under considerable stress, evidently by David in Jerusalem (verse 11), probably before Absalom rebelled.

The background to the psalm is the same as Psalms 3 and 4. Absalom's plot, leading up to an attempted revolution, didn't work. Absalom forfeited his life; so did Ahithophel and many other people.

These psalms also reflect the history recorded in 2 Samuel 13. Amnon had raped Tamar, Absalom's half-sister. Absalom took revenge by murdering Amnon. David was then told that all his sons had been killed. When he learned the facts, that only one had been killed, it didn't assuage his grief. No one can take the place of a son or daughter.

David was especially grieved because he knew that the moral chaos in his family was probably the result of his own immorality with Bathsheba and his violence toward Uriah. He was beginning to receive fourfold for what he himself had done. This was apparently the occasion for the writing of this psalm.

Structurally, we have in this psalm a perfect example of inverted parallelism. Parallelism, as you will recall, is the Hebrew structure of poetry in which parallel ideas are repeated. This psalm begins and ends by describing the righteous person (verses 1-3; verses 11, 12). Verses 4-6 speak of the evil person, an idea that's repeated in verses 9 and 10. The center verses, 7 and 8, contain personal references.

"Give ear to my words, O Lord," begins David in verse 1, "consider my sighing." "Sighing," or "meditation," as the *King James Version* puts it, means "a softly uttered thought." It's as if David is groaning in his prayer. This verse and verse 2, "Listen to my cry for help," communicate a sense of urgency. David is appealing to God to listen to him. He's crying for help.

The psalm makes other petitions also, such as those in verses 8, 10, and 11, and it's well for us to note them for use in our own prayer life.

In verse 2, an earthly king addresses God as his King. David was probably thinking of God as the King of the theocratic kingdom of Israel. Other psalms allude to this as well. Psalm 94, for instance, which was not a psalm of David, but of the sons of Korah, speaks of God as King. We find a similar thing in Psalm 10. The idea was that God was ruler of the kingdom He Himself had set up in the nation of Israel. In one sense, Israel had no king. God was the King, so that David viewed himself as a minirepresentative of the Lord. Though David was on the throne, in prayer he addresses the One who is really King—the One who is his God as well.

Verse 3 says something very practical to us. I was once chatting with a young man about spiritual living and asked him if he prayed. He was somewhat startled and told me yes. When I asked him when he prayed he said whenever he could catch a few minutes. I then shared with him the importance of seeking God's face early in the morning. That's the practical message of this verse.

Psalm 3 is a morning prayer of trust in God, Psalm 4 an evening prayer, and Psalm 5 is another morning prayer.

Job 1:5 also refers to rising up early in the morning. Mark 1:35 tells us that despite His busy life, our Lord Jesus Christ prayed early in the morning. And Daniel prayed in the morning, at noon, and at evening. Actually, one needs to be in an attitude of prayer all day long.

The language is very graphic here in verse 3. In the margin of some Bibles, the expression is, "In the morning I will direct my sacrifice to Thee and eagerly watch." The idea is that prayer is a priestly sacrifice that should be made with care. The word in Hebrew refers to arranging the wood for an animal sacrifice on the altar.

Even while David was in exile, he could still pray. In Psalm 141:2 he says there was no way he could come into the Tabernacle in Zion while Saul was chasing him. He couldn't possibly participate in the ritual worship of the nation. But he wanted his evening prayer to be like the incense which was burned in the Tabernacle.

You and I have been called to be priests, all of us. We see this especially clearly in 1 Peter 2:9 and Revelation 1:6. The sacrifice we offer is the sacrifice of praise (Heb. 13:15).

So David lays his sacrifice on the altar, and imagines his prayer ascending to God like smoke from an offering. "I wait in expectation," he says. Micah 7:7 adds to the thought: "I keep watch for the Lord, I wait in hope for God my Savior; my God will hear me." I think Micah had Psalm 5 in mind when he wrote those words.

David was a great poet, and he used powerful words. We see this in verses 4-6, which bristle with words like *evil, wicked, arrogant, hate, wrong, bloodthirsty,* and *deceitful.* These traits stand in sharp contrast to the character of a person like David, who, even though he fell, could rise again.

"Lead me, O Lord," says David, in his first petition since the second verse. How does God lead? This isn't spelled out in a single verse, but Psalm 32:8, 9 says God will instruct us, and we are not to be stubborn like a horse or a mule. God teaches us the way we should go through His Word. Psalm 119 spells out that truth in nearly every verse; that psalm contains more than 170 verses, and all except a few refer to the Word of God.

Verses 9 and 10 speak further about the wicked people David mentioned earlier. "Destruction" may refer to Absalom, who killed Amnon, or to his comrades, such as Ahithophel, a deceitful person who pretended to be David's counselor while all the time plotting against David. Ahithophel helped start a rebellion that resulted in the destruction of thousands of lives.

Verse 9 gives a graphic picture of someone who is dead inside. The throat is "an open grave" and a channel of "deceit." The wicked may utter flattery with the tongue, but it is ultimately corrupt.

I would like to say something about what are often called the *imprecatory* psalms—that is, psalms in which David calls down wrath upon his enemies. Such imprecations don't seem to be in harmony with the New Testament, where we're told to love our enemies. Commentators who have thought deeply on the Psalms have made differing statements about this, some of which I don't agree with. C. S. Lewis, for example, that great Christian scholar to whom all of us are indebted, was quite misguided with reference to this element in the Psalms. He felt the imprecations flaw the Psalms. I don't think they're a flaw at all.

First of all, these imprecations are not dictated by a personal thirst for revenge. Second, they exhibit a special hatred of certain forms of evil. Third, they are expressive of the worthiness of God's cause. Fourth, they look to God as the executor of justice. Fifth, they reveal judgment in the moral government of the world. That is, there is such a thing as right and wrong, and wrong should be put down. These imprecations regard sin and punishment as being organically connected. If a person is a gross sinner, he or she should be punished. And in the absence of any final judgment, which you don't find clearly stated in the Old Testament, the writers expect and call for the punishment of sin in this life and in this world. Finally, these imprecatory psalms disclose an earnest desire that God's will should be done on earth.

So David was not calling for personal vengeance in these imprecatory psalms, but rather was filled with a sense of righteousness and a zeal for justice on earth. To him, it was unthinkable that anyone should get away with abomination. We know from the fuller teaching of the New Testament that God does hold people accountable for what they do, and that sooner or later wicked folk who prosper in this life are going to be judged by a holy God.

The imprecatory psalms call down this wrath of God upon the sinful. They are a cry for justice and righteousness. In both the Old and New Testaments God says, "It is mine to avenge; I will repay," and we rest in that.

Verse 9 of Psalm 5 paints a word picture that is reproduced in Romans 3. Paul was telling the Jewish moralists that their own writers had said people are sinful (Rom. 3:13).

In verse 10, David protests rebellion against God rather than rebellion against him as a king. The early history of Israel contains other examples of this. For example, the story of Korah in Numbers 16. The people were grumbling about Moses and Aaron. God put the people to death, not because they rebelled against Moses, but against God Himself. Absalom and his cohorts were really rebelling against God, and in doing so they struck at God's anointed king, David.

The psalm ends with a military picture, and finally, an expression of praise.

David was thinking in terms of arms because he could see the rebellion brewing; no doubt men were sharpening their swords around the country. But David makes it clear that he was surrounded with God's favor as with a shield, a defensive weapon. God was David's shield, as David had stated in Psalm 3. How good it is for all of us to take refuge in the Lord.

PSALM 6

Psalm 6 is titled, "For the director of music. With stringed instruments upon an eight-stringed lyre. A psalm of David." There is not complete agreement about the translation of the Hebrew words, given here as "With stringed instruments." But the point is that the psalm gives musical direction to the choir leaders. It is a psalm of David.

This is the first of seven penitential psalms. The penitentiary was invented by the Quakers in the hope that the people locked up there would become penitent. Penitential psalms are psalms in which the writer confesses his sins and pleads with God for help. Sometimes they are called the Lenten psalms, meaning psalms that are read in services leading up to Lent, just before Easter. The church calendar used in many Christian denominations is very ancient, and probably has its roots in the calendar of the people of Israel.

The other six psalms usually recognized as penitential are 32, 38, 51, 102, 130, and 143.

I would add to the list Psalms 3, 13, 23, 25, 30, 31, and quite a few others if at least one verse in the psalm can be seen as giving it the flavor or character of a penitential psalm. For instance, in this psalm in the first few verses the words *rebuke, discipline, anger,* and *wrath* are used, words which all imply great guilt. And David calls God "Jehovah" in verse 1, as if to say that he had no hope in any other source but the God of the covenant, the God of promise.

Psalm 6 is like Psalm 38 in that David had been quite ill and viewed his illness as having been sent from God. He saw this as in some way connected with his sin (6:2) Our Lord told the disciples that they would be pruned or chastened in order to bring forth more fruit. We read in Hebrews 12 that whom the Lord loves, He disciplines. Sometimes, though by no means always, that discipline could take the form of physical illness.

41

Physical illness is by no means always the chastening hand of God. If someone is sick, we can't look at that person and say he or she has done something wrong. But if there is some serious illness in your life, you as a Christian might ask yourself, Is there something in my life that God wants me to think about? Lying on your back is a great time to do some soul-searching. When I was a young man in my midthirties I spent three months in bed. They were very formative months in my life, and I shall always look back to them with thanksgiving. Among other things, including lots of time to read and study, there was time for prayer and the soul-searching that precedes praying. Praying took the form of confession a good part of the time.

David learned what many Christian people learn, and that is that God sends us infirmities to cure our enormities. There is no reference to illness in the historical books, but there are a number of allusions to it in the Psalms, for example, 18:5; 22:14; 25:18; 30:2, 9; 31:9, 10.

David's prolonged illness enabled Absalom to devise his plans. And David sought God during this time.

"My soul is in anguish," says David in verse 3. The expression "my soul" conveys deep anguish as David wonders whether or not God is going to lift His hand from him. In John 12, our Lord uses the same expression, anticipating the hour of His death.

Many times in the Psalms *soul* is the equivalent of the personal pronoun. Instead of saying "myself," the psalmist would say "my soul."

"Return" (verse 4, KJV) doesn't mean God has gone away, but that the psalmist has been far away from God. He is imploring God to again bless his life. Psalm 90, an ancient psalm written by Moses, expresses a similar thought which David echoes here.

Verse 5 reveals the ignorance of the future that clouded Old Testament times. The Old Testament writers saw only shadows of a life after death. They could not say with Paul, "Absent from the body, present with the Lord. To live is Christ; to die, to be with Christ, is far better."

So David, with his limited knowledge, speaks here about Sheol, the Hebrew equivalent of Hades, that is, the grave.

42

Verse 6 is an example of Hebrew poetry. How does David make his bed "swim" (KJV)? He waters his couch with his tears. This is parallelism, and it occurs again in the next verse. "My eyes grow weak with sorrow; they fail . . ."

In verse 8, David is no longer praying, but speaking directly to those who do iniquity. "Away from me . . ." Why? "The Lord has heard." Assurance of God's favor helps us renounce evil.

PSALM 7

The title of this psalm is, "A *shiggaion* of David, which he sang to the Lord concerning Cush, a Benjamite." *Shiggaion* is an ancient Hebrew word that probably means "a wild, passionate psalm." It is related to the structure of the psalm and the music to which it was set. We know from the title that this psalm was written during an early period in David's life in the palace, while Saul was still king. First Samuel 24:1-9 sums up what the psalm tells us.

First Samuel 18:6 begins the story of Saul's pursuit of David. Saul looked at David's triumphs with suspicion and jealousy (verse 9). In verses 10-28 we see the wrath of Saul developing toward David. In chapter 19, his hatred turns into official policy.

Note these facts: all of King Saul's advisors were of the tribe of Benjamin. David was of the tribe of Judah (1 Sam. 10:1, 9; 20; 21; 22:6). Saul was a man of Benjamin, meaning he was a descendant of Joseph's younger brother (1 Sam. 9:1).

First Samuel 22:7, 8 apparently records the beginnings of the work of this person called Cush, evidently someone who was going to inform on David and would warp and twist what David said. First Samuel 24:9 quotes the essence of the words of Cush, which we find referred to in Psalm 7.

There's no one named Cush in the Old Testament historical accounts of the life of David; so we cannot identify the actual person. Some scholars have theorized it was another name for Saul himself, because he was obviously a very powerful and menacing person. I think Cush, a Benjamite, someone from the same tribe as Saul, was probably one of David's aides or advisors. This man feared that David posed a threat to his own position. So he continually told Saul that David was trying to get Saul, that David wanted the kingdom. Of course Saul was deeply suspicious to begin with, and this Cush fed his fears that David was out to get him.

In 1 Samuel 24, a fascinating chapter, we read that David could have run his spear into Saul, but didn't. David would not put to death the Lord's anointed. He refused to attack a person whom God had put on the throne. He was going to let circumstances remove Saul and give David the throne as God had promised.

Reading in 1 Samuel we think David was always in complete control of the situation. He seems as cool as ice when he cuts the piece of cloth off Saul's robe (24:11). But the turmoil he felt in his heart is revealed in this psalm. We see here his deep anguish and at the same time his terrible indignation against those people who spoiled his relationship with Saul, people such as Cush.

The psalm's structure is: one paragraph of five verses that ends with "Selah"; two paragraphs (verses 6-11 and 12-16); and a concluding doxology.

The first few verses give David's appeal to the Lord for help. He also describes the one who is pursuing him.

In verse 1, he asks for preservation from a crowd of people and in verse 2 he switches from the plural to the singular (KJV). David had been a shepherd, and early in his life he killed a lion (1 Sam. 17). So David understood about the savagery of lions. His psalms contain a number of references to David's enemies as lions (Psalms 22, 35, 57).

Verses 3-5 present David's denial of the specific sin with which he was being charged. He was being accused of planning a rebellion against Saul, of being a traitor in order to take over the kingdom. David denies that. It sounds here like David was bragging about being innocent of all wrong. The point is, he was innocent of that specific charge. He's not claiming sinlessness of soul, but that he did not do the thing for which he was being accused.

In verse 3, David is saying, If I am guilty, let me get what I've got coming. At no time in David's life did he deny the justice of God's chastening in reponse to genuine sin. In Psalm 51 we see that clearly. He's confessing a very real sin there. But notice the "if"—what they were saying here about him was untrue.

45

The Hebrew in verse 4 is difficult, and scholars are not quite sure how it should be rendered. It could be translated, "who has plundered him who without cause was my adversary." That is in keeping with Hebrew poetry, meaning, "if I have rewarded evil to my friend Saul, if I have plundered him who without cause was my adversary." However, many scholars translate it as it reads in the *King James Version*, in which case this is a reference to 1 Samuel 24:4, 7 and 1 Samuel 26.

In both of those chapters David could have killed Saul. David's own men were telling him to run him through and be done with it. Not only would David not do it, but he kept them from doing it too, because Saul was the Lord's anointed.

Verse 5 means, "If I have wronged Saul, let him destroy me." Of course David is affirming his innocence, so he says, "Arise, O Lord" (verse 6), meaning, vindicate me, save me, and take over as judge.

When we see David's references to righeousness and integrity, we should be very careful not to accuse David of being somewhat of a Pharisee. That's not what he was at all. Throughout the psalm when he speaks of his personal righteousness and integrity, he's denying the specific charge that was laid against him. He is saying, I am not guilty of what they said I am guilty of; I'm not plotting against Saul. He is simply contrasting himself with those who were truly wicked, like Cush.

Verses 6-8 appeal for God's intervention and also for vindication by God.

Verses 9 and 10 give an expression of faith in God.

Verse 9 speaks of the evil of the wicked person. We all fall; we all commit sin. However, there's a difference between those who are committed sinners—meaning they aren't interested in God, they don't seek God—and those who do seek God and pursue Him even though they fall continually. That's a great difference.

The word *righteousness* occurs 130 times in the Book of Psalms. *Sin* and *iniquity* appear sixty-five times; *good* and *evil* appear about forty times each; and *judgment* and related words appear more than one hundred times. We have in these words what we would call ethical concepts. Even though the standard set forth in the Book of Psalms is not quite the same as the Lord sets forth in the New Testament, where He Himself is the model of righteousness and holiness, still the ethical standard in Psalms is supremely high. David is very conscious that God is a righteous, holy judge. So he expects God, who is righteous and holy, to do righteous and holy things and to bring the wicked to the bar of judgment. He expresses this confidence in verses 10 and 11.

In verses 11-13, God is seen as judge. The language here is quite descriptive. David pictures God as a soldier or warrior. David had his little ragtag army around him when Saul came after him with several thousand soldiers. There were two armies—a guerrilla army, so to speak, which was only taking defensive action and not fighting Saul at all, and a real army coming against them. David speaks of God as the one genuine soldier on his side, opposing the armies of Saul.

Verse 12 is lifted from Deuteronomy 32. David often refers to that Old Testament book. There we have the song of Moses and God speaking through Moses. "If I sharpen . . ." This tells us that David knew his Bible. He had a very small Bible. He didn't even have the Psalms—not all of them anyway, just some as he wrote them. He didn't have any of the Proverbs because they were written by his son. He didn't have the minor prophets. But he knew the Pentateuch well, and he refers to it continually.

The picture we get of God here is one who is against the wicked person who had slandered David, and against his wicked armies. God was taking up the cudgel on behalf of David.

PSALM 8

Up to this point we've been taking about the life of David as revealed in the books of Samuel and 1 Chronicles, and have been able to relate some of the psalms to specific incidents in his life. But we do not have a hint as to when Psalm 8 was written, though it may be one of the nature psalms which David wrote while spending a lot of time in the open air. Until David went to the palace of Saul he was a shepherd, and so was out in the open and able to see what was happening.

We have a number of nature psalms, psalms that have quite a bit to say about the world around us. Psalm 19, for example, speaks about "the heavens" and describes the sun as if it were a bridegroom coming out of his chamber rejoicing. Another psalm says the trees of the field clap their hands, a figure of speech for the leaves waving in the wind. As the shepherd boy heard the wind blowing the leaves, he said the trees were clapping their hands, as if a choir of people were praising God. This beautiful nature psalm, Psalm 8, is a meditation on Genesis 1. It takes the psalmist back to Eden, and he stands as it were beside Adam and Eve before the Fall.

Psalm 8 is quoted three times in the New Testament: Matthew 21:16; 1 Corinthians 15:27; and Hebrews 2:6-8. It starts off with a wonderful description of praise. The psalmist is simply overwhelmed with the majesty of the name of the Lord, Jehovah.

"Above the heavens" (verse 1) may refer to outer space.

Verse 2 uses an expression that the Lord interprets for us (Matt. 21:16). The Lord quotes this verse as if this were fulfilled when small children, who were never trained theologically, who couldn't read or write, just little kids, saw what Jesus did and began to say, Hosanna, hosanna. They called Him, actually, the Messiah. The psalm predicts that God will bring praise from the mouth of infants and nursing babes.

In verse 3, David is looking up into the sky. He sees the moon, he sees the stars that twinkle in the outer darkness, and he calls these all the works of God's fingers. Elsewhere in the Old Testament salvation is the work of God's outstretched arm. For God, making a cosmos, a universe, tens of thousands of universes, galaxies without number, innumerable stars all far bigger than the earth, all that is the work of His *fingers*. He simply flicked them out there the way we would tiddly-winks. But to save lost humanity—that was much more difficult. It took the Incarnation; it took the death of God's Son on the cross. That was the work of God's outstretched *arm*.

David sees the moon and the stars which God has appointed, or fixed, in their places. Then he says, "What is man . . . ?" If you were to read the work of scientists or even those who write about science in a poetic vein, you would probably find them looking into the cosmos and seeing billions and billions of stars. They can't count them. Then they talk about the insignificance of the human race upon this little miserable planet, Earth. They send their spacecraft probing into outer space looking for life, thinking that they are going to find superior intelligence. They talk in terms of billions and billions of light years, the density of the moon, the density of the stars, this and that to the power of ten, all the rest of it, and then they speak of humanity as a little creature, an insect, who has evolved here on earth. Not David. David saw these immense things and, knowing that human beings are the apex of Creation, said that if the things God's fingers have made can be so great, then how great are human beings! How much more incredibly significant humans are than all of these things.

Human beings were made "in the image of God" (Gen. 1:26). The glory and majesty God never gave to the creatures, the animals, the dogs, the wolves, the bears, the elephants, He has given to men and women, boys and girls. Human beings are greater than the moon and the stars. Verses 3 and 4 show that God considers the human race His chief work. He views human beings, as it were, as His vice-regents.

David has gone back to the Garden of Eden. As he sits outside and sees the twinkling stars, mere matter, he looks into his own soul and sees there an expression of the image of God.

First Corinthians 15:27 quotes Psalm 8:6 regarding the subjection of all things to Jesus Christ. This will be true someday. But right now, Hebrews 2 may reflect your own thoughts. We do not yet see all things subjected to Christ—the Fall intervened between Creation and David's own time. The subjection God planned is not in force today. We can't control the animals. We run from lions and other wild beasts. We are tormented by microbes, tiny bugs the naked eye cannot see, but which infect us and affect us. We do not see all things subject to Him, but we do see Jesus, and in Jesus we see that psalm fulfilled. One day the world to come will be subjected to the Son of Man, who is also the Son of God and who, having become human and having suffered death on our behalf, calls us into friendship with Him to be coheirs with Him of that coming world.

I'm inclined to think David wrote this psalm as a mature person reflecting on what he had seen when he was a shepherd. I don't think a seventeen- or eighteen-year-old boy is capable of this kind of psalm. I believe David could not have written this psalm until he had been anointed by God not only as a king, but also as a prophet.

PSALM 9

In this psalm, the writer is agitated because of the presence of evil in the world.

No one really knows what "Muth-lebben" in the title means. It could be an old familiar tune, or a musical instrument about which we know nothing.

The following psalm, Psalm 10, seems connected to this one by similar themes.

Psalm 9 was probably written after the defeat of certain enemies of David (vv. 5, 15, 17). He was now king. David had won some key battles, but the war was not finished (2 Sam. 5:6, 10).

In 2 Samuel 5:17-25 we read about a battle David had with the Philistines. Second Samuel 6:3-8 describes yet another battle, a very fierce one with the king of Zoba, Hadadezar. Zoba has been identified as being north of Damascus. The Syrians of Damascus came to help this king, so David had to take on, and actually killed, 22,000 Syrians.

Then, in 2 Samuel 10, we have David fighting the Ammonites on the east bank of the Jordan River, the area now called Jordan. Near the end of the chapter we find him again battling the Syrians, and in Chapter 21 he's fighting the Philistines again, the last account of a battle by David with the Philistines.

The historical event to which Psalms 9 and 10 refer took place some time between 2 Samuel 5, when David was able to capture Zion, and Chapter 21, when we read that the Lord had finally delivered him from all his enemies. He had subdued the Philistines, he had subdued everybody, and he was now at peace. There were no more wars until after the days of Solomon.

Psalm 9 consists of ten strophes (verses of poetry) of two Biblical verses each. The structure in Psalm 10 is basically the same.

51

Note also that Psalm 9 is very similar in its opening to the closing of Psalm 7.

The "Most High" God in verse 2 is *Elohim*. Quite a bit of study has been done on the concept of the Most High God, and many anthropologists maintain that no tribe exists today that does not have a concept of the Most High God. We find reference to such a God early in the Bible. Abraham knew the Most High God. It was only later, in Moses' time, that God used the name *Jehovah* of Himself.

This psalm is similar in form and language to Psalm 10, as I mentioned. There is a "Selah," meaning a pause, at the end of verse 9, suggesting they went on to sing Psalm 10 before stopping the music.

Both psalms are alphabetical acrostics. There are nine of these—Psalms 9, 10, 25, 34, 37, 111, 112, 119, and 145. Best known, of course, is Psalm 119, in which every paragraph begins with a different letter of the Hebrew alphabet. Then each line begins with the respective letter. Here each line begins with the successive letter of the Hebrew alphabet. The reason for writing an acrostic was probably to make it easy to remember the psalm.

The theme of Psalm 9 is the righteous versus the wicked. Whereas in Psalm 9 David is troubled about wicked people outside the nation of Israel, in Psalm 10 he's concerned about wicked people within the nation. David wasn't so stupid as to think that Israelites were all great people and Gentiles were all evil. He knew that there were people just as evil within the nation. He takes up these two ideas in these two successive psalms. He's telling us that God is judge, and He will deal with the nations in His own time.

You and I can start off any prayer with verse 1. As Christian people, we can think of God Most High and can also thank Him that He allows us to call Him Father. When Jesus was raised from the dead, He told Mary to go tell the disciples that He was going to ascend "to my Father and your Father." We can call Him "Our Father who art in heaven."

Verses 3-6 obviously refer to the battles we mentioned. David is thanking God for victory. These statements can also be taken as prophetic, telling us what is going to happen. God will judge the nations. There are many passages in the Old Testament where this is mentioned, and also in the New Testament (for example, in the Book of Revelation and in Matthew 25). The nations *will* stand before Him.

What David emphasizes and what is of permanent value to you and me (apart from the historical incident in his life that inspired the writing of the poem) is in verse 7. We live in days when evil nations—for example, those that stir up rebellion and trouble around the world—are exporters of terror, paying for the bombing of cities and peaceful citizens. Nations like this seem to be able to do what they want with none to rebuke them. David is telling us that the memory of the wicked will perish, but the Lord will abide forever.

The Second Coming is not just designed to snatch the Church away and make things cozy for Christians. The Second Coming is one of the great moral imperatives of the Bible. Why? Christ's coming assures us that He will one day judge the world in righteousness and execute judgment for the peoples with equity. When that happens, the Lord will be a stronghold for the oppressed (verse 9).

It doesn't always appear to be true that the Lord has not forsaken those who seek Him (verse 10), but it is true, and David makes that very clear.

Verse 12 is a commentary for David's time, but also includes principles for today. God avenges not ony nations that shed blood, but also avenges the victims of murderers. You and I live in a country where blood is shed every day. God says in Genesis that the blood of the victim calls out from the ground, and here we read that He is an avenger.

David acknowledges in verse 18 that appearances sometimes defy the affirmations in his earlier verses. Sometimes it seems as if evil is on the throne and good is on the scaffold. But that's not the case. The Lord remembers His people. There will come a time when it will be quite evident that the needy are not forgotten.

The world may seem to be topsy-turvy now, as evil nations flourish and evil people prosper, but this will be corrected. The disorder of this age will be repaired.

PSALM 10

We're not quite sure whether this psalm was written before or after David was free from the oppressions of Absalom. We do know he was already king. It was not until David captured Zion, having been made king, that Zion became the center of praises (9:11).

Some feel that verse 14 infers that David was fleeing from Absalom. But most expositors, including myself, believe that David, having been crowned king, was engaged in warfare with other peoples, possibly the Phlistines (2 Sam. 5:17-25), or the Ammonites (2 Sam. 10), or the Syrians, or again the Philistines in David's last battle with them (2 Sam. 21).

In Psalm 9 David was obviously concerned with the Gentile nations opposing him. They were seen as personifications of wickedness. In Psalm 10 "the wicked" may be wickedness within the nation, within Israel itself. It may be that David is remembering some of his own troubles when he was being pursued by Saul or other enemies within the nation.

Verse 1 presents a recurring theme of the Psalms, especially in the third book of the Psalms in Psalm 73, and also in Book 4 beginning with Psalm 90. The Israelites were puzzled by the fact that God seemed so inactive in the face of wickedness. He seemed to have withdrawn and not to be taking any action.

The idea is repeated in verse 11. God seems to be hiding as wicked people succeed in their wickedness.

Verses 3 and 4 give a precise description of the wicked. Psalms 14 and 32 do likewise. The philosophy of life that says there is no God lends itself to the ungodliness of the wicked person. If there is no such thing as accountability before a living God, people will do whatever they can do or think they can do without being caught by the authorities. Psalms 36 and 73 express a similar idea, as does Romans 3.

No one could be more eloquent in his descriptions of wicked people than David—he was surrounded by them all his life. This was true not only in the days when Saul was pursuing him and when he, David, was being helped by wicked people such as Joab and others, but also after David became king. He was then surrounded by flatterers and evil people anxious to shed blood. May God help you and me be different than this through the power of Jesus Christ.

Romans 3:14 quotes this psalm (verse 7). Paul was writing to Jewish people who boasted in their religious privileges. Paul went back to the Old Testament, mainly to the Psalms, and showed how the Jews' own writers, David and others, testified to their hypocrisy and their essential evil, so that the Jewish people were no better than anyone else.

Verses 5-11 give a frightening description of the evil person, who is graphically pictured as a savage animal waiting for prey. Many times the Bible uses animal imagery to describe sinful people, and generally savage animals (though 2 Peter 2:22 mentions a dog and a sow).

A prayer begins in verse 12. There's already been one prayer in verse 1. Many Bible scholars would say that this is a sub-Christian prayer. Are we not urged to pray for our enemies? While it's true that we should pray that God would turn evil-doers from their wickedness and save their souls, we can also petition God for justice. This is a valid part of our prayer life.

We generally have the idea that Christian prayer is nothing but soft sentimentality or sloppy *agape* (a Greek word for love). But the Apostle Paul told the saints in Thessalonica that it is only just for God to repay with affliction those who afflict His people and to give relief to those who are afflicted (2 Thess. 1). We don't have to sniff at the psalmist as if he, poor crude person, knew nothing about forgiveness or love. He was someone with a sense of outrage at injustices and the apparent tolerance of this on God's part.

In verses 16-18 the psalmist seems to be telling God, "in spite of what they say about You not seeing anything, and in spite of what I see (You don't seem to be doing anything about their wickedness), You are the one in charge."

During our Lord's Millennial reign on earth, this will be fully

55

true—He will rule! In the meantime, He is the vindicator of the orphan and the oppressed (verse 18).

No one gets away with sin. They may think so, but "the Lord is King" (verse 16).

PSALM 11

Psalms 11, 12, and 13 form a group because they are similar in theme: David's cries to God for salvation from his enemies. The titles tell us that these are David's psalms, and the autobiographical material contained in each shows an intensifying of David's sense of persecution—to the point where, in Psalm 13, he's convinced he's going to die.

I think the background of these psalms is the early persecution of David at the hands of Saul, the time before it became necessary for David to flee the court and hide in such places as the cave of Adullam. First Samuel 15, 16, 18, and 19 give us the account of the Lord's rejection of Saul, the secret anointing of David to be the new king, David's appearance at court to play his harp to soothe the troubled Saul, and Saul's increasing rage and jealousy over the new anointed of the Lord, David, whom he views as his rival. Twice David has to flee for his life from Saul's presence. Saul knows that as long as David is around, his own son Jonathan will not be able to inherit the throne—and he himself will become increasingly unpopular. So Saul plots again to bring David to his death, this time by demanding what he thinks is an impossible bride price. However, David not only meets it, but escapes alive.

Psalm 11 is David's reaction to these experiences. In it, he hasn't yet reached the stage of despair he gets to in Psalm 13. Rather, Psalm 11 opens in verse 1 with David protesting to someone—perhaps Jonathan—who is urging him to flee to the mountains like a bird because of the danger posed by Saul's hatred.

Jonathan answers in verses 2 and 3 in a graphic yet poetical way to tell David there are those who are trying to kill him—and probably at night. If the person who is supposed to represent righteousness—that is, the king, the embodiment of all the

57

nation stands for—has been corrupted, what can the righteous do?

David's response beginning in verse 4 is an afffirmation of faith in the stability of God's rule. Jonathan had said, "the foundations are being destroyed," but David replies, "the Lord is in his holy temple." Everything David says here is absolutely true. But he must have had occasion to wonder many times in the coming years, when he was being chased like a partridge upon the mountains, whether God was indeed in His holy temple on His heavenly throne. David was to find that this psalm did not express all the pain of experience that he was to endure in years ahead. Yet even in those deeper expressions of pessimism and gloom, he never sank completely to the point of despair. There was always an expression of hope in God.

Verse 6 is a fascinating, and I think scientifically impressive, reference to Sodom and Gomorrah (Gen. 19:24). Some feel that what happened at Sodom and Gomorrah was a massive explosion of some kind—which would have been followed by a burning, scorching wind, just as the blast of an atomic bomb is followed by a burning wind. At any rate, the fiery coals, burning sulfur, and scorching wind are symbols of God's wrath.

The expression "portion of their cup" (verse 6 in the KJV) is a common one in the Bible; I think this is the first use of it. In contrast to this cup of the wicked, David speaks in other psalms, such as the Twenty-third, about his own cup overflowing. In the Garden of Gethsemane, our Lord talks to God about His cup—of sorrow and grief and the bearing of our sins on the cross.

In verse 7 David concludes that the upright will see God's face. This is the highest blessedness in the Old Testament. In the New Testament, 1 John 3:2 expands this idea by telling us that when we do see God's face, "we shall be like him, for we shall see him as he is."

PSALM 12

Psalm 12 takes us a bit further than Psalm 11 in David's cry of despair. In Psalm 11, David has just protested Jonathan's assessment of the situation as being too severe. But now, having experienced a little more of Saul's oppression, David begins Psalm 12 with this cry: "Help, Lord, for the godly are no more"! Godly people are those filled with genuine piety; the faithful are those steadfast in their belief in God and in their obedience. David's lament is that these people have vanished.

This prayer comprises the first part of the psalm, from verses 1-4. In it, David graphically describes the corrupt people—those who prevailed at the time—and by whose speech he as a godly person is appalled. He says they are all liars, and "their flattering lips speak with deception." In other words, they don't speak truthfully, but with a syrupy, honeyed speech that was filled with hypocrisy.

"May the Lord cut off all flattering lips" (verse 3) is pretty strong language. It's as if David is imagining the smooth talkers in a courtroom scene—where their fast talking would win them the case against their helpless neighbors unless God intervened.

But God will intervene, as His answer in the second part of the psalm, verses 5-8, shows. "'I will now arise,' says the Lord." He is speaking in direct answer to continuous pleas for Him to do just that: "Arise, O Lord!" (Psalms 3:7; 7:6; 9:19; and 10:12). God says that because of the devastation of the weak and the needy, He will arise, and He will "protect them [the weak and the needy] from those who malign them" and set them in the safety for which they long.

By contrast with the lies of the flatterers described in verses 2-4, God's words are "flawless, like silver refined" (verse 6). The allusion to the "furnace of clay," or earth, seems to mean that God's word is tested by contact with the earth. It will judge the people on the earth.

Verse 7 is a great affirmation of faith: "O Lord, you will keep us safe and protect us from such people forever." "Such people," or "this generation" (KJV) is used in a bad sense, not only here, but in other psalms as well (Psalm 78:8, KJV).

But verse 8 again ends the psalm on a sad note. I think that David is once more pointing to Saul in saying, "when what is vile is honored" (that is, Saul, the person on the throne), then "the wicked freely strut about." That's true in any society. If the people at the top—in positions of authority where legislation is prepared—are corrupt, then there is no way that corruption can be restrained. This is indeed a sad comment upon the spiritual morale of a nation where the person on the throne is corrupt.

PSALM 13

Psalm 13 shows David at his most intense pitch of anguish in this three-psalm cycle as he finds the strain of living on the thin line between life and death almost intolerably exhausting. Never knowing from moment to moment when Saul will fling the spear at him again, David cries out in verse 1, "How long, O Lord? . . . How long will you hide your face from me?" It is the familiar cry of the anguished human soul, sounded as early as Job (Job 13:24; Job is often considered to be the oldest book in the Bible), and repeated in other psalms besides this one (Psalm 89:46). In the face of God's apparent lack of answer to their pleas, these writers cry out in their pain: "Are you playing hide and seek with me, God? No matter how hard I try to find you, I can't! Is this going to go on forever?"

David describes his torment by saying in verse 2 that he has "sorrow in [his] heart" "every day" because of what feels to him like the "triumph" of his enemy over him. In fact, 1 Samuel 18 describes the deterioration of Saul's soul, the approach of madness, and his attitude of hostility toward David—all of which made David's situation one of intense strain.

This strain is so great that David pleads with God to answer him before it is too late, and he "sleep[s] in death" (verse 3). "Give me spiritual renewal," he's saying, "or I'm a dead man." In fact, David's fear of "sleep[ing] in death" may have been quite literal, because in 1 Samuel 19:11-15 we read that Saul plotted to have David killed right in his own bed.

Yet in spite of the circumstances—the intensity and seeming endlessness of his trouble—verses 5 and 6 present an amazing contrast: David's inner peace. David was quite aware that God had "dealt bountifully" with him (verse 6, KJV)—in allowing him to escape the spear that Saul was forever flinging at him. "He has been good to me," says David of God, and several expressions in 1 Samuel 18 bear this out. We read that "in

61

everything [David] did he had great success" (1 Sam. 18:14), so much so that all the people loved him, as did Saul's own children—his son Jonathan and his daughter Michal. And so we have this paradox: in the midst of his stressed circumstances, David can still say, "I will sing to the Lord."

PSALM 14

I think that Psalm 14 speaks of the same period in David's life that we find discusssed in the preceding psalms: the time when because of Saul's moral corruption, the entire nation of Israel was morally corrupt. When, as David has already said in Psalm 12, the godly person had ceased to be. There was such a spirit of atheism that the very people who called themselves the Lord's people said there was no God. God preserve us from that.

I think the specific occasion for this psalm is Saul's pursuit of David to the town of Keilah, described in 1 Samuel 23:7-14. Even though David had just rescued these people from their enemies, the Philistines, God tells David in no uncertain terms that they mean to hand him over to Saul, who is hot on David's heels.

So, in verse 1, David explodes about this type of person: "The fool says in his heart, 'There is no God.'" David isn't speaking about an individual here, but rather a class of people. Nor is he talking about those who are merely obtuse or slow to learn. The Hebrew word, *nabal,* translated "fool," speaks of moral degradation. It's used of those who, having known the truth, have turned away from it and become spiritually corrupt.

This verse is describing a particular kind of atheist (see also Isa. 32:6). This is not the statement of seekers, or of agnostics, or of those who have never really learned of the existence of God. Rather, it's the statement of people who have turned away from God. These people are similar to the corrupt people of Noah's day (Genesis 6:11, 12). They became apostate—that is, they cast off their belief in God. Inevitably, these types of apostates also become corrupt in their manner of life, having cast off the restraints. Consequently, they can be described as "corrupt" and doers of "vile" deeds.

63

When David says in verse 1 that "there is no one who does good," he does not mean that there's no such thing as a good person on earth. He is not making a sweeping generalization about every living person on earth at any time. Rather, again he's talking about this particular apostate class of people. That's something to remember when you come to Romans 3, where Paul uses this same passage with great force in talking to his own people, the Jews of his time.

Verse 2 again suggests in very powerful language a comparison in David's mind of his times—under the oppressive spiritual conditions of the days of Saul—with the days of Noah. Whereas the fool looks within and sees no God, God looks down at these people and finds none with understanding.

"All have turned aside" (verse 3) again points to apostasy, as David piles up and repeats these expressions. The word "corrupt" here literally means "rancid," used of fruit or milk. David speaks of human nature when it is turned away from God as if it were sour, rancid, rotten. Something that was originally fresh and good and beautiful has become rotten. This is not speaking about the Fall. This is speaking about people who start out acknowledging the existence of God even though they are still unconverted. There is a goodness in many of them with reference to their actions which the world acknowledges. But when these kind of people become apostate, turning from God and denying God's very existence, they become a thousand times worse than they were.

The construction in verse 4 is ambiguous. Some would translate this, "who eat up my people while they eat bread" or "even as they eat bread" in the sense of "at the same time." At any rate, this same class of corrupt, wicked, evildoers go along and have fairly prosperous lives—but they are really devouring the people. "My people" could be the godly people David represented. These wicked people do not call upon the Lord.

But, says David in verse 5, even while these wicked folk are eating my people, God is going to surprise them, for "God is present in the company of the righteous"! God is among those whom the wicked devour. God is with the righteous. It may be that David is thinking of his ancestors, God's people, being devoured by the Egyptians in the land of Egypt, and of God's surprise deliverance then. He is also, of course, certainly thinking of himself and people like him, a small minority in Saul's court in Saul's day, the righteous company who were being oppressed by Saul and others.

Verse 6 is elliptical; that is, some words have been left out. We use elliptical expressions in our speech today, for example, "Going home?" to mean "Are you going home?" This verse is saying that you evildoers may try to frustrate the plans of the poor, but in vain, because the Lord is their sure refuge.

Many believe Psalm 14 is really a psalm of six verses: a two-part structure of three verses each. They feel that verse 7 is probably a later addition, made by an editor after the Babylonian captivity, to which this verse seems to refer. This could well be; we certainly have hymns in English in which an additional verse is added by a later editor or writer.

On the other hand, it's also possible that the expression in verse 7, "when the Lord restores the fortunes of his people" (in the KJV, "when the Lord bringeth back the captivity of his people"), refers to David's flight from Absalom later in his life. (The KJV expression "bringeth back the captivity" seems to be an idiom used in the Old Testament for relief from affliction, as when God restored Job to prosperity in Job 42:10.) The reference to "Zion" might seem to support the idea that David did write the whole psalm, but later on, since Zion was captured by David after he became king.

PSALM 15

This psalm is used in the liturgy of some Christian churches to mark the Day of Ascension.

The occasion of its writing was, I think, David's bringing the ark of God into Zion. The "holy hill" verse 1 is a reference to Zion, which was once a fortress in part of what is now Jerusalem. Second Samuel 5:6-10 tells how David captured that stronghold of Zion, or Jerusalem; 2 Samuel 6 tells how he brought the ark of the covenant there.

The structure of this psalm is as follows: it begins with a question in verse 1; verses 2 through the first part of verse 5 give the answer; the last line of verse 5 is an observation that concludes the entire psalm.

"Lord, who may dwell in your sanctuary: Who may live on your holy hill?" asks verse 1. God, of course, is the One who can determine who is His guest, who has fellowship with Him; and in verses 2-5 we have a description of His guests.

God's guests are the godly. These middle verses of the psalm describe the godly in both positive and negative terms: positive, meaning what they do; and negative, meaning what they do not do. The suggestion is that true godliness consists both in doing things and in refraining from doing others.

Eleven items describe the godly: 1) they walk with integrity; 2) they walk with righteousness; 3) they speak the truth from their hearts; 4) they have no slander on their tongues; 5) they do no wrong to their neighbors; 6) they don't pick up a line of rumor and spread it around; 7) they're not chummy with the apostate; 8) they honor those who fear the Lord; 9) they keep their oath even when it hurts; 10) they don't put out their money at interest; and 11) they don't accept bribes against the innocent.

These are very high ethical standards. There isn't much reference in this passage to matters of worship or religion. The person described as fit to be a guest of God in His holy hill is the one who is truly righteous.

Now let's look at these qualities more specifically. "Whose walk is blameless" in verse 2 is a reference to Abraham. God told Abraham to walk before Him and have integrity. Psalm 14 talks about the wickedness of people who don't walk with God, and Psalm 12 tells of the same evil people as speaking falsely. These people are in direct contrast to the kind of person who is qualified to enter into the presence of God.

Verse 3 draws attention to the tongue, as do much of Psalms and Proverbs. In contrast to wicked people, who misuse their tongues, godly people speak the truth in their hearts. They don't slander or spread rumors.

In verse 4, David could be referring to his wife, Michal, who "despised [David] in her heart" (2 Samuel 6:16). She didn't honor David, who feared the Lord.

Leviticus 5:4-6 sheds light on the phrase, "keeps his oath even when it hurts." In the Old Testament, if a person made a vow hastily he could offer a tresspass offering and break the vow—unless it was a vow in which he was supposed to help someone out. If breaking the vow would hurt someone, there was no way he could break it.

Verse 5 describes the godly as someone who "lends his money without usury." It's against the law in the United States to charge more than a certain amount of interest. The loan sharks are those who are guilty of taking usury, meaning they charge excessive interest, and in that way rob people. Taking usury was prohibited among the people of Israel because in an agricultural community, taking interest on the money had the effect of impoverishing the poor. I think the circumstances that evoked that Old Testament law were very different from circumstances in our own country today, where we rent out money at reasonable interest rates—rates that do not impoverish the person who borrows the money. (Of course, the person could borrow more than he could handle, and no matter what the interest rate, could never pay it back.)

People who measure up according to the eleven items will

never be shaken. That's moral stability. David is saying that this is the kind of believer he wanted to be, as well as the kind of king. May God help us to measure ourselves according to this standard.

PSALM 16

If you look in the margin of your Bible, you might find many explanations of the Hebrew word in the title: *miktam*. There are six psalms with this same title: Psalm 16, and Psalms 56—60. No one knows exactly what *miktam* means. It may mean simply an epigrammatic poem, or it may mean an atonement psalm. But I think the word "golden" is as good a translation as you can find; this is a golden poem.

In 2 Samuel 7:1, 12, and 29 we find a hint as to the occasion of the writing of this psalm. It was a time of comparative peace in David's life. In response to his request to be able to build the Temple, God spoke to David of something better—the permanence of David's house. This had a deeper meaning to David than simply the prospect of having descendants to sit on his throne. It signified eternal life. It had the same meaning as God's calling Himself "the God of Abraham, Isaac, and Jacob." God did not mean that He was the God of these individual people, but rather that He was a living God and these were living people—alive still because He had shown them the paths of life.

Psalm 16 is structured in three parts: verses 1-4, 5-8, and 9-11. Or you may divide it verses 1-4, 5-6, and 7-11—a small part in the center flanked by two longer parts.

The psalm begins with David affirming that his greatest value in life is the object of his worship—the Lord Himself. The thought in the first two verses of this psalm, "Apart from you I have no good thing," reiterates the desire expressed in the first two verses of Psalm 15, to dwell in God's sanctuary and live on His holy hill.

In verse 3 David links the living God with the saints, of whose eleven godly characteristics he's just given a description in Psalm 15. He says they are "the glorious ones in whom is all [His] delight." I wonder if we can say the same about the Lord's people? Let's think about our attitudes toward Christian people.

The word "saints," by the way, does not refer just to people whom the Church has canonized, but to all the people of God set apart for Him. I wonder if David was thinking of Jonathan when he wrote of saints. We read in 1 Samuel 23:16 that "Saul's son Jonathan went to David . . . and helped him find strength in God."

David could have been thinking of the people of Keilah in verse 4, the evil people against whose betrayal God warned David by supernatural intervention (1 Sam. 23:9-13). Verse 7 seems to suggest this, too, as David says, "I will praise the Lord who counsels me." Even at night, he says, his heart instructs him. The *King James Version* uses the word "reins," which means "kidneys," here instead of "heart." But the sense is the same. The heart, or kidneys, were viewed as the seat of the emotions. Even today medical science is discovering how closely linked the health of our inner organs is with the health of our emotional state. These writers of the Old Testament, with their more integrated view of the human being, already knew that.

If you're familiar with the New Testament, you'll know that in verses 8-10 we have a messianic passage.

A messianic psalm is one that looks forward to the coming of the Messiah and says something about His person or His work. Technically, a messianic psalm is one that is mentioned in the New Testament. We know when we find such a quote in the New Testament that that psalm was definitely referring to the Lord.

This passage in Psalm 16 is quoted in Acts 13. There, Paul says bluntly that although David wrote the psalm, he was not talking about himself when he said, "Nor will you let your Holy One see decay." We know this, says Paul, because David did die, was buried, and decomposed. He did undergo decay. But "the one whom God raised from the dead," meaning Christ, did not undergo decay. Peter made the same point earlier, in Acts 2:22-32. So Psalm 16 is a messianic psalm predicting the resurrection of our Lord Jesus.

Jesus Himself, chiding the slow-learning disciples on the Emmaus road, pointed back to the messages about Him contained in the Old Testament Scriptures. He noted that "Everything must be fulfilled that is written about me in the Law of Moses, the Prophets, and the Psalms" (Luke 24:44).

Some have made quite a study of the messianic psalms, classifying them according to their treatment of Christ the Messiah in His person, His offices, and His works. Briefly, these may be outlined as follows:

Messiah's Person: He is presented as the Son of God in Psalm 2; the Son of Man in Psalm 8; the Son of David in Psalm 89; and as very God in Psalms 45, 102, and 110.

Messiah's Office: The Messiah is Prophet—Psalm 22:2, 25 and Psalm 40; Priest—Psalm 110; and King—Psalms 2 and 24.

Messiah's Work: He offers Himself in Psalms 22 and 40; Psalm 23, as compared with Hebrews 7 and 13, shows His resurrection and ascension; Psalm 8 as compared with 1 Corinthians 15 shows Him restoring all things.

As for the inner life of the Messiah, see Psalm 16. Psalms 22, 69, and 40 depict His thoughts in His agony on the cross.

PSALM 17

This psalm can be divided into three parts: verses 1-5, 6-12, and 13-15.

The title of the psalm is "A prayer of David." Only four other psalms have that title: Psalms 86, 90, 102, and 142.

This psalm seems to have been written during the time that David was being pursued by Saul (1 Sam. 23). It was obviously written before David's sins of adultery and murder.

In verse 3 David says, "though you test me, you will find nothing." He is not claiming complete innocence, but rather saying he's not guilty of conspiracy against Saul.

The expression "the apple of your eye" in verse 7 cannot express the tenderness of the Hebrew equivalent. David was very conscious that God loved him.

Verse 12 is one of the ways David describes Saul—as a lion. It's not the strength of the lion David is thinking of either, but its ferocity, as it lurks in hiding places waiting to tear and rend its victim. Saul's victim, of course, is David. Despite this image of Saul's viciousness, David lamented Saul's death when it happened (2 Sam. 1).

In verse 13, David asks God to rescue him by His (God's) sword. David would not use his own sword against Saul, the Lord's anointed (1 Sam. 26:10, 11).

Verse 14 is again an allusion to the kind of wicked people David has described in Psalms 7, 9, 10, 11, 12, and 14.

Verse 15 is very similar to the end of Psalm 16. This psalm is also similar to Psalm 10, having been written at about the same time. In each, David was contemplating the possibility of death. God gives him the assurance, which he expresses in these psalms, that God would raise him to life again. David could say that God was the source of his riches and his joy, and that he looked forward to seeing Him after death.

PSALM 18

Psalm 18 is the longest psalm attributed to David. There are longer psalms, like Psalm 119, but this is the longest that bears a title indicating David's authorship.

Psalm 18 is a song as well as a poem-prayer. It was composed in order to be accompanied with music, probably on the lyre, and possibly to be recited.

I think it was composed by David to be a public celebration, or giving of thanks, for his victories over Saul and his other enemies. Just such a public celebration is described in 2 Samuel 6 and 1 Chronicles 16, when David brought the ark of the Lord to Jerusalem. It's quite possible they began the Tabernacle service described in 1 Chronicles 16 with this psalm, Psalm 18. First Chronicles 16:8-22 does record a psalm that Asaph and his relatives recited then—the first fifteen verses of Psalm 105. Psalm 18 could also certainly have been recited then.

This public celebration ushered in a time of peace in David's life, when "the Lord had given him rest from all his enemies around him"(2 Sam. 7:1). This seems in keeping with what the title of the psalm describes: "when the Lord delivered him from the hand of all his enemies and from the hand of Saul."

I favor this earlier time of writing rather than a later one, because David could never have written verses 20-24 after his adultery with Bathsheba and his murder of Uriah. This psalm could have been read publicly again, at a later date—for instance, after David quelled the minirevolutions that sprang up in the wake of his adultery and murder (2 Sam. 21:18-20). But I don't believe it was written later.

So we can read this psalm as David's expression of thanksgiving to God for having preserved him during those long years of exile when Saul was trying to kill him; for the times when he had to conquer the Philistines; and then, for those early days of his reign when he had to establish his rule completely by bringing the family of Saul to heel and teaching all of Saul's friends to acknowledge him as king.

Psalm 18 is not directly messianic, meaning it is not quoted in the New Testament with reference to Christ, but it is indirectly messianic. There are various places in which we see David as the ideal type of the Messiah who was yet to come; for example, in verse 34: "He trains my hands for battle; my arms can bend a bow of bronze." This was true of David, but will be even more true of Christ in a future day. The description David uses of himself in the title, "the servant of the Lord," not only echoes David's own sense of a special calling, but is one that is used prophetically of the Messiah.

Incidentally, Jonah uses this psalm in prayer while in the belly of the fish. This teaches us that we can use the words of Scripture in our own prayer to God. The more we study and assimilate these psalms into our own minds and vocabularies, the more at ease we will feel with them when we pray.

The psalm is structured first with five stanzas of three verses each, then followed by five more stanzas of increasing length.

"I love you, O Lord, my strength," begins David in verse 1. The word "love" is a very powerful word meaning to "love" very tenderly, as with a mother's love. David's use of it shows his spiritual maturity, his sense of intimacy with God.

In verse 2, David switches to the third person to speak of God. At other times he uses the second person, as if he were speaking directly to God.

The word "rock" used in verse 2 means more than just power and stability. The Lord is not only the rock, but also the fortress built on that rock. He is my personal deliverer, says David.

When David speaks of God as his "shield," he is going back to the time God revealed Himself to Abraham in Genesis 15:1: "Do not be afraid, Abram. I am your shield."

In the expression "horn of my salvation," "horn" is a symbol of strength and dignity. Zechariah uses "horn of salvation" in Luke 1:69 as he speaks prophetically of the coming Messiah.

Verses 4-6 are a prime example of Hebrew poetry, which works by repetition. "The cords of death entangled me," says David, then repeats it slightly differently: "the snares of death confronted me." All true poetry, such as this, is thought distilled, highly condensed, and expressed in beautiful literary images. Here the image "cords of death" speaks of a hunter's snare. David is saying that death was a hunter which almost snared him. Death was the hunter, and he was the game. He sees himself in a field, pursued by a hunter, a helpless quarry whose escape is cut off by rushing rivers of water. What a terrifying image! As we read this powerful poetry, we can feel with a chill something of David's overwhelming distress in the years Saul pursued him.

I was confronted by death, says David in verse 6, so I confronted God. I went before Him. The word "temple" as used here stands for the very presence of God in heaven.

Verses 7-15 present a beautiful picture of a storm. But it's not just any ordinary storm; God Himself came down in it to do battle and rescue David from being destroyed by his enemies. In verse 10 we have God swooping down upon the wings of the wind. The word "flew" is used in only one other place—Deuteronomy—of an eagle swooping down. Verse 11 implies that God was hiding in the clouds. The sound of the wind blowing was almost like the sound of chariot wheels. In verse 12 it's as if the clouds were lifting and the sun was shining through. God's "arrows" in verse 14 would be lightning. In verse 15, David is thinking of the crossing of the Red Sea: the "foundations of the earth were laid bare," meaning dry land—the bottom of the sea—was visible. Throughout this whole passage, David sees God acting on his behalf. It's all very reminiscent of Exodus 14 and 15, the crossing of the Red Sea and the song of triumph that follows. Exodus 15:3 says, "the Lord is a warrior"—and that's the same thing David is telling us in this powerful nature poem.

In verse 16, "he drew me out of deep waters" is an allusion to Moses, whose name meant "drawn out of the waters," possibly because of his being pulled out of the water as an infant by Pharaoh's daughter. David is looking back into the history of the people of Israel. He sees the deliverance of the Israelites from the armies of Pharaoh, and he thinks of his own deliverance from Saul in similar terms. Saul was the modern Pharaoh who pursued him—right up to the sea itself—where he was surrounded by torrents of water, that is, "torrents" of ungodly

75

people. He was vastly outnumbered by Saul (v. 17). But God drew him out of these "deep waters."

"He rescued me because he delighted in me," says David in verse 19. Was he simply boasting? I don't think so. David repeatedly expressed his satisfaction in God's love for him, and that's what he's doing here—simply expressing a fact. God loved him and wanted to preserve him.

In verses 20-24 David gives the reason for God's intervention on his behalf. He describes his innocence. In general, David's life was characterized by obedience to the Lord—the one great exception being the Bathsheba/Uriah incident. In this description of his innocence, though, he has not yet committed that sin. He is protesting specifically the charges laid against him by Saul and Saul's companions, who accused David repeatedly of attempting to overthrow and kill Saul. David denies these charges. He tells how the Lord didn't let him down—He didn't let Saul kill him on those false charges. This could be called a moral intervention on behalf of David.

In verse 23 David describes himself as "blameless," a word first used in Genesis 17:1 when God tells Abraham, "I am God Almighty; walk before me and be blameless."

Verses 25-30 are a general statement about the dealings of God and His moral character. "To the faithful you show yourself faithful."

"But to the crooked" (verse 26) "you show yourself shrewd." This word "shrewd" means that the Lord deals with crooked people in such a way as to bring them into confusion and thereby overthrow them and their counsels.

By contrast, God keeps David's "lamp burning"—that is, God gives him life and prosperity. There's a similar passage in Job 29:3, which may have been in David's mind as he wrote this. The word "lamp" which David uses is the one used for the golden lampstand in the Tabernacle. It's also used in 1 Kings 15 as a symbol of life and prosperity.

David ends the paragraph in verse 29 by talking about the special energy and ability God gives him. "With my God I can scale a wall" may be referring to his capture of Zion (2 Sam. 5).

David sums up God's way in verse 30: "As for God, his way is perfect." When things go wrong in life, instead of blaming God, all we need to do is to quote this verse.

Verse 31, "Who is the Rock except our God?," leads back to Deuteronomy 32:31. Again and again we find references in these psalms to the book of Deuteronomy.

Verse 33 describes God making David like a "deer." Actually he's referring to a mountain goat or antelope, which is sure-footed and can leap from one rock to another without ever losing its footing. David is saying that while others trudge laboriously up the hill trying to catch me, I can bound from place to place. He's crediting the Lord with giving him the tremendous physical stamina, speed, and agility he had—and needed—to stay one jump ahead of Saul's pursuit.

David could say that God has trained his hands for battle; but it's God's "gentleness" (verse 35, KJV) that makes him great. God dealt gently with David, and David assimilated that gentleness. Some have thought of David as ferocious and bar-baric, but I don't care for that idea. David was a gentle person. He wanted to show kindness to the house of Saul for Jona-than's sake. His relationships with Jonathan and with a woman like Abigail show us something of the gentleness of this man. He was capable of tremendous ferocity, yes; he had to be. But he was also a gentle person; a gentleness acquired in imitation of the God who had been gentle and gracious in all of His dealings with David. By the way, I think this is the only place in the Bible where this particular term, "gentle," is used of God.

"You broaden the path beneath me, so that my ankles do not turn" (verse 36). This refers not only to David's experiences as a warrior, but also to his moral life.

In verses 37 and 38, David seems to be gloating over his crushing of his enemies. But this description has to be under-stood in the light of the Old Testament. We can't judge these Old Testament characters by New Testament standards. David was the anointed of the Lord, a representative of God. There-fore, those who were pursuing him to death were opponents of God Himself. David is not so much gloating, therefore, as he is triumphing in the spirit of the Lord.

In this whole paragraph, verses 37-42, David is expressing what he feels is God's victory over those who were opposed to God's will and the establishment of righteousness in the king-dom of Israel. C. S. Lewis points out the value of these portions of the Psalms that seem to gloat over the death of the wicked.

77

They serve to remind us that there is such a thing as evil, and that someday God is going to overcome it.

Verses 43-45 anticipate the rule of the Lord as head of the nations. David is talking about his role as conqueror of the nations surrounding Israel. As such, he is a precursor of the Messiah Himself, the One who will indeed be the head of the nations.

Verses 46-50 continue this theme of David's—and Messiah's—rule over the nations. The Pharisees and other religious leaders living in the days of Jesus seemed to have lost any vision of the rule of Messiah over the nations. That wasn't David's way.

Because they were surrounded by pagan nations who worshiped lifeless idols, David and other Israelites were very conscious that they worshiped a living God (verse 46).

David sees himself in verse 49 as a king, the representative of God ruling among the people of Israel, but also as one who would sing praises to the Lord's name among the Gentiles. It's as if he could look ahead and see the One who would finally unite all nations—Christ. David here is a type of Christ, who will unite all nations, meaning the Gentiles, with believing Jews in His Church. The Apostle Paul quotes this verse in Romans 15:9 as he describes how this union is already taking place.

A *type,* by the way, is a representation of something or someone that is expected to come. Thus, David and other people were types of Christ.

God "shows unfailing kindness to his anointed, to David and his descendants forever" (verse 50). David is thinking here of the promises God made to him via the prophet Nathan in 2 Samuel 7, about his throne being established forever. Ultimately, of course, this beautiful verse describes the eternal reign of the coming Messiah, Christ.

PSALM 19

Psalm 19 is the basis for the hymn by Joseph Addison, "The Spacious Firmament" (On High), set to the music of Franz Joseph Haydn. It's a very familiar psalm; many people who know the Twenty-third Psalm also know the Nineteenth.

This psalm presents a comparison and a contrast between what may be termed "natural religion" and "revealed religion." Verses 1-6 speak of natural religion, that is, as shown by nature. God expects people to look at creation and conclude that these things had a Creator (Romans 1:20). Verses 7-12 describe religion as revealed—by God's law.

Natural religion "declares the glory of God," but does not reveal the will of God. I can look up and see the sun; I can study astronomy and know something about the immense distances between the stars; I can look at a "flower in the crannied wall," as Alfred, Lord Tennyson did, and be amazed; I can think in terms of teleology (that is, design—the intricate design we see in nature), and be profoundly impressed with God's attributes, such as His power, wisdom, ability, and incredible skill; I can do all these things, but I still don't know the will of God. That's why He's given us His law, or His Word.

It's His law that reveals His will. He does this for our conversion—that we may be brought to Him. We also find instruction and guidance in the Word of God, so that we can live in a way that pleases God.

Psalm 19 was written about the same time as Psalm 18. In Psalm 18, David mentioned a mission that God had given him to the heathen. In Psalm 19, he begins to think about the groundwork that had been laid with these people. They have all had the witness of nature to the Creator God (Acts 14:14-17; 17:27). Unfortunately, sin has so perverted humanity that not many people come to the correct conclusions as they view creation. Instead, they tend to devise pantheism or some other

79

idolatry. So David then begins to think about God's Word, His law, by which the conversion of the nations will ultimately be effected.

"The heavens declare the glory of God," begins verse 1, using a name for God, *El*, that denotes His majesty and power. (In the second part of this psalm, the name *Jehovah* is used seven times. The Old Testament uses several names to denote various characteristics of God. But whichever name is used, the Bible is talking about one and the same God.)

Verse 2 says that creation, the heavens specifically, continuously "pour forth speech." The phrase "pour forth" is used of religious utterance in Psalm 78:2. Speech is communication. The second part of the verse says the heavens "display knowledge." Knowledge is comprehension of that which is communicated by speech. The cosmos is viewed here as a great communicator, communicating messages from God in a way that can be comprehended.

Romans 10:18 quotes verse 4, "Their voice goes out into all the earth." Paul takes the imagery of the psalm, about the voice of creation speaking to all nations, and applies it to Christ, and to the apostles who preach the word of God.

In verses 4 and 5, the sun is a symbol of youthful vigor. It's like a bridegroom coming out of his chamber.

In part two of the psalm, in verses 7-10, there are six references to the law: the law of the Lord, the statutes of the Lord, the precepts of the Lord, the commands of the Lord, the fear of the Lord, and the ordinances of the Lord. "Statutes," or "testimony" (KJV), is used in the Old Testament primarily of the Ten Commandments (Exod. 25:16). The fear of the Lord and the ordinances of the Lord are allusions to some aspect of the law (Psalm 119).

Verses 10-13 describe the effects of the law; in verses 12-14 we find David applying the law to his own heart. He prays that he will be kept from "willful" or "presumptuous" (KJV) sins (Num. 15:30). Even that willful sin David did commit was forgiven him (2 Sam. 12:9).

David calls God his "Redeemer" in verse 14. Job did also; and he looked forward to vindication because his Redeemer would return to earth and vindicate him (Job 19:25).

PSALMS 20
AND 21

Psalms 20 and 21 are very closely connected. Psalm 20 is a prayer by the people for the king as he sets out on a military expedition. Psalm 21 is an expression of the thanksgiving and joy of the people when the king returns victorious.

These two psalms are both songs ascribed to David. He was called the "sweet psalmist," or singer, and writer of songs of Israel. David wrote Psalm 20 for public recitation. It was sung by the priests and the people in the Tabernacle in a way that later became the Temple service (1 Chron. 16:4-6; 25:6, 7). Both of these psalms relate to the time described in 2 Samuel 10:17-19, when David as king was defeating his enemies. The reference in verse 7 of Psalm 20 to "chariots" and "horses" seems to allude to the seven hundred charioteers and the forty thousand "horsemen" of the Arameans who were killed in this battle (2 Sam. 10:18).

"Some trust in chariots and some in horses, but we trust in the name of the Lord our God," says the psalm. When David went out to kill Goliath, he said he came in the name of the God of Israel. It was in that name and everything connoted by it that he slung his stone and managed to kill the Philistine. That same spirit is echoed in this psalm.

Later, the people of Israel departed from that and became spiritually degenerate. Deuteronomy 17:16 warns that the king was not to multiply, or build up, an army. But Israel departed from God's standards.

The United States is very different from Israel. We are not a Christian nation, and it's foolish to think that we are. Still, we may find certain principles in this psalm. One is that the nation that trusts in the Lord need not build up massive armed forces.

81

Of course, there must be a balance between defenselessness (in the sense of having no armies or navies) and an arms race that impoverishes the country. The temptation is always to cut back on every social program, on foreign aid, and on other programs which do not seem to benefit the country, and to pour money into the most sophisticated kinds of weapons. In this psalm we see quite a contrast: the people of Israel said they did not trust in equipment, but in the name of the Lord.

Practically speaking, that proved to be very efficient, because as the armies of the Syrians poured into Israel with their chariots and their horses, these very swift, capable, Israelite infantrymen cut them down. I think there may be a principle here, too. The United States (and its opponents) increase highly sophisticated weapons that depend upon computers to operate. But then they find either that their people can't figure out how to operate the equipment or that the equipment is defective. Ask any technician or engineer and he'll tell you that "Murphy's Law" holds true: anything that can go wrong will go wrong—at the worst possible moment. That's what seems to happen with much of the equipment modern armies get.

PSALM 22

This prophetic psalm anticipates all the circumstances of the crucifixion with accuracy and great detail. It is a psalm of David, but many of the details in it cannot have applied to David. Instead, David was writing as a prophet, anticipating the sufferings of our Lord Jesus. No one can doubt that this is a messianic psalm, because we find references to it in all the Gospels. For instance, Matthew 27:35, Mark 15:24, Luke 23:34, and John 19:24 all refer to verse 18: "They divide my garments among them and cast lots for my clothing." This incident did not happen in David's life, nor in the life of any other Old Testament character. Consequently we view this psalm as prophetic.

How does prophecy happen? Acts 2:29-31 is a marvelous passage on inspiration, describing the way the Holy Spirit of God uses the knowledge that a person has and guides that person in interpreting and applying it. Second Peter 1:20, 21 helps us account for this marvelous psalm, in which David says such things as "they divide my garments among them" and "they have pierced my hands and feet." First Peter 1:10-12 says that when the Holy Spirit moved people to speak, He didn't always give them the enlightenment they would have liked to have had about what they were saying. They were very conscious that they were predicting sufferings and glories to follow—but whose? They tried to find out in whom and when these things would be fulfilled.

Not surprisingly, there is less of David's personal experience in this psalm than in his others. The time of writing probably can by assigned to David's flight from Saul. But the predominant theme here is Christ as the sufferer; and in particular, the sufferer who was being crucified.

The purpose of this psalm is to inspire worship. You may recall that on the night the Lord was betrayed, He asked His disciples to do certain things in order to remember Him. He gave them a loaf of bread and said it was a symbol of His body, which was to be broken for them. He also gave them a cup. He sanctified both these things to the permanent use of God's people. We call the Lord's Supper a number of things; but it is a remembrance feast, at which time by taking these symbols (and, of course, by our prayers and praises) we do "proclaim the Lord's death," as Paul reminds us in 1 Corinthians 11:26. This psalm is a great help in doing that, because we get insights here into the human feelings of that great human sufferer, our Lord Jesus Christ. He became human, and as such He expressed these things.

The psalm opens in verse 1 with that terrible cry of affliction, "My God, my God, why have you forsaken me?" In His consciousness as the second person of the Godhead, Jesus could not have said, "My God, my God." But here He was speaking as a human being who was being offered up as the representative of the human race. David might have said this more than once, in despair, as he was fleeing from Saul. In David's case it would have expressed a certain amount of befuddlement or amazement, but as used by Christ the cry directs attention to the cause of the affliction (Matt. 27:46; Mark 15:34).

"The words of my roaring" (verse 1, KJV) could have reference to a bull.

Verse 2 expresses thoughts similar to those found in Jeremiah 14.

The idea in verse 3 seems to be that if God is continually receiving the prayers of His people, He can answer the prayers of the one who represents the people now, the psalmist.

"I am a worm, and no man," cries the psalmist in verse 6. The word "worm" is used in Job, and in Isaiah 41:24, the connotation in Isaiah being helplessness and humiliation. I am a "reproach of men" (KJV), he wails, using a phrase that has reference to Psalm 69:9, and which Paul applies to the Lord in Romans 15:3.

"They shoot out the lip" (verse 7, KJV) is a cumbersome way of saying, they make mouths at me. Or, to put it colloquially, they are giving him the "Bronx cheer."

"From birth I was cast upon you; from my mother's womb you have been my God" is the great expression of faith in God found in verses 9 and 10. Jesus early expressed His faith in God (Luke 2:22, 40, 49, 52).

Verses 12, 13, and 16 contain animal imagery: bulls, lions, and dogs. These animal images we find in the Bible are not complimentary to the animals. The bull is a symbol of great strength and pride. But applied to the human being this spells ungodliness. The lion is a symbol of fierceness. The rabble that surrounded Jesus are depicted as dogs. These verses give us a sense of wonder at Jesus' love, that He was willing to endure this human bestiality in order to make atonement for us.

Verse 16's phrase, "they have pierced my hands and feet," is a remarkable prediction of the crucifixion.

Verse 22 changes from despair, helplessness, and hopelessness to a sense of satisfaction. "I will declare your name to my brothers; in the congregation I will praise you." We know this is a reference to our Lord's triumph because we find verse 22 quoted in Hebrews 2:12.

Verse 31 is a commentary on "He has done it," which is the Lord's second last cry from the cross.

PSALM 23

The language is exquisite and the imagery is beautiful in this, perhaps the best known and loved of David's psalms, Psalm 23.

"The Lord is my shepherd," begins verse 1. And immediately we think, "Ah—David wrote this when he was a young man herding sheep." But as we read further we conclude that that couldn't possibly be. For one thing, David refers in this psalm to his "enemies." He didn't really have those until he met Goliath—and Saul. For another, he speaks of walking "through the valley of the shadow of death," and of God preparing a table before him "in the presence of [his] enemies," in the wilderness. I believe the tone of this psalm is not that of the innocent young shepherd boy, but of David, the man who had committed a great sin with Bathsheba, and who now saw his traitorous son, Absalom, leading a rebellion against him.

The story is given in 2 Samuel 11—17; 2 Samuel 17:27 in particular describes the scene. David and his people had fled to the wilderness. Not far off were the armies under Absalom, waiting to attack. The big battle would take place the following day. David didn't know at that time that he would be victorious and Absalom would be killed. He suspected, rather, that things would be the other way around. So this psalm is an expression of his great faith.

In verse 1, then, "The Lord is my shepherd," the emphasis should be on *my*: the Lord is *my* shepherd, not Absalom's. Shepherd imagery is used powerfully in Scripture to speak of God. Psalm 80:1 describes God as the "Shepherd of Israel," and the beautiful Isaiah 40:11 says, "He tends his flock like a shepherd: He gathers the lambs in his arms and carries them close to his heart; he gently leads those that have young." In John 10:14, Jesus calls Himself the "good shepherd."

Verse 3 is one of the reasons why I believe this psalm was

written after David's sin of adultery and murder. "He restores my soul" speaks of daily cleansing, something which David would, as an older man, feel the need of. This restoration and reconciliation that we get when we come in confession to God is very precious. Apart from it I doubt that we could survive. Everyone needs this restoration, whether from a great sin, or from the stresses that show us how far we drift from God day by day. We need constantly to be brought back.

"Even though I walk through the valley of the shadow of death, I will fear no evil" (verse 4). "The valley of the shadow of death" may signify to some a terminal illness. Others would say the whole world is the valley of the shadow of death, and we humans are in it from the beginning of our lives to the end. But we can go through life fearless, filled with courage. This bravery is not the recklessness or bravado of people who care nothing about their lives. We do care about our lives, and we regard them highly. But we fear no evil, because the symbols of divine protection—God's "rod" and God's "staff"—comfort each of us.

"You anoint my head with oil" (verse 5) is a recollection of David's own anointing, which took place under Samuel. Saul was the people's choice, but David was "a man after [God's] own heart" (Acts 13:22). So Samuel anointed David at God's direction, in a kind of private coronation. Later it took place publicly. Absalom would not be king because David had been anointed. Here David is saying, in effect, "I'm the king" (verse 5), and therefore, "I'm going to go back to Jerusalem" (verse 6). "I will dwell in the house of the Lord forever" is an expression of confidence in God, and genuine conviction that he would return to Jerusalem.

PSALM 24

This psalm of David is divided into two parts. The first part, from verses 1-6, consists of three little stanzas of two verses each.

The second part, from verses 7-10, has only two stanzas. It refers to the time when the ark, a symbol of the presence of the Lord, was brought into the sanctuary (2 Sam. 6). This was a holy occasion, and perhaps to commemorate it later, David composed this psalm, as well as Psalm 15.

"The earth is the Lord's," begins verse 1. Christians who have a sense of ecology often point to this verse. They remind us that we have twisted the command of Genesis 1 to "subdue the earth," trying to find in it justification to exploit mineral substances in the earth, to pump out every possible drop of oil, to dig every pound of coal, to cut down every tree. This verse does remind us that "the earth is the Lord's," and everything in it belongs to God. We are simply stewards of God's gifts. God expects us to acknowledge His Lordship (Acts 14:15). If people do what they want to with God's creation, it's only because He permits it—yet at the same time He gives them testimonies of His own goodness (Acts 14:24).

But the verse also points out that not only does the Lord own the earth and everything in it, He also owns the people. And He will someday call them to an accounting for how they have used or abused His earth. We need to respect the earth—the trees, the soil, the water, the air—and do what we can to preserve this creation of God, as well as acknowledge God's proprietorship of it.

Verse 3 reminds us that God dwells in a "holy place," and in verses 4 and 5 David describes the character requirements for those who would serve God. These requirements are both external and internal. "He who has clean hands" is an external requirement; "a pure heart" is an internal one. The next pair of

88

phrases reverses the order: "who does not lift up his soul to an idol" is internal; who does not "swear by what is false" is external. "Cleanness of hands" refers to perfect honesty in dealings with God and with others—a very important quality if one is going to serve God. The equivalent in the New Testament, integrity, could summarize most of what David says.

The word "generation" (v. 6) is used in the Bible to describe character, not as a statement of chronology.

Verse 7 begins the second part of the psalm. This is probably an antiphonal psalm, meaning there was singing by one part of the choir and response by the other. For example, verse 7 is singing; verse 8 is response. Verse 10 is a mass of voices answering. This psalm was sung as David and the priests approached the sanctuary with the ark (1 Chron. 16).

These verses make constant reference to "the King of glory." The King of glory was not David. If these are the words sung at the time of the arrival of the ark at the sanctuary, they as prophets were looking beyond the immediate to something that was even greater than the immediate. That was the arrival of the King of glory, the Lord Himself.

In this second part the psalmist does go beyond the immediate and speaks as a prophet, looking forward to the time when earth—and heaven itself—will receive their king during the Millennium. Traditionally, the Church believes that this section of the psalm anticipates the ascension, as if the Lord were returning to glory after His sojourn on earth.

The Lord Jesus Christ is the King of glory, the glorious King.

PSALM 25

Psalm 25, which is a psalm of David, is similar in tone to Psalm 34. We are not sure of the occasion of writing, but it is probably after David's sin, which places him in his late middle or old age, since David speaks in verse 7 of the "sins of [his] youth." The psalm may have been written at the time of Absalom's rebellion, as verses 2, 3, 12-15, 17, and 19-22 seem to indicate.

Psalm 25 is one of nine acrostic psalms (Psalms 9, 10, 34, 37, 111, 112, 119, and 145 are the others). In the Hebrew language, the first letter beginning each stanza is different.

Two prayers are found in the structure of this psalm: verses 1-7 and 16-22. The middle portion of the psalm, verses 8-15, is made up of two paragraphs of four verses each.

The psalm begins with an idiomatic expression: "To you, O Lord, I lift up my soul" (verse 1; see also Psalms 86:4 and 143:8, and contrast with Psalm 24:4). It means, "I'm directing all of my affections, all my being, to the Lord." The emphasis is not so much on lifting up his soul as on the object of its lifting up: "To *you,* O Lord."

In verse 2, David prays that his enemies not triumph over him. Who were David's enemies after his sin? As was pointed out in the last psalm, the major enemy David faced after his sin was his own son, Absalom.

Those who "are treacherous without excuse" (v. 3) seems also to be an allusion to Absalom and his friends.

Verses 4-7 are a great help for one's prayer life. These verse are full of such injunctions as "show me," "guide me," "remember," and "remember not." This is powerful writing—and makes for powerful praying. I also like to collect references in the Psalms to the way of God, the paths of God, God's truth, and the like to enhance my prayer life, since Psalm 103:17

reminds us that "the Lord's love is with those who . . . remember to obey his precepts."

I wonder if Paul was thinking about verse 7 when he warned Timothy about the sins of youth. Of course, Paul also told Timothy not to let anyone look down on him because he was young (1 Tim. 4:11).

"Forgive my iniquity, though it is great," prays David in verse 11, again alluding to the sin with Bathsheba and Uriah. David had already received forgiveness for this, but he was coming back to God for reassurance. David did not have 1 John 1:9, as we do.

The "snare" David mentions in verses 12-15 probably refers to the trap Absalom and his friends were laying for David. But, says David, affirming his faith in God, "My eyes are ever on the Lord" (verse 15). God would save him from Absalom.

"Turn to me and be gracious to me," he prays, "for I am lonely and afflicted" (verse 16). We all know something of loneliness. I think the Lord Jesus was probably the loneliest human being who ever lived. Who could communicate with Him on His level? Some of His disciples had a little more insight than the others, and were part of an intimate group— Peter, James, and John. But even they failed Him in His terrible loneliness in Gethsemane. An angel came and strengthened Him.

In verse 18, David links deliverance with forgiveness.

The psalm ends with the cry in verse 22, "Redeem Israel, O God, from all their troubles!" Because of this verse, some scholars believe this psalm is set later than I believe it is. They refer to 2 Samuel 24, and suggest that this was the setting: the time when the people were filled almost with hatred for David because of the pestilence that came upon them as a result of his having numbered them. Joab protested, but David did it, and as a result, many thousands of people died.

PSALM 26

Psalm 26 is related to Psalm 24; in fact, Psalms 15, 25, and 26 were all composed shortly after the ark had been brought from the house of Obed-Edom (1 Chron. 15:25). In these psalms we see not only similarity of theme, but similarity of language.

Psalm 26 is structured as follows: an introductory verse, three stanzas of three verses each, and a concluding stanza of two verses.

"Vindicate me, O Lord, for I have led a blameless life," says David in verse 1. As David sets up the sanctuary worship, he is answering the question he has asked previously: "Lord, who may live on your holy hill?" (Psalms 15:1 and 24:3). His answer is that *he* can. But David is not being arrogant. He is simply referring to an early period in his life: the time when, during Saul's persecution, he kept himself pure by not killing Saul and by trusting God. David was a genuinely godly person. It is true that later he did commit a terrible sin; but the general direction of his life was toward God.

In verses 4-6 David continues to describe his life of purity, saying he doesn't "sit with deceitful men." Does that sound stuck-up? Think instead of Psalm 1:1. David is saying that his preference was for the place of the Lord, as he makes explicit in verse 8: "I love the house where you live, O Lord."

"My feet stand on level ground," says David in verse 12. Only young people can say things like this. Later on in life, David would discover when he was tested by circumstances and by the properties of a sinful nature that it wasn't always so easy to keep his footing. As we get older, we realize that we stumble; then we feel more at home in Psalm 25.

"In the great assembly I will praise the Lord," concludes David. Some Christian people today think that the major thing in Christianity is to maintain communion with God. There is a sense in which this is true; but we maintain communion with God in order to be something for other people as well. Whatever David thought of God he wanted to proclaim in the congregation. He wasn't going to go off and be a hermit. He was going to bless God and speak about these things publicly (Heb. 10:25).

PSALM 27

Psalm 27 is entitled, "A Psalm of David." These titles are all very ancient, given by rabbis before the era of Christ and Christianity. I think the psalms with titles are more easily understood than those without. But, of course, internal study of the content confirms the title.

This psalm may have been written at one of two times: early in David's life, when he was fleeing from Saul; or else later, during the time of Absalom's rebellion.

The earlier time may be indicated by verse 4: "One thing I ask of the Lord . . . that I may dwell in the house of the Lord all the days of my life." David's great anxiety when Saul was pursuing him was that his blood would "fall to the ground far from the presence of the Lord" (1 Sam. 26:20). David's greatest hope was to live out his life and die where the Lord had placed His Name—in the sanctuary.

But it's also possible that the psalm was written at the later time, the time of David's flight from Absalom. Psalm 3 is echoed in this psalm, and it is titled, "A psalm when David was fleeing from Absalom." This psalm (verse 4) also recalls Psalm 23, which definitely belongs to the time of David's flight from Absalom.

Perhaps the ambiguity is helpful. We can feel comfortable using this psalm at any period in our lives, whether we feel ourselves under pressure or pursued by enemies. Many people in various parts of the world in our day have lived under circumstances not very different from the tension under which David wrote this psalm.

Psalm 27 has a two-part structure: verses 1-6, and 7-14.

"The Lord is my light and my salvation," begins the psalm in verse 1. This is the only Old Testament passage where the Lord is actually called "light." Other Old Testament passages suggest the idea, such as Isaiah 60:1 ("Arise, shine, for your light has come") or Micah 7:8. In the New Testament, the theme of light is developed: Christ is the light (John 1:8; 1 John 1:5; Rev. 21:23, 24). This is an example of a theme in the psalms being extended into the New Testament, something which happens with other themes, too. Verse 1 is similar in some aspects to Psalm 3.

Verses 2 and 3, "when evil men advance against me," could relate either to Saul's trying to catch David (1 Sam. 26) or to Absalom's attempt to overthrow his father (2 Sam. 17 and 18). Psalms 3 and 23 are somewhat similar to these verses; they are both linked to the Absalom event.

Verse 4 is a good prayer: "One thing I ask of the Lord, this is what I seek . . ."

Verse 7 introduces a shift of thought. This is somewhat characteristic of David: as soon as he looks within he gets a bit gloomy. But he is able to reassure himself just as quickly of God's presence still with him.

Verse 8 is a dialogue between David and the Lord. David's heart tells him to seek God's face. In Psalm 24, "face" is a figure of speech that stands for the favor of God, for God's having fellowship with us. Many times in the Bible we are told to seek God's face (Jer. 29:11-13; Zeph. 2:3). How do you seek the Lord? In His Word. That's where He reveals Himself. He reveals Himself in the person of His Son, and the Word of God is the testimony of Christ. We also seek God by prayer, when we ask Him to illumine us and help us understand His Word.

When David prays in verse 9 that God not "hide" His face from him, it wasn't that God didn't want David. God had told David to seek His face.

"Though my father and mother forsake me, the Lord will receive me" (verse 10) is an expression of the extent of David's faith in God. In Isaiah 49:15, God expresses a similar thought: as strong as mother-love is, My love for you is stronger.

Verses 1, 4, 11, and 14 of this psalm, Psalm 27, are all excellent ones to memorize.

PSALM 28

The language, the tone, the feeling, and the words of Psalm 28 all indicate it was written under circumstances very similar to those of Psalm 27. I think this is one of a series of psalms that David composed when he was fleeing from Absalom. Psalm 27 also shows similarities to Psalm 3. We know that Psalm 3 was composed during Absalom's rebellion because of the title.

There are two possible ways to understand the structure of this psalm. As a two-part structure, the psalm can be seen as a prayer from verses 1-5, and as the answers to the prayer in verses 6-9. A three-part structure would be verses 1 and 2, verses 3-5, and the final paragraph.

"To you I call, O Lord my Rock," begins David in verse 1, thus expressing his faith in God. The word "rock" is reminiscent of Psalm 18 and many other psalms. But here David also expresses some apprehension lest God refuse to hear him: "Do not turn a deaf ear to me." I think he is remembering that God turned away from Saul and refused to hear him. David was convinced that his own sin was by comparison far worse than the sins that Saul had committed.

His fear continues as he says, "For if you remain silent, I will be like those who have gone down to the pit." By this David means those who are now in the place of the lost, and with whom God did not speak during their lifetime because of their sinfulness. David is not speaking of the righteous dead.

In verse 2, David "lift[s] up [his] hands" as he cries for mercy to the Lord. The lifting up of hands was a Hebrew custom accompanying prayer, much as we see in some groups today, and we find references to it throughout the Old Testament (Exod. 9:29; Psalm 141:2; Lam. 2:19). David lifts up his hands toward "your Most Holy Place." He may have been thinking of heaven, the abode of God, or he may have had in mind the sanctuary in Zion. Many churches today like to build facing east and west, so that the sanctuary of the church will be at the eastern end. This practice derives from this ancient custom.

The theme of treachery that we see in verse 3 (and that runs through these psalms) relates this psalm to the time of Absalom's rebellion. David was very conscious of these treacherous people, "who speak cordially with their neighbors but harbor malice in their hearts." He feared becoming like them if God remained silent to him.

"Repay them for their evil," says David in verse 4. He was not asking for action on his own behalf, but was calling on God to set things right in the kingdom and not to turn a blind eye to what was patently wrong. It is a call for justice. David had a very high sense of the righteousness of God and the evilness of evil. Some of us may think this does not quite match the standard Jesus set, and that may be true. But on the other hand, we do find in this part of the Bible—and in other parts, too, including the New Testament—a strong sense of the rightness of God's justice. The Apostle Paul echoes David's words when he says that it is only right for God to repay with wrath those who afflict God's people (2 Thess. 1:6, 8). So let's not be prissy about our view of David in these psalms, calling him spiteful or vengeful. He wasn't. He was righteous—in the profound sense of the word.

In verse 5 David says of those who don't acknowledge God's works that He will "tear them down and never build them up again." Second Samuel 18:17, 18 describes how the traitorous Absalom, because he had no sons to name as successors, built a monument to himself. But he was "torn down"—literally, from the tree—and buried under his meaningless monument.

Verses 6-9 seem to have been added to the psalm after Absalom's defeat. I think the sudden transitions we often see, from a prayer beseeching God's help to a note of praise, indicate that David first wrote one part and later another part of a psalm.

Verses 6 and 7 are good memory verses: "Praise be to the Lord, for he has heard my cry for mercy," and following.

In verse 8, David is speaking of himself as king when he

97

refers to God's "anointed one." In verse 9, he is acting as a priest when he intercedes for God's people. "Carry them" is the same expression found in Isaiah 40:11, where God the shepherd "carries [the lambs] close to his heart."

PSALM 29

Psalm 29 is a nature psalm. Although there are longer descriptions of a storm, such as Joseph Conrad's *Typhoon*, I think one could search literature in vain for one that would excel this one in Psalm 29.

This is a psalm of David. Certainly David would have seen a summer storm or even a winter one while watching his sheep as a youth. But just the fact that shepherds are in the open is by no means conclusive in dating the writing of this psalm. All his life—at least until the very end when he was sick in his palace—David had access to the countryside because he lived in an agricultural country where the towns and cities were extremely small. He could have seen storms at any time, and with his powers as a writer, he could have described them. I am inclined to think this is a psalm of David's mature years, after he was king, and after he had set up the order of worship in the sanctuary in Zion (1 Chron. 16 and 25).

"Ascribe to the Lord glory and strength," proclaims verse 1. How does one give, or ascribe, glory and strength to God? By acknowledging that He really does have these qualities. Here David is calling upon the "mighty ones" to do this ascribing. "Mighty ones" may mean angels, as it does in Psalm 103:20 where David says, "Praise the Lord, you his angels, you mighty ones." Or David could be calling on the mighty ones of earth—powerful humans—to see the Lord's work and recognize their own insignificance by comparison.

"Worship the Lord in the splendor of . . . holiness," says verse 2. The "splendor of holiness" can also be interpreted "holy vestments," that is, the special robes and garments the Old Testament priests were commanded to wear (Exod. 28). This Old Testament custom is the basis for the rich robing of the ministers or priests in some churches today. In other churches today the minister wears an ordinary business suit. These

99

churches feel that the "new wine" of the gospel of Christ is to be poured into "new wineskins" (Matt. 9:17). That is, that the Church Christ was founding would take new forms other than those found in Judaism.

Verse 3 begins the vivid, magnificent picture of a storm coming closer and closer.

"The voice of the Lord breaks the cedars," declares verse 5—an unforgettable picture of lightning. All nature is affected by this terrible storm; even the deer calves before its time. While on earth everything seems to be chaotic under the thunderous noise of the storm, in heaven "all cry 'Glory!'" The point of view in heaven is often very different from the point of view of those exposed to the elements here on earth.

Verse 10 is the whole message of the psalm. It's telling us that the Lord Jehovah is able to protect His people when the storms of life come. And in the terrible storm of God's wrath that is going to come in the future, He is mighty to save. (The word "storm" is a symbol for judgment in the Bible.)

There may be stormy winds blowing in your life. But "the Lord sits enthroned over the flood." God can give you strength at this time; He can not only bring you through the storm, but He can "bless [you] with peace" (verse 11).

In the awful storm of the wrath of God which is going to come, God will lift out of that terrible flood those who have put their trust in Him—just as He did Noah of old.

PSALM 30

The title of Psalm 30 tells us David wrote this at the time of the dedication of the Temple (1 Chron. 22:1, 6). The Temple is known as "Solomon's Temple," but strictly speaking it was as much David's, because he gathered the money and the materials to build it. Then he committed these things into the hands of Solomon, prepared this psalm, and sang it. Sometimes today a poet will be asked to write a poem for a national occasion, and that's what David seems to have done here.

The psalm is structured in three parts: verses 1-5 give a note of praise; 6-10, David's prayer of confession; and 11 and 12 his testimony on behalf of the Lord.

"I will exalt you, O Lord," sings David in verse 1, "for you... did not let my enemies gloat over me." Coming as this psalm does after the rebellion of Absalom, David indeed had cause to be thankful to God for preservation from his enemies.

Verses 2 and 3 echo David's sense of thanksgiving for preservation from disaster. Perhaps they are referring to David's disastrous numbering of the people (1 Chron. 21). No one really knows why this was such a terrible thing, but even Joab, an unspiritual person, was appalled at David's suggestion. I think David was doing what we'd call "registering people for the draft"—and this was in direct violation of God's command in Deuteromony 17:16 that the king should not "acquire great numbers of horses" or troops. Whatever the sin, it so angered God that He struck Israel with a plague (1 Chron. 21:14).

In verse 3 David is saying, I who brought the whole thing on Israel, I was sick and I began to die, but when I cried out to the Lord, He healed me. Many of us can look back in our lives and say we were close to death. If the Lord had not intervened, we would not have survived. So we thank God for it.

God's "anger lasts only a moment," says David in verse 5, referring to the anger of God that expressed itself in the pestilence. "Weeping may remain for a night," he continues, "but rejoicing comes in the morning." There are people who have shed tears for many years. But morning is coming—with death, or with the Lord's return.

In verse 6, David is confessing to the sin of presumption. Second Samuel 24, which parallels 1 Chronicles 21, describes David planning the sin he is now confessing. In this verse of this psalm, David uses of himself the very language he had used in Psalm 10 to describe the characteristically wicked: "When I felt secure, I said, 'I will never be shaken.'" This sin of presumption led to the active sin of making a census.

In verse 7, David describes the results. When God favored David, He made his "mountain stand firm." "Mountain" here refers to Mt. Zion. It was by God's favor that it was strong. But when David sinned against his great God, God "hid [His] face," and David was "dismayed."

David pleads with God in verse 9: "What gain is there in my destruction? . . . Will the dust praise you?" "Dust" here probably refers to the body. David did not have the light of the New Testament as we do. When he thought of death, his immediate anticipation was of his body turning into dust. We who have the New Testament know that when we die we will be with the Lord. Still, it's true that "night is coming, when no one can work" (John 9:4). Death does make a change in the kind of service we can render to our God.

PSALM 31

Psalm 31 is a messianic psalm from which Jesus Himself quoted in His words on the cross: "Father, into your hands I commit my spirit" (verse 5; Luke 23:46).

David wrote this psalm, and I believe it was during the later period of his life, when he was fleeing from Absalom. Some believe the psalm dates from an earlier time, when David was fleeing from Saul. They think the "besieged city" of verse 21 refers to Keilah. When Saul heard that David had gone to Keilah, he gloated, "David has imprisoned himself by entering a town with gates and bars" (1 Sam. 23:7), and he set out to besiege David. But if we read a little further, we discover that David used the ephod and escaped. Saul's siege never took place.

I believe this psalm belongs to the period of the flight from Absalom because of the sense of extreme imminent danger (verse 2), the general tone of depression (verse 9), and the plotting to take David's life (verse 13)—likely a reference to Absalom and Abimelech's conspiracy. During Absalom's uprising, David had indeed become a "dread" to his friends. But the final evidence again is David's deep consciousness of sin: "my strength fails because of my [guilt]" (verse 10), a consciousness he did not have before his sin with Bathsheba and Uriah. That was the sin which led, ultimately, to this revolt of Absalom.

The psalm is structured in five stanzas: verses 1-5; 6-8; 14-18; 19-22; and 23, 24.

"In you, O Lord, I have taken refuge," begins David's prayer in verse 1. Because he was being pursued by his enemies, it was natural for David to think of God as his refuge or fortress. In Psalm 3, the first of this group, David refers to God as his shield. "Let me never be put to shame" means, don't let me lose this terrible battle with Absalom.

103

"Be my rock of refuge," pleads David in verse 2, using a "Davidism"—a favorite expression of his, "rock." Verses 3 and 4 also show familiar themes of David's; "for the sake of your name lead and guide me" (verse 3) is very reminiscent of Psalm 23.

Jesus quoted the first part of verse 5 on the cross as the final act in His life: "Into your hands I commit my spirit." Because of His work, all of us have the opportunity of praying the second part of the verse, "Redeem me, O Lord, the God of truth."

In verses 6-8, David goes on to say that loving and worshiping the Lord is the only worthwhile thing in life.

Verses 9-13 bespeak a tone of distress and exhaustion that, I think, help to mark this as the psalm of an older man. David speaks of being worn out; of the trial this experience is on his body as well as on his soul.

But in this psalm we find expressions of faith as well as of grief: "I trust in you, O Lord" (verse 14). These expressions of faith in verses 14, 15, and 24 make wonderful memory verses.

"Let your face shine upon your servant" (verse 16) is a reference to the high priestly benediction of Numbers 6:25.

In verses 17 and 18, David prays that he will be spared defeat, and that the wicked will be "put to shame"—that is, defeated. David was praying here as a godly person; Absalom's insurrection was not only against him, but against all the godly people in the land. We can see that David was a godly person, that he did have a firm sense of justice, by his reaction to the prophet Nathan's story. David was outraged at the injustice done the poor man. The fact that David was personally capable of sin did not mean that he was fundamentally wicked. Rather, he was a fundamentally godly person who fell into sin.

"Be strong and take heart, all you who hope in the Lord," says David, the godly person, to close this psalm.

PSALM 32

Psalm 32 was a favorite of Augustine's, who read and recited it frequently. It is reported he had it on his wall so he could see it from his deathbed.

The title is a *"maskil,"* *maskil* meaning a teaching psalm. Verse 8 makes reference to this: "I will instruct you and teach you in the way you should go." Although this was a psalm of confession as well, David's intent was also to teach.

We can see his intent to teach in the care with which he constructs the psalm. He didn't just blurt out his confession, but carefully composed it so it would serve as a model for those who would use the psalm. And many did—and do. In David's own time, many listened to it or recited it in the sanctuary. For many centuries the psalm was used in synagogues at the end of the Day of Atonement. The Day of Atonement was a very solemn annual occasion in which the high priest went into the sanctuary and offered a particular sacrifice (Lev. 16).

The psalm has six stanzas of two verses each. Three of these strophes end with the word "selah": verses 4, 5, and 7. "Selah" is interpreted as a call for a pause. Some think it was a musical note meaning "stop here, because we are going to pause in the singing of this." Others believe "selah" means "stop here and think about what we are saying."

"Blessed is he whose transgressions are forgiven," proclaims verse 1. If there is some dark secret in your life that has drained away your spiritual vitality, read this psalm, make your confession to God, and then enter into the blessedness of the person whose sins are forgiven.

Verse 8 in the *King James Version* reads, "I will guide thee with mine eye." I don't believe the "mine" here is referring to God, but rather to David. David is saying that as someone who's learned the hard way, he will look out for and instruct others so they don't make the same mistakes. First Corinthians

10:6 expresses the same idea: "Now these things occurred as examples, to keep us from setting our hearts on evil things as they did."

"Many are the woes of the wicked," says verse 10. Some people think the only way to have fun is to sin—that the wilder they are, the happier they'll be. David knew that wasn't so. Rather, as he concludes in verse 11, the righteous are the truly happy ones: "Be glad, you righteous; sing, all you who are upright in heart!"

PSALM 33

This psalm has no title, and there are no references within it to designate an author. But it does occur right next to Psalm 32, and in some ancient manuscripts these two psalms are run together as if they were one. I do think David was the author; much of the language sounds like his. Someone has suggested this may even be one of the songs of deliverance mentioned in Psalm 32:7, and indeed, verse 3 says, "sing to him a new song."

The psalm has an opening stanza, verses 1-3, and a closing stanza, verses 20-22. In between are eight stanzas of two verses each. The first stanza is a call to praise, the middle eight stanzas cite the praiseworthiness of Jehovah, and the last stanza is a response to the initial call to praise.

"Sing joyfully to the Lord, you righteous," verse 1 invites. Sometimes we talk to God as if we had been storing up complaints all day long. But here we find that "it is fitting for the upright to praise him."

Verse 5 says that "the earth is full of [God's] unfailing love." Those who have eyes to see this unfailing love can see it. The Apostle Paul told the pagan people among whom he was preaching that God "has not left himself without testimony; He has shown kindness" (Acts 14:17).

Verses 4-9 talk about God's divine power in creation, "He spoke, and it came to be" (verse 9), while verses 10-19 talk about His divine providence—God acting in history.

"Blessed is the nation whose God is the Lord," says verse 12. Although our nation is not the chosen people of God, nevertheless it's still true that whatever nation chooses God is blessed. But our nation and other nations of the world need to learn the lessons of verse 16: "No king is saved by the size of his army."

Verse 20 is a good memory verse: "We wait in hope for the Lord; he is our help and our shield."

The psalmist closes with a prayer in verse 22: "May your unfailing love rest upon us, O Lord, even as we put our hope in you."

PSALM 34

Psalm 34 is a good one for people who have fears.

This psalm was written, as the title tells us, "when [David] feigned insanity before Abimelech, who drove him away, and he left." This takes us back to the time of David's flight from Saul (1 Sam. 21:19—22:1). In trying to escape Saul, David fell into the hands of Philistines from Gath, where Achish, that is, Abimelech, was king. (I don't think there's a contradiction in the names here—one may have been his personal name, the other his dynasty name.) Since David had already killed quite a few of the Philistines, including Goliath—who was from Gath itself—he became frightened when Achish's aides recognized him, and feigned insanity in order to escape. The ruse worked. This psalm was written after David had made good his escape. It's very similar to Psalm 32.

"This poor man called, and the Lord heard him." Along with verse 4, this verse, 6, is a reference to the danger David was in at Gath, and from which he was delivered.

"Taste and see that the Lord is good," says David in verse 8. The word "taste" is used in Scripture for experiential knowledge—and David had just experienced God's goodness. Peter expresses the same idea in the New Testament in 1 Peter 2:3.

"The lions may grow weak and hungry," says David, alluding to the aides of the king of Gath, "but those who seek the Lord lack no good thing."

In verse 11, David seems to be making a contrast between fearing God and fearing people. "Come, my children, listen to me, I will teach you the fear of the Lord." He had been terribly afraid of Achish and had done something stupid. Now he remembered it with shame. I like to think David did actually present this psalm to his own children. In Proverbs 4:3, 4, Solomon talks about his father (David) teaching him when

Solomon was just a boy. And verse 12 sounds very much like something we'd find in Solomon's book of Proverbs.

"Keep your lips from speaking lies," David urges in verse 13. He's thinking of the lie he told to the King of Gath: he, David, the anointed of the Lord, acted insane with his words. The Bible has much to say about avoiding the sins of the tongue; for instance in James 3:2-10, or in 1 Peter 3:10-12, where Peter quotes this very psalm. But all these things are meant to encourage us, not to make us feel miserable.

"The Lord is close to the brokenhearted and saves those who are crushed in spirit" (verse 18). This signifies something stronger than sorrow for sin. Everything that resists the entrance of the Word of God, everything that resists the working of the grace of God must be broken and crushed in the presence of the Lord. The Lord is close to that kind of person.

"He protects all his bones, not one of them will be broken," reads verse 20. David may have been thinking here of the paschal lamb, not one bone of which was to be broken (Exod. 12:46). In John 19 we read that the soldiers did not break Jesus' legs, as they did those of the others crucified, because Jesus was already dead. John says this happened to fulfill the Scripture, "Not one of his bones will be broken," a reference perhaps to this psalm, or to the Exodus passage.

Verse 21 is a great encouragement, describing as it does the eventual downfall of the wicked. No matter what the literal cause of their death may be, those who turn away from God are actually suicides—because refusal to turn to God means the loss of one's soul. David had lived long enough to see this verse come true: "evil will slay the wicked." Many of God's people can bear witness to the same thing today. But others live out their lives apparently seeing the opposite: the seeming triumph of evil. However, we know that ultimately "The Lord redeems his servants" (verse 22).

PSALM 35

This psalm is the very sober prayer of a deeply distressed person. It's David, as the title tells us; a David pursued by Saul and his aides, who were unjustly attempting to destroy him. This psalm has all the marks of that early flight period rather than the later flight from Absalom. It has David's sense of personal righteousness and innocence, rather than his later sense of wrongdoing after Bathsheba and Uriah. It has no references to Zion, his stronghold later as anointed king. And it has internal comparisons with Psalm 34, which we know was written during the time of flight from Saul. (Both psalms mention lions, as well as the angel of the Lord.)

"Contend, O Lord, with those who contend with me," begins David in verse 1—which is almost exactly what he said to Saul in 1 Samuel 24:12, "May the Lord judge between you and me." David knew he was innocent of the treason Saul accused him of, but Saul wouldn't listen. David, however, wouldn't kill Saul because Saul was the Lord's anointed. So David was calling on God for justice—for vengeance. Vengeance was very much part of David's thinking as an Old Testament person: he had little concept of a judgment in an afterlife, and he wanted to see justice done here and now. Vengeance is not a Christian point of view.

David calls on God to be his warrior for him: "take up shield and buckler; arise and come to my aid" (verse 2). David's seeing God in these very human terms is called *anthropomorphism,* and it's part of the way the poetry of these psalms works. This particular anthropomorphism, seeing God as a warrior, is also found in Isaiah 59:17. And in Ephesians 6, Paul takes this warrior imagery and applies it to Christians, whom he says need to equip themselves to do spiritual battle.

In verse 5, "the angel of the Lord" is God Himself. He pursues David's enemies so they are like "chaff before the wind." Once they were the pursuers, but now they are the pursued, finding their path "dark and slippery" (verse 6).

Still, David sees himself as a pursued animal, for whom his enemies have laid traps and snares (verse 8). But when God rescues him, his "soul will rejoice in the Lord" (verse 9).

Verse 10 in the *King James* refers to "bones." The Old Testament Hebrews regarded the bones as the place where one felt pain or pleasure most sharply. So David says, "All my bones shall say, Lord, who is like unto thee, which deliverest the poor from him that is too strong for him?" David certainly had experience of being delivered from one "too strong" for him— Goliath. David was able to defeat Goliath with the help that came from the Lord.

When we read verses 11 to 13, we can't help but think of our Lord, who also was persecuted without a cause. Some of this is messianic, in that it does anticipate sufferings much greater than David's, the sufferings of our Lord Jesus. At no time was anyone able to point the finger at Him and say that He sinned or was not compassionate. Yet they repaid Him with evil (verse 12).

"They slandered me without ceasing . . . they maliciously mocked; they gnashed their teeth at me" (verses 15, 16). David had once eaten regularly at the king's table (1 Sam. 20:27). But when he began to fall from Saul's favor and was absent, they slandered him. In other words, the court jesters, whose job it was to amuse the king, told dirty jokes about David for a laugh.

"O Lord, how long will you look on?" David prays in verse 17, distressed that the persecution goes on week after week, year after year.

"I will give you thanks in the great assembly" (verse 18), the same expression as in Psalm 22:25, means that David longs to go back to Jerusalem to thank God and to be part of the nation.

"They gape at me" in verse 21 might refer to big-mouthed people who were scornfully laughing at David.

"Awake, and rise to my defense!" David says in verse 23. David was so convinced of God's justice that he couldn't understand why God didn't seem to be doing anything. So he calls out for this warrior to stop taking a break! But God did not do anything until it was the right time—until David was disciplined by years in the wilderness and had become fit to be the king of God's people.

PSALM 36

Psalm 36 is a beautifully vivid portrait of good and evil personified. Yet, surprisingly, it also manages to be calm and contemplative at the same time. David seems at peace.

No personal allusions help us place this psalm in David's life; nothing except this sense of peace. Therefore, I'd place it after the death of Saul, but before the sin with Bathsheba and Uriah and the subsequent revolt by Absalom. David seems to have the time to reflect upon the eternal matters he writes about in this psalm. He does not seem distracted by pursuits from enemies, nor by the deep sense of personal sin that troubled him in his later years.

The psalm contains three stanzas of four, five, and three verses each: verses 1-4, 5-9, and 10-12. The breaks are very apparent.

Verse 1 begins by personifying crime as dwelling within the heart of a wicked person. It speaks to him, uttering suggestions to which he listens and, as a result, loses all fear of God and sense of His presence.

Verse 2 is rather obscure, but we can be helped by reading it from a modern translation.

Verse 4 describes the ultimate stage of the wicked person's degeneracy—apathy. Not only is he indifferent about moral matters, he actually welcomes evil.

Verse 5 expresses the Hebrews' love of nature and their profound appreciation of its beauty, as do so many of the psalms. Here, the voice of the Lord in nature is in sharp contrast to the voice of sin in the evil person.

The mountains and oceans of verse 6 are symbols of God's unshakable righteousness. Does that remind you of Romans 11:33, "How unsearchable are his judgments"? There's nothing superficial about God. This reference to the mountains of God also reminds me of Chinese paintings in which towering mountains dominate the picture. These paintings seem to have captured the idea of the mountains' grandeur and splendor revealing something of God's grandeur and splendor.

"O Lord, you preserve both man and beast," says verse 6. We also find in Psalm 106 God sustaining human beings and animal life. And one of the reasons that He should spare the city of Nineveh, God reminded Jonah, was that it was full of people and animals.

Verses 5-8 can become for us a means, a vehicle, whereby we can convey our own prayers heavenward.

"Both high and low . . . find refuge in the shadow of your wings," says verse 7. In the Old Testament, the "shadow of your wings" is probably a reference to the ark of the covenant, which had winged cherubim on its lid. They symbolized the holiness of God. Their outstretched wings overshadowed the lid on the ark, where blood was sprinkled on the Day of Atonement. This expression, "in the shadow of your wings," might stand then for the place where sacrifice was offered—the place of atonement, and by extension, of refuge. Ultimately, that is at the foot of the Cross. The expression is usually found in the context of a reference to the sanctuary. Thus, it is an Old Testament way of saying, at the Cross.

"For with you is the fountain of life; in your light we see light" (verse 9). As David composes this poem, he imagines himself going into the sanctuary, and he anticipates all these things—which were beautifully fulfilled in Christ. Christ is "the life" (John 14:6), and from Him flows "the river of the water of life" (Rev. 22:1).

"Continue your love to those who know you, your righteousness to the upright in heart" (verse 10), is a good prayer for us to echo.

"May the foot of the proud not come against me," David concludes. David was always very conscious of his enemies' pride. It was this that inspired them to do such terrible things.

PSALM 37

Psalm 37 is a psalm of David. There are no allusions in it to the circumstances of his life except the one remark in verse 25: "I was young and now I am old." Indeed, the psalm lacks the passionate anxiety or deep regret of some of David's earlier psalms, sounding instead a note of calmness and gravity more characteristic of age. At this point in life, David has two certainties in his mind. One is the divine retribution that will come on the wicked, and the other the eventual prosperity of the righteous.

The psalm is an acrostic, an alphabetical psalm, in which verses or groups of verses begin with succcessive letters of the Hebrew alphabet.

David's first words are calming: "Do not fret," he says, "because of evildoers" (KJV, verse 1). Do not be "envious of those who do wrong." David seems to have known the book of Job fairly well. In this psalm he attempts to reply to some of the questions Job raises. When Job looked around at the wicked, he said, "When I think about this, I am terrified; trembling seizes my body" (Job 21:6). What they were doing did not seem to square with his ideas of the righteousness of God. David, however, was more assured. Over the course of a lifetime, he had seen a number of things that convinced him that generally speaking, the wicked do not prosper, but the righteous do.

Again, we need to understand the Old Testament context here. David's point of view is almost purely Old Testament in that he had little idea of a future judgment. If righteousness were going to be accomplished, and if God's divine retribution was going to be meted out, it had to be in the here and now. Psalm 73 expresses the anxiety of the psalmist when he saw what he felt was the divine order in disarray.

David is also speaking as a member of the nation of Israel, which was called God's chosen people. God had set up a cov-

116

enant with this nation in which they were promised material prosperity to the extent to which they obeyed God, and punishment and suffering if they ignored Him (Lev. 26:3-46; Deut. 30). During David's time, the principles he elucidates in this psalm operated fairly well. Later, of course, it didn't seem to work this way, because someone like Jeremiah, probably the finest person of his day, suffered terribly. So we need to keep this Old Testament context in mind when we read this psalm.

Having said all that, though, the promises of verses 3, 4, 5, and 7 are just as sure today as when David wrote them. "Delight yourself in the Lord and he will give you the desires of your heart" (verse 4). These verses, with their beautiful verbs "trust" (verse 3), "delight" (verse 4), "commit" (verse 5), and "be still" (verse 7) are wonderful material to memorize.

"Do not fret," David repeats twice (verses 7 and 8). It's as though now, as an old man, he looks back upon the turmoil and anguish of his younger days as he "fretted" himself over evildoers like Saul. He says in effect, "I shouldn't have been so agitated by the activities of the wicked! After all, there's no future for them! Sooner or later, they'll come to naught."

"Refrain from anger" can be understood in this context of "do not fret"—don't get worked up over it.

"The meek will inherit the land," says verse 11, a phrase very reminiscent of the Sermon on the Mount (Matt. 5:5).

Verses 16 and 17 are a conclusion. Though this refers to the land of Israel, I think these principles do prevail, generally speaking, in the world. That is, the wicked do come to naught, and it's the righteous in whom God is interested, and for whom He does care and extend His help. It's equally true, though, that the righteous do suffer. Jesus said we would. "In this world you will have trouble. But take heart! I have overcome the world" (John 16:33).

Verse 21 describes the wicked as borrowing and not repaying, while the righteous "give generously." Poverty in the Old Testament was seen as punishment, and prosperity was seen not only as a reward for good, but as an opportunity to confer benefits and be a blessing oneself. To be a blessing to others is as great a blessing as anyone can enjoy.

Verse 25 again must be understood in the context of the Old Testament nation of Israel and Deuteronomy 30. It helps to

117

explain the tension between David's assertion and the facts of the modern world, where many righteous people apparently have been forsaken, and their children have gone begging bread.

The last few verses of the psalm are a personal testimony. It's quite possible that in them David is again talking about Saul. As we read the narrative of Saul in 1 Samuel, we are sometimes tempted to feel sorry for Saul. But then we read David's psalms, and we realize that Saul was not so much pitiable as pitiless. He was a truly wicked person who attempted to kill David without a cause. The man was driven mad by his own sinful jealousy.

"The future of the wicked will be cut off," says David in verse 38. After David became king, he looked around for Saul's offspring. There weren't many of them left. He did find Jonathan's son, Mephibosheth, who was Saul's grandson. Jonathan's posterity survived, but Saul's direct posterity did not. Neither did Absalom's, who died without any descendants.

The psalm ends with an encouraging note. The long view of this psalm is that, sooner or later, the wicked have no future whatsoever, but the righteous do. Reading this psalm can give us a tranquillity of spirit in these troubled times. Fret not.

PSALM 38

Psalms 38 and 70 both have the same titles: "A psalm of David for a memorial" (or in other versions, "A petition"). A memorial means to bring to remembrance.

In Psalms 38 through 41 the penitential note was uppermost in the psalmist's mind. It's astonishing how many of David's psalms have this dark shadow of guilt over them. When he committed the sin against Bathsheba and Uriah, David blighted his life. First Kings 15:5 tells us that this sin against Uriah was the major sin in his life. The penitential psalms are very beautiful in that nowhere in them does David ever blame anyone else for his sins. He blames himself.

"O Lord, do not rebuke me in your anger," says David in verse 1. This was written after the complete awakening of his conscience to the terrible guilt he had incurred by the murder of Uriah, an awakening brought about by the prophet Nathan's parable (2 Sam. 12:12, 13). The results of David's sin were manifested in many ways: disarray in his family, the incest of his son raping his daughter, the avenging murder of that son by another son, the estrangement of his friends and relatives (verse 11), and the near triumph of his dangerous enemies. Absalom nearly seized the kingdom because David had lost his grip in the aftermath of that sin against Uriah. In this psalm we read about the agonies of mind and body David suffered as a result. Among the penitential psalms none bear deeper marks of a time of utter frustration of heart and spirit than does Psalm 38.

The psalm is structured in three divisions: verses 1-8, 9-15, and 16-22. Each division has strophes of two verses each.

PSALM 39

The title of this psalm indicates that it is "for Jeduthun," who was likely the choir director. Psalm 40 was also dedicated to this person. This psalm was meant to be used in the Tabernacle worshp.

Like the preceding psalm, this one is a penitential psalm, written after David's conscience awakened to the deadly guilt he had contracted in the seduction of Bathsheba, but especially in the murder of her husband, Uriah. The introductory theme of this psalm seems to be the silence that David maintained in the wake of that event. Evidently David's silence distressed his friends and encouraged his enemies.

The structure, in my opinion, is three-part: verses 1-6, 7-11, and the final prayer of verses 12 and 13. Others divide it differently.

"I will put a muzzle on my mouth as long as the wicked are in my presence," David says was his beginning stance (verse 1). In this psalm, we are looking into the soul of a godly man, who although he was suffering the consequences of his own sin, still contrasts himself with the perpetually wicked. I think that David's resolution to keep quiet was tied to his consciousness of his own sin. He felt he had failed as the teacher of Israel. So he kept silence even through the horrendous things that followed shortly in his own family—when he should have instead spoken up and done something about it. But this powerless silence, where he was reduced to a mumble, seems to have been one of the effects of his sin.

However, the silence policy did not work. "When I was silent and still, . . . my anguish increased. . . . My heart grew hot within me," he says in verses 2 and 3. In other words, his desire to speak up and say something became so burning that finally he did. "Then I spoke with my tongue" (verse 3). Despite his embarrassment over his sin, he just had to speak. What he had to say is recorded from verse 4 on.

"Show me, O Lord, my life's end," prays David in verse 4. He is talking about the fleetingness, the brevity of life. He is realizing the truth: all of us are terminal cases. When I talk to someone in the hospital who is a whole lot closer to dying than I think I am, I like to talk about heaven. I think heaven will be infinitely better than the Garden of Eden.

In verse 6, David continues the theme of life's brevity, saying that each of us is a "mere phantom." He's telling us that we are really insubstantial—just a breath.

"But now, Lord, what do I look for? My hope is in you," says David in verse 7. He has characterized life itself as simply an uproar over nothing. Now he makes the point that his hope is in God. We who have the New Testament understand more fully the faint allusion David makes here to life after death. We know that "the trumpet will sound, the dead will be raised imperishable, and we will be changed (1 Corinthians 15:52).

"Save me from my transgressions," prays David in verse 8. He didn't soften his sins by calling them mistakes.

In verse 10, David acknowledges that the sickness he was suffering was God's dealing with him. Does this mean that when people get sick it's the hand of God? No; although it can be. Anyone who is wise will examine his life to see if God is trying to get his attention.

"Look away from me" is a prayer for God to turn His anger away from David. It's a prayer for God's hand of discipline to be lifted, and for physical healing to occur.

PSALM 40

Psalm 40 is closely linked to the three psalms that precede it, and to the one that follows it. If we read Psalms 38, 39, 40, and 41 together, we see similar themes among them. I think all four were written around the same time—just before the rebellion of Absalom, a time when David was physically ill.

The title indicates that this psalm is "For the director of music"—probably Jeduthun, the person mentioned in the title of Psalm 39 (see also 1 Chronicles 16:41).

The structure of Psalm 40 can be simplified by saying that in verses 1-5, David is remembering his grief. His patience, which he expresses in Psalm 39, has been rewarded, and God has given him a song. Verses 6-10 express the source of his new joy—obedience to God's law and also public acknowledgment of God's righteousness. Whereas David had been quiet before in the presence of the wicked, now he is speaking up. Verses 11-17 start off with an expression of apprehension. David is afraid he is going to lose this newfound joy, and prays that God will sustain him.

"I waited patiently for the Lord," begins David in verse 1. Some students of Hebrew prefer to translate "patiently" as "with all my heart," or "intently," or even "longingly." The idea is one of intense concentration on his prayers. David repeatedly tells us to wait patiently (Psalm 37:7), which means to wait expectantly, in intense yearning for the assured deliverance of God.

"Slimy pit" in verse 2 is best translated "pit of destruction." Here David is picturing himself as a heavily armed warrior who had fallen with a loud crash into a pit. There he lay, immobilized, because of his terrible sin. To kill him, his enemies had only to run him through with a spear or shoot him with an arrow. But God did not abandon David to that muddy, miry destruction. Instead, God gave David "a firm place to stand"—

122

a rock, which was God Himself. The rock is a symbol of stability (Psalm 27:5; 37:23). God also "put a new song in my mouth," says David in verse 3. May God give you a new song today.

"Blessed" is the person, says David in verse 4, "who does not look to the proud." In general, this is a reference to apostasy; in particular, David probably has in mind Absalom and his co-conspirators, who were proud, brutal, treacherous, and unscrupulous (2 Sam. 15-18).These were people like Ahitophel (2 Sam. 15:12), who pretended to be David's friend, but took the first opportunity to drive the knife into his back, so to speak, by aligning himself with the rebellion.

Verses 6-8 are prophetic. They express David's convictions, and they also have a long-range application to Christ, as Hebrews 10 makes clear. David's overall point in these verses is that ceremonial religion is absolutely useless if the heart is not involved (see also Psalm 51:16, 17; Isaiah 1:11-15; Hosea 6:6; and Micah 6:6-8).

Specifically, in verse 6, David says, "Sacrifice and offering you did not desire, but my ears you have pierced," or "opened" (KJV). David is saying what Samuel had said, and what the prophets also said: instead of sacrifice, You want an ear that is open to hear the law of God. "My ears you have pierced" could be an allusion to the ear-piercing ceremony described in Exodus 21:6 and Deuteronomy 15:16, by which a willing servant was bound to his master for life.

Verse 6 is quoted in Hebrews 10:5, but slightly differently: "Sacrifice and offering you did not desire, *but a body you prepared for me.*" This variation in wording could be because the Hebrews quote was taken from the Septuagint version of the Old Testament. The Septuagint was the translation by about seventy scholars of the Hebrew Old Testament into Greek. The idea seems to be that the "opening," or "piercing," of the ear consecrates all of the bodily faculties to the service of God.

David drives home his point by mentioning four different kinds of sacrifice: a slaughtered animal ("sacrifice"), a meal offering—a highly symbolic oblation ("offering"), a "burnt offering," and a "sin offering." The first two were required by Old Testament law to enter into a covenant relationship with God;

123

the second two to remain in it. But in contrast to these, David says, "Your law is within my heart" (verse 8). He meant he had an inner willingness to do the will of God. He was not just going through the motions. In Hebrew psychology, the heart was the seat of the personality. Truly godly Israelites like David anticipated what was spelled out in Jeremiah 31:33 about heart religion: " 'I will write [My law] on their hearts,' . . . declares the Lord."

"I proclaim righteousness in the great assembly," says David in verse 9, referring to Psalm 39:1, 2. In that psalm, he told how he had planned to keep quiet, he had been so conscious of his sin. But that hadn't worked, so now he says, "I do not seal my lips."

In verse 11, David is praying that God will not withhold His mercy from him, even as he, David, has not withheld his praise from God.

Verse 12 again sounds a note of desperation; David says he "cannot see"—that is, he cannot see any hope in life. But in verse 13 he turns to the Lord: "Be pleased, O Lord, to save me."

Verses 14-17 are repeated as Psalm 70, although they probably appeared in Psalm 70 before Psalm 40. At any rate, they became a song for the choir director in their own right.

"Be pleased, O Lord, to save me; O Lord, come quickly to help me" (verse 13). Someone has described this as a deep sigh. David is praying that the Lord not delay in His coming. This reminds us of the promise in Hebrews 10:37, that "He who is coming will come and will not delay"—meaning there the Second Coming of Christ. Another application is to the here and now. The God who comes to meet our needs does not delay.

124

PSALM 41

This psalm is the last in the first book. Each of the books ends with "Praise be to the Lord, the God of Israel, from everlasting to everlasting. Amen and Amen." This formula is found in this psalm as verse 13.

Psalm 41 is also one of the series, beginning with Psalm 38, written about the time of Absalom's conspiracy. We see in this psalm references to David's serious illness, and to his enemies as false friends. In psalms written after the rebellion of Absalom had been quelled, the allusions to false friends disappear. They were no longer there, because David had already dealt with them.

"Blessed is he who has regard for the weak," begins verse 1. In these first few verses, David mentions a visitor, possibly Zadok the priest, or Hushai, or maybe Ittai (2 Sam. 15:19, 21, 32-37). It seems to have been someone who had remained faithful to David during the rebellion, and now was come to visit the sick man. These first few verses may be the visitor's prayer for the sick man, David, or it may be David's prayer for this visitor.

We can always say the first part of verse 3 to any sick person: "The Lord will sustain [you]," but we can't always say the second part. Sometimes a person has a terminal illness, and it would be deceitful to say he or she is going to get better.

In verse 4, David links his dangerous illness to his sin. He sees a definite cause-and-effect relationship between the two events—something he also mentions in Psalms 38, 39, and 40.

Verse 6 says, "Whenever one comes to see me, he speaks falsely, while his heart gathers slander; then he goes out and spreads it abroad." Although we aren't sure if the "he" in this verse refers to the visitor of verses 1-3, whoever it is is a traitor. This verse might be a reference to Ahitophel, once a close friend and counselor of David, who betrayed him in the Absalom

125

uprising (2 Sam. 15:12, 31). David suffered greatly from that betrayal.

In John 13:18, Jesus quoted this verse to the disciples to let them know there was a traitor in their midst—Judas. However, Jesus carefully left off parts of the verse. He did not call Judas His close friend, or say He had trusted Him. No, Jesus knew from the beginning who Judas was and what he would do (John 6:70). But that painful, bitter experience of the betrayal of David had provided a type of the betrayal Jesus would experience at the hands of Judas.

"In my integrity you uphold me and set me in your presence forever," says David in verse 12. This is David's intimation of his hope of eternal life in the Lord's presence. He looked forward to the presence of the living God who had helped him all his life.

PSALM 42

This psalm begins Book II, which consists of Psalms 42—72. Books I and II were the original collection of the psalms by David and his singers. Although Book II ends with the statement, "This concludes the prayers of David son of Jesse," there are other psalms of David in the following books.

Books I and II have certain similarities. For example, the last psalm in each book is a prayer of a sick old man (cf. 41 and 71). The explanation may be found in 1 Chronicles 16:37-43. David organized two choirs, one in Zion, the other in Gibeon. Hence the need of two hymnbooks—books I and II of the Psalms.

Psalm 42 was not written by David, but rather is by the Sons of Korah, as the title tells us. It is a *"maskil,"* which scholars believe was a skillful teaching psalm. "For the director of music" indicates it was set to music.

Originally, Korah and his associates were Levites who aspired to the priesthood as well. God rebuked them for that, and they met death at God's hand in punishment for their rebellion (Num. 16:1-33). But here, Korah's descendants (apparently there were some left) repudiate their forefathers' actions. They write in this psalm and others that bear their name about their delight in God, and in the place where He has put His name.

As a Levite, the author of this particular psalm was one to whom was committed the service of the sanctuary. This particular "Son of Korah" may even have been a close associate of David. I say this because of the similarity of the language of this psalm to the language of David's psalms.

The occasion for the writing of Psalm 42 was probably the flight from Absalom. I think this Levite fled with David, and in this psalm expresses his feelings as a Levite in exile, a fish out of

127

water. His chief concern is his longing to get back to the center of his life as a Levite: the sanctuary.

"As the deer pants for streams of water, so my soul pants for you, O God," says the author in verse 1. The word "pants" here could be translated as "longs." The Levites repeatedly expressed their longing desire for a place to worship God during the early days of the Israelites' wanderings. They understood that God needed a permanent place of worship: it was only at the sanctuary that blood could be shed (Lev. 17:3-11). Once the Israelites crossed the Jordan River into the Promised Land, the Tabernacle was set up at Shiloh. Later, David brought the ark to Zion and set up the permanent place of worship, the sanctuary, there. That was the chief sanctuary, though there was an auxiliary one in Gibeon. All godly people living in ancient Israel longed for that dwelling place of God in Zion and wanted to go back there, no matter how far away they had gone.

Since Christ came, there is no longer the one place where God "dwells," but rather, God indwells each believer in the person of the Holy Spirit (John 14:16, 17). Jesus also said, "Where two or three come together in my name, there am I with them" (Matt. 18:20).

"My soul thirsts for God, for the living God," says the psalmist in verse 2. "When can I go and meet with God?" Again, he is expressing his longing for the sanctuary, the place where he could meet with the living God.

Verse 3 expresses the people's amazement that the king and his retinue would flee here to the other side of the Jordan from Absalom.

In verse 4, the writer reminisces about things of the past. Think of him as a Levite, one who has spent all his life ministering in the sanctuary. Now he is forced away from it because of his loyalty to David. Yet he really has no part in the rebellion; he longs only to go back to celebrate the sanctuary. Again, how different it is for us today, when God calls upon us to worship Him everywhere—"in spirit and in truth" (John 4:23).

"Deep calls to deep," says the writer in verse 7. He's talking about sorrows as if they were a tempestuous sea, or a torrential rain roaring down a ravine. The psalmist could hear the roar of his grief in his own soul.

"At night his song is with me," says the psalmist in verse 8. At night, all of our worries are magnified. But if we learn to turn to God and hope in Him—as Paul and Silas did in their midnight jail vigil (Acts 16:25)—then we will have songs in the night.

PSALM 43

Psalm 43 is either an appendix to Psalm 42, or else is part of it.

The occasion of both Psalms 42 and 43 was probably the rebellion raised by Absalom. No one would have reacted to a rebellion with more horror than would the descendants of Korah. They knew that their forefather had lost his life by rebelling against the authority God had placed in Moses and Aaron. These people were not about to rebel against God's anointed king.

Whereas Psalm 42 refers to God as the "God of my life" (verse 8), Psalm 43 refers to Him as the "God of my strength" (verse 2).

"Send forth your light and truth," pleads the writer in verses 3 and 4. He may be referring to the *Urim* and the *Thummim*, lights the high priest Aaron wore on his vest. Aaron used them to find God's guidance. At any rate, the psalmist is praying for God's guidance—back to God's "holy mountain."

In verse 4, the author says that God is his "joy and delight." How many of us can say that?

The psalm ends on a hopeful note, as the psalmist affirms his confidence that he will yet return to the sanctuary: "I will yet praise him, my Savior and my God" (verse 5).

PSALM 44

This is one of the psalms that is very true to life. We tend to pick nice, sweet verses out of the Psalms, such as verses 1 and 2 of this one. Then we come to verses 9-19, where we have a dirge, or lament, in which the psalmist bemoans God's seeming desertion of His righteous people. These are questions that everyone asks sooner or later. The Psalms help us think our way through these problems. They encourage us by telling us we aren't the only ones who've asked these questions.

The author of Psalm 44 was probably one of the "sons," or descendants, of Korah. Some believe the author was David, who composed this for the sons of Korah, in order that it might be sung by these Levitical singers.

I think the occasion of writing was a terrible, crushing defeat of the army of Israel. Verses 9-11 picture just such a military tragedy. Yet the nation had been faithful to the covenant (verse 22). Since the only time this could really be said of Israel was during David's reign, I believe this battle was an invasion by the Edomites while David was fighting elsewhere against the Syrians (2 Sam. 8:13, 14; 1 Kings 11:15). The army under Joab lost so many soldiers that he had to go back to attend to the burials. Ultimately, under David and Joab, the Israelites did slaughter the Edomites. But first they suffered a terrible defeat, described also in the title of Psalm 60.

The structure of the psalm shows us that it was more than a lament or a prayer; it was composed in such a way as to be sung or chanted. The structure is verses 1-8, and verses 9-16; then there is a dramatic change in tone and we have verses 17-19, and verses 20-28.

"We have heard with our ears, O God; our fathers have told us what you did in their days," says the psalmist in verse 1. He is striking a note sounded over and over again by Old Testament writers: when things were going wrong in their times,

131

they looked back at the history of God's dealings with the nation in the past. This means that in order for us to understand the Bible today, we have to know its history—meaning from Genesis to Revelation. We cannot just snatch verses from here and there and expect to be sustained in times of trouble. We must understand the sweep of God's dealings with humanity.

Deuteronomy 33:17 is a prediction of God acting in a military capacity. Here in verse 5 is a word picture that echoes that: a wild ox pushing its enemy backwards.

Verses 9-16 are a graphic description of a military defeat: "our adversaries have plundered us" (verse 10).

"You sold your people for a pittance," laments the writer in verse 12. But in fact, as we find out in the New Testament, there was a terrible price for our redemption (1 Pet. 1:18, 19). God pays everything; we pay nothing.

Verses 17-22 are a remarkable assurance of innocence. Not that the individuals or the nation were innocent of sin, but that the nation had not slipped into apostasy—the kind of sin which later in its history led to captivity. The God who gave them away was nevertheless the One who redeemed them—free of charge to them, but at great cost to Himself.

In verse 22 the psalmist is still appealing to the fact of their national innocence of apostasy. This seems to echo Job 31:24-28. The psalmist is saying, all this has come upon us, not because of our sin, but because we represent You. The enemy who attacks us is really striking at You. Paul uses this verse in Romans 8:36, giving it a slightly different twist. The psalmist says, what is happening to us is because we belong to You. Paul says, because we belong to You, this is what's happening to us. Yet, Paul adds, we are "more than conquerors through him who loved us."

When the psalmists speak of God as "sleeping" (verse 23), they are saying He seems to have suspended His exercise of justice and righteousness. "Why do you hide your face?" asks the writer (verse 24), in phraseology reminiscent of Psalm 35.

"Rise up and help us," pleads the writer. "Redeem us because of your unfailing love." Repeatedly the psalmist appeals to the Lord's own stake in you and me. He appeals to the character of God.

Is there trouble in your life? Do you feel God has let you down? Then do what the psalmist did: review evidences of God's loving-kindness and care to you. Begin with Calvary and move to your personal life. Then say, "Lord, that's who You've always been, that's who You are according to the testimony of my friends, that's who You are according to the testimony of the many people who've gone on before. I trust You to be my help now." This is faith. Our faith is nourished by developing a strong sense of God's acting in the past, so that we begin to count on Him to act consistently with His character in the future—again, and again, and again.

PSALM 45

Psalm 45 is a messianic psalm referring exclusively to the Messiah. The theme is the marriage of an anointed king, with verses 1-9 describing him, and verses 10-17 describing the bride.

The bridegroom is portrayed as very handsome and gracious. He's a conqueror. He's a divine person bearing the name of God and is seated on an everlasting throne. Who is this king?

In my judgment, the ancient Hebrew rabbis were correct in thinking that this king was the Messiah. We simply cannot fit any human beings into the descriptions this psalm gives—for instance, the reference to His universal dominion.

The one who wrote this psalm wrote under the inspiration of the Holy Spirit of God. Yet at the same time, the writer was still human. He wrote of what he knew, and his concept of the King and the bride is limited to a certain extent by his experience. His concept of sovereignty is kingship; of conquest, the girding on of a sword (verse 3). Nor, of course, does the Messiah have a literal "bride." Rather, that is a figure of speech for the Church. So bear in mind that while this psalm is an anticipation of the King who will reign forever in righteousness, it is at the same time poetry written by someone living in the days of David.

T. Ernest Wilson, in his book *The Messianic Psalms* Loizeaux Brothers), says this is the central messianic psalm, because it sets forth the messianic bridegroom. Psalm 91, says Wilson, portrays the prophet, Psalm 110 the priest, and Psalm 45 the King. In Mr. Wilson's view, this psalm gives a prophetic picture of the Lord Jesus coming out to reign after the marriage supper (described in Revelation 19). But when He comes He won't find the world waiting for Him, so He brings a sword, to put down rebellion, and a scepter, the symbol of His rule.

The title of this psalm indicates it is to be sung "To the tune of 'Lilies.'" This suggests to many scholars that the four psalms which have this title were to be used in the springtime, possibly at Passover. The winter is gone, and this is a time of celebration. Other scholars think the word "lilies" could have been a symbol for brides or bridesmaids.

The choir director in the title was probably the grandson of Samuel, a man named Heman, who was the director in Gibeon (1 Chron. 6:33).

"My heart is stirred . . . I recite my verses . . . my tongue is the pen of a skillful writer," proclaims verse 1, using every faculty to extol the glory of the King.

Verses 2-8 extol the King's moral glory: the excellency of His person, the equity of His rule, the eternity of His throne, and the ecstasy of His heart. Wilson says His moral glory was in perfect balance: gentleness and indignation, grace and truth, wisdom and simplicity. We, by contrast, are creatures of extremes. Even Moses, who was called the meekest person in all the earth, spoke rashly on one occasion. But in Christ, every grace was manifested in perfection.

The second item of glory was His official glory: the sword, the scepter, the throne, and the anointing. Each one has significance. He will gain the Kingdom not by the power of the gospel, but by conquest (Zech. 14; Rev. 19). The scepter, which represents power and authority, is the shepherd's rod. It becomes an iron rod for His enemies, but a golden scepter for His people. The idea of the golden scepter comes from the book of Esther.

Verse 7 refers to the anointing. You may recall that David was anointed to be king three times: first in the house of his father, Jesse; second, over the royal tribe of Judah when Saul was dead; and finally, over the twelve tribes at Hebron. The Lord Jesus was anointed twice while here on earth: first, at the beginning of His public ministry, and then again at the end. The anointing with "the oil of joy" in this verse could be a reference to His anointing of the Holy Spirit.

Verses 8 and 9 describe the King's glory as a mediator.

The second part of this psalm describes the beauty of the bride: first, her name; second, her attendants; third, her attire; and finally, the bridal procession. This is a beautiful and hopeful picture of the glorious purity of the Bride of Christ, the Church.

We have in the description of the king-bridegroom in this psalm the moral glory of Christ as a human, His official glory as a King, His divine glory as God, and His mediatorial glory as bridegroom to His Church.

PSALM 46

This psalm is the first of a series, consisting of Psalms 46, 47, and 48, that expresses confidence in God in time of national danger. In Psalm 46, the presence of the Lord God is seen as being in the midst of His people and the city. In Psalm 47, the Lord is viewed as King of the earth, a fact demonstrated by Israel's victory. Psalm 48 speaks of the safety of Zion, the city, as a result of the Lord's presence there. Psalm 48 is an almost complete reversal of Psalm 44, in which the psalmist bemoaned the apparent defeat of Israel's armies.

The title of Psalm 46 indicates that here, again, is a poem set to music to be used in the service of the sanctuary. We don't know whether the descendants of Korah actually wrote the psalm, or if it was written for them by those who served in the sanctuary at Gibeon.

The title notes something additional: "According to *alamoth.*" The word can be translated "virgins" or "maidens." Consequently, scholars believe this is a composition written for soprano voices. The Old Testament contains several references to all-women choirs, such as Exodus 15:20, 21, where Miriam led the women in singing, tambourine-playing, and dancing.

Some assign the occasion of this psalm to the time of Sennacherib's threat to Hezekiah (2 Chron. 32). Others, however, would assign it to the time of Jehoshaphat (2 Chron. 20:1, 17). I personally think it was written in the same time frame as Psalm 44, when Israel's armies suffered a crushing defeat. I believe this psalm describes the retreat. Another possible occasion of writing might be the events described in 2 Samuel 10, a glorious victory over the people who had drawn up in battle to defeat the people of Israel.

If we compare Psalm 44 with 2 Samuel 8 and 10, we can see why there was so much enthusiasm at the time of victory. The

137

Israelites were first dismayed at their setback; now we find them pouring out their hearts in praise to God.

The psalm is structured in three parts, each of which ends with "selah." The three parts are verses 1-3, verses 4-7, and verses 8-11. Because the last two stanzas end exactly the same way in verses 7 and 11, I think in all likelihood that the same refrain should be at the end of stanza one also (following verse 3). It was probably dropped in the copying of the psalm.

"God is our refuge and strength, a very present help in trouble," begins verse 1. This psalm is the source of Martin Luther's great hymn, "A Mighty Fortress Is Our God."

"There is a river whose streams make glad the city of God," says verse 4. The river is a symbol of tranquillity and serenity, of God's presence in His mighty Spirit. Its steadfastness stands in sharp contrast to the earthquakes, upheavals, and other natural convulsions described in verses 2 and 3.

Verse 5 describes how God is in the midst of the city. The idea of God dwelling in their midst was very precious to Israel. The Church today feels the same way.

"God will help her at break of day," continues verse 5. I think the writer was thinking of Exodus 14:27: "Moses stretched out his hand over the sea, and at daybreak the sea went back to its place." This verse is a description of the Egyptians' destruction in the Red Sea after the Israelites' safe crossing. In the mind of the psalmist, the morning was a time when God acts to deliver—after the long night of anxiety. In our own lives this is often true. We've gone through a night filled with worry, and in the morning we've seen evidence of God helping us.

I believe verses 8 and 9 are prophetic of the end of all things, when God "makes wars to cease to the ends of the earth." The Devil is the one who stirs up wars; but God hates war, and can bring it to an end.

"Be still, and know that I am God," is the ringing cry of verse 10. "I will be exalted among the nations, I will be exalted in the earth." Isaiah 2:11-17 bears similarity to this and verse 11, so that some scholars believe the early chapters of Isaiah reveal a close familiarity with Psalms 46—48.

PSALM 47

Psalm 47 is really a continuation of the previous psalm, Psalm 46. The clue to this is the word "selah," meaning to pause, at the end of Psalm 46. We naturally pause when we get to the end of a song (which this psalm is); since it tells us directly to pause, that must not be the end. Wherever we find the word "selah" as the last verse of any psalm, it's an indication that the following psalm is really part of the one we've just read.

This psalm celebrates the victory described in Psalm 46, a victory over a very menacing enemy.

The psalm's beautiful imagery says much about God as the one who is Lord of the universe. He is called "King of all the earth," and "Lord Most High." When we collect the various titles of God given in Psalms 46—48, we get quite an impressive insight into His awesome power and the fact that He has not yielded the earth to the evil one.

The psalm speaks prophetically of the Ascension. Having done what He came to do (described in Psalm 46), Messiah goes back up to where He came from—"God has ascended" (verse 5). This picture of God ascending was fulfilled literally in our Lord Jesus Christ (Eph. 4:8).

The psalm is structured in two strophes, with verse 5 as a connecting link.

After urging us to "shout to God with cries of joy" (verse 1), the psalm begins by reminding us "how awesome is the Lord Most High!" (verse 2). We need to be reminded of this need for reverence before the awesome God, we who sometimes tend to think carelessly of Him. People like Moses and David had a balanced sense of both God's awesomeness and His approachability. The writer to the Hebrews reminds us that "since we . . . have a high priest who is [able] to sympathize with our weak-

139

nesses, . . . let us then approach the throne of grace with confidence" (Heb. 4:15, 16).

God is "King of all the earth," proclaims the psalm, twice. God as King of the earth is a subject that occurs frequently in the Old Testament (Isa. 2:2; Zech. 14:9).

"God reigns over the nations," says verse 8, looking forward to the time of the Messiah. This verse will be fulfilled in the future when God reigns from Jerusalem.

Verse 9 makes it clear that this is a prophetic psalm. Abraham was the founder of the Jewish race, and we read about the inital promises God made to him in places like Genesis 12:2.

God is not always exercising control, but is nevertheless in control. He is waiting for the day when His purposes are going to be fulfilled. Only God Himself knows why He allows rebellion on the earth or in your heart. We do know that God is going to ultimately bring rebellion to an end and reign in righteousness through Jesus Christ.

PSALM 48

In Psalm 46, God is in the city, and the city is safe and the enemy defeated. Psalm 47 celebrates the triumph of God's glory. Now, in Psalm 48, we see the beauty of the dwelling-place of God—that is, the city. All these psalms are both lyrical (that is, set to music) and prophetic.

Verses 1 and 2 describe "the city of our God, his holy mountain . . . Mount Zion." "A city on a hill cannot be hidden," states Matthew 5:14. Jerusalem was in fact on a hill; it was and is a beautiful city, even though nearly two thousand years have passed. The ancient Israelites thought of it as the perfection of beauty, and had a fascination with it. We can read these verses in the light of the Millennial reign of Christ, and the holy city that is going to be rebuilt in Jerusalem (Isa. 2).

The city is symbolic of God's great power. When the enemies of Israel "saw her," they "fled in terror" (verse 5). Obviously, the enemies did not literally see Jerusalem, for that would have meant an invasion of the land. The "her" they saw was the power of God.

What do you think about when you go to church? The psalmist says in verse 9 that "within your temple, O God, we meditate on your unfailing love." This singing of songs of joy in verses 9-11 was because the city of Zion was safe, even though it had been threatened.

"For this God is our God for ever and ever; he will be our guide even to the end" (verse 14). The "end" here may refer to death; but even beyond that, God is our guide—for ever and ever. "God . . . gives us the victory [over death] through our Lord Jesus Christ" (1 Cor. 15:57).

PSALM 49

There is no specific occasion to which we can trace this psalm. It belongs to any age of the history of the people of Israel, though it probably was written during David's reign. It was incorporated into this second Book, which was used as a songbook at Gibeon.

Some have described this psalm as the most perfect development of Hebrew thought on the deepest problem of existence. It affirms clearly the doctrine of the future state of compensation, and assures the reader that for those who don't know God, there really is no future at all. By contrast, though the righteous may have nothing in this life, nevertheless for them there is a future. This psalm sounds very much like the book of Job, and also like Psalms 37 and 73.

The psalm begins in verses 1-4 with a lofty proclamation, a request for people to listen.

"Why should I fear when evil days come?" asks the psalmist in verse 5. He goes on to describe the wicked, and says that no matter how rich they are, they can't prevent death: no one can "redeem the life of another" (verse 7). Death for us believers has been neutralized by Christ's death. We will emerge from the grave in new bodies. Or, it may even be our own generation that won't see death at all, but will be caught up at the Rapture of the Church. The point the psalmist is making, though, is that death is like a jailer, out of whose power one human can't "redeem," or rescue, another. The only redeemer is God Himself.

Human beings are "like beasts that perish" (verse 12). But if we know the Savior, then physical death is simply an interlude, a door leading into heaven.

In verse 14, death is pictured as a shepherd herding all humanity to the grave.

"But God will redeem my soul from the grave; he will surely

take me to himself" is verse 15's triumphant assertion. We can use it as our own testimony. If the Lord does not return, my body will eventually go down to the grave. But God will redeem me, body and soul (1 Cor. 15:42).

PSALM 50

This is the first of the psalms attributed to Asaph, and the only one of his in Book II. Psalms 73—83 of Book III are all attributed to him. Asaph was a musician, a prophet, and a "seer" (2 Chron. 29:30) serving in the sanctuary at Zion. He lived a long time. He may have been David's age at the time he was inducted as a musician; we don't know. But he did outlive David; he lived some years after the coronation of Solomon.

All of Asaph's psalms are characterized by solemnity and what could be called a lofty judicial tone. In some of them, such as this one, God is seen as speaking personally to the people. Another interesting feature of Asaph's psalms is that he uses the word *El* for God—the singular, rather than the plural *Elohim*. He seems to do this deliberately, to express God's manifold characteristics.

The central idea in this psalm is the inadequacy of mere outward sacrifices, as opposed to heart involvement and purity of life. This is especially significant coming as it does from one who spent his entire life in the sanctuary.

The structure of the psalm is verses 1-6, the introduction of God; then two main strophes in which God speaks, verses 7-15 and verses 16-23. Seeing a psalm's structure like this is helpful to us in analyzing and understanding it.

"The Mighty One, God, the Lord, speaks and summons the earth," says verse 1, using three names of the deity: *El, Elohim,* and *Jehovah*. The use of these three names helps set the psalm's tone of deep solemnity, as well as showing God's completeness. *El* is God in His might. *Elohim* is God in the manifold attributes of His being. *Jehovah* was the covenant name God gave to Himself.

Verses 2-6 describe a scene reminiscent of Mt. Sinai: "a fire devours before him, and around him a tempest rages" (verse 3). In this psalm, God is going to speak to Israel again as His

144

covenant people, as He did in Moses' time (Exod. 24:7, 15-18).

Verses 7-17 give the main thought of the psalm. God calls the people together and tells them He is going to testify against them. He does this on the grounds that He is their God, the One with whom their ancestors had made a covenant. Your sacrifices, says God, are well and good. They are important. But mere sacrifice without inner reality is unacceptable. Throughout the Old Testament we hear this emphasis on an inner approach to God: Psalm 40:6-8; Psalm 51:16, 17; Isaiah 1:11-15; Jeremiah 7:22, 23; Hosea 6:6; Micah 6:6-8; Mark 12:33. But habitually in ancient Israel they adhered to the sacrifical system even when their hearts were far from God. We Christians don't have much to brag about today, either. We find it just as easy to keep the machinery of the church going even when we may be neglecting very seriously the important commandments of the gospel. Take, for example, those that have to do with love of our brothers and sisters in the Lord, and in general toward our neighbors. The heart of Christian living is to do the will of God from the heart. May God help us think about our true priorities as Christians.

In verses 16-23, God speaks to a different kind of people— the wicked. In the Old Testament, the wicked were a special class. David never calls himself wicked. He distinguishes between himself and the characteristically wicked, even though he almost exhausts the Hebrew vocabulary in finding words to describe his own sinfulness.

The first characteristic of the wicked is inner alienation from God: "You hate my instruction and cast my words behind you" (verse 17).

Because God did not immediately punish sin, these wicked people came to the awful conclusion that He was like them— indifferent to, or even approving of, sin (verse 21). But God will swiftly disabuse that notion: "I will rebuke you," He says. These verses describe the holiness of God, not a very popular notion today, when we instead prefer to think of God as a Santa Claus in the sky. God is loving; and He is also light. He's holy.

145

PSALM 51

Psalm 51, a very beautiful and powerful psalm, has occupied the attention of fine Bible students from time immemorial. It tells us a great deal about the character of God, as well as about the nature of humanity. It is the first of the seven penitential psalms.

The occasion for Psalm 51 is indicated in the title: "A psalm of David. When the prophet Nathan came to him after David had committed adultery with Bathsheba." This incident is described in 2 Samuel 12:1-14. The prophet Nathan pointed the finger at David, and David said, "I have sinned against the Lord" (2 Sam. 12:13). This confession of David's was a most remarkable one. There was not another king anywhere in the world in those days who would actually have confessed to having taken another man's wife and then killing that man. Behavior like that was regarded as the divine right of kings. But David's essential godliness is revealed in the fact that, when confronted with his sin, he admitted it.

In this psalm, we read the details of David's confession. Verses 1 and 2 are a prayer for mercy and forgiveness; verses 3-6, confession; verses 7-12, a prayer for inner cleansing; verses 13-17, a prayer for God to preserve him; and verses 18 and 19, a prayer for Zion.

"Have mercy on me, O God," prays David in verse 1, "according to your unfailing love." David uses two very strong words here: "mercy," or the quality of graciousness, which is kindness, and "unfailing love," an even stronger word referring to the abundance of tender sympathy with which a mother assures her child of her love.

"Blot out my transgressions," continues David in the same verse. He's asking God to erase his transgressions, to wipe them clean. The plural, "transgressions," is significant, because David committed more than adultery. The adultery was

146

crowned with the most heinous sin of all: David plotted with Joab, and then murdered the woman's husband, Uriah. This murder was the worst of the sins, the most desperately wicked thing that anyone could have done in Israel, and David's prayer indicates that he knew this.

In verse 2, David is asking for deliverance from the imputation of guilt. He uses three different words for his sin, all with slightly different meanings. "Transgression" is a violation of God's law, "iniquity" means inner depravity, and "sin" means defilement. Transgressions are like a mighty load which must be taken away. His iniquity, he prays, will not be charged against him. Sin is to be covered. When David prays, "wash me," he's using the same verb used in Leviticus 13:6-24 of lepers. In the Bible, leprosy was a symbol of inner defilement. So David is asking God to wash him in order to remove his leprous condition of defilement.

All that David had to offer to God was his confession (verse 3). There's nothing more we need do than confess our sins (1 John 1:9).

When David says in verse 4, "Against you, you only have I sinned," he means that whatever guilt he had toward people was nothing compared to his offense against God. What he did was sin because God had declared it so. It wasn't against society's rules at the time; any of David's contemporary kings in the Middle East at that time would have been amazed at his confession of sin.

"You are . . . justified when you judge," continues verse 4. David is saying to God, in effect, whatever You do to me is right because I have earned Your punishment. David justified God by admitting that he had no hope whatsoever but in God's free forgiveness. Having said that, he found that God justified him by taking away the guilt of his sin.

In verse 5, David is speaking about his own inward sin. He is not saying that his mother was a sinner or that the act of conceiving him was immoral.

"Surely you desire truth in the inner parts; you teach me wisdom in the innermost place" (verse 6). This verse echoes the description of the godly in Psalm 15:2, the person who may live on God's holy hill.

"Cleanse me with hyssop, and I will be clean," says David in

147

verse 7. This is a beautiful prayer; David was a great poet even when he was in great distress. Hyssop, mentioned in Exodus 12:22, Leviticus 14:6, and Numbers 19:18, eventually came to stand for blood and the whole cleansing ceremony. David was praying, in effect, that God would cleanse him by blood sacrifice. We are not sure if David understood this or not, but he was anticipating the death of our Lord Jesus, apart from whose death there is no cleansing from sin.

"Do not take your Holy Spirit from me," prays David in verse 11. He's thinking of how the Spirit of the Lord left Saul, and praying he won't be rejected, as Saul was.

In verse 12, David prays that the joy of God's salvation will be restored to him. Psalm 32 talks about David having lost his joy.

In verses 16 and 17, David expresses one of the most profound truths of the Old Testament: God wants us to put the emphasis where it belongs—obedience first. If you come to God brokenhearted because of some sin in your life, then come in assurance that God will not despise this.

Some call the prayer for Zion in verses 18 and 19 a liturgical addition. But I think that David's use of the word *Elohim* for God throughout the psalm explains the prayer at the end and shows it to be an inherent part of the psalm. David felt that he as king had jeopardized Israel's covenant relationship with God by his sin. So instead of addressing himself to Jehovah, the God of the covenant, David approaches Him as Elohim. In these verses at the end, David tacitly acknowledges his fear that the foundations of the nation had been shaken by his personal sin.

PSALM 52

While Psalm 51 was written long after David had been made king, Psalm 52 is one of several psalms that hark back to David's earlier days—the days of exile when Saul was hounding him. I'm inclined to think that those who put the psalms in this order did so to contrast a truly godly person who committed sin (Psalm 51) with truly wicked people (the theme of Psalms 52—54).

The truly wicked person referred to in this psalm was Doeg, who not only betrayed Ahimelech to Saul for helping David, but personally murdered Ahimelech and eighty-five other priests, plus their families (1 Sam. 21:7; 22:9-19). David was remarkably restrained in this psalm, considering Doeg's terrible character.

"Why do you boast of evil, you mighty man?" asks David in verse 1. He goes on to describe the plotting, deceit, and falsehood of Doeg, who had, in fact, inflamed Saul's paranoia by telling Saul he had seen David, but then lying and adding quite a few other things to the tale.

But David is confident that God's loving-kindness will prevail, not evil. Ultimately, "God will bring you [Doeg] down to everlasting ruin" (verse 5).

Meanwhile, "I am like an olive tree flourishing in the house of God," says David. His words are a great personal affirmation of faith in a time when terrible distress and evil seemed to prevail.

PSALM 53

The same theme as Psalm 52 runs through this psalm: the despicable activity of the evil person who does not know God. I think it's this similarity of theme that caused Psalm 53 to be placed here, even though it was actually written later than Psalm 52. Psalm 53's reference to "Zion" shows that it was written after David had become king, because Zion did not become his city until then.

Psalm 53 is also a kind of reworking of Psalm 14: verse 1 is very similar. "The fool says in his heart, 'There is no God.'" Here David is again describing the kind of wicked people who populated Saul's court. As a consequence of turning away from God, they became corrupt and committed abominable injustices (verses 1b-4).

I think this psalm was placed here in order to link it with Doeg, and also to show that the reason for the abominations he and his kind committed was their refusal to acknowledge God.

PSALM 54

The occasion of the writing of Psalm 54 is given as part of the title: "When the Ziphites had gone to Saul and said, 'Is not David hiding among us?'"

This incident is further described in 1 Samuel 23:14-19. David had just escaped betrayal at the hands of the people of Keilah, and had fled to the Desert of Ziph. There his best friend, Jonathan, had come to offer him encouragement. The friendship between Jonathan and David is very beautiful, because, you see, Jonathan was Saul's son. Yet Jonathan had a magnificent and great heart. He was willing to accept David as the next king, and he says so again to David in this meeting at Horesh in the Desert of Ziph: "You will be king over Israel, and I will be second to you." Jonathan told David, in effect, to trust God, and if you do, He will deliver you from my father.

Then the two friends made a covenant; this was the last time David saw Jonathan.

I love the way the Spirit of God has put this: "the two of them made a covenant before the Lord"; then "the Ziphites went up to Saul. . . ." It's as if God is saying, yes, the Ziphites are going to betray you, but you have a friend who sticks closer than a brother, and he is the king's own son.

This is the background for the psalm.

This triad, Psalms 52, 53, and 54, corresponds to Psalm 11, the first of the psalms written when David was fleeing Saul; Psalm 12, when he's distressed by the terrible chaos in the kingdom; and Psalm 14, where he describes the terrible kind of people who came to power when Saul was king.

151

PSALM 55

In Psalm 55, I think we jump ahead again to events later in David's life: in particular, David's betrayal by his trusted counselor, Ahithophel, during Absalom's rebellion (2 Sam. 15:12, 31-37). Because of the sin in his life, David had lost his grip on the country as its king, and his own son Absalom took the opportunity to stage an uprising. Ahithophel, who had been David's friend, became one of the conspirators. In the account in Samuel, it seems David's only cause for concern was that because of Ahithophel's sharp and shrewd advice, Absalom might actually succeed. But in this psalm, David pours out his soul, and we learn how he was so torn by this betrayal of a friend that he could scarcely bear it. Jonathan was long gone, and Ahithophel seems to have taken the place of Jonathan as the friend of David. Yet he betrayed him. David, who was such an intensely loyal, true, loving person, was incapable of understanding what could have led a person to do such a terribly wicked thing.

David expresses his pain in the first several verses: "Listen to my prayer, O God. . . . My heart is in anguish within me" (verses 1, 4).

In verse 6, David is feeling very frightened and wishes he could fly away from his troubles on wings like a dove.

"Confuse the wicked, O Lord, confound their speech," prays David in verse 9, echoing his own words in 2 Samuel 15:31. In fact, God did confound Ahithophel's wisdom through the wisdom of David's counterspy, Hushai (2 Sam. 17:5-14).

Verses 10 and 11 describe the breakdown of law and order that happened in the wake of Absalom's attempted takeover. We see the same thing in the modern world: when a government is shaken and loses control over the people, crime increases.

In verses 12-14, David cries out about the pain of his betray-

152

al—by a friend. "A man like myself, my companion, my close friend," he calls Ahithophel in verse 13. It is this closeness that makes the betrayal so unbearable.

In verse 15, David gives vent to his fury: "Let death take my enemies by surprise."

"I call to God, and the Lord saves me," says David in verse 16. God did deliver him (2 Sam. 17, 18).

"My companion attacks his friends," says David of Ahithophel in verse 20. "He violates his covenant." A covenant in those days was a pact between friends. David and Jonathan had a covenant. After the death of Jonathan, David sent for Mephibosheth to be kind to him for Jonathan's sake. That must have been part of the covenant. David and Ahithophel apparently had a covenant, too, although we don't know the terms of it. But Ahithophel certainly violated it.

The important thing is not to become embittered by those who let you down or even betray you when you had expected better from them. Forgiving them even when they do not confess is far better in the long run for you. Still, there's nothing more painful than to be betrayed by a friend.

PSALM 56

The title of Psalm 56 tells us it's a psalm of David, "to the tune of 'A Dove on Distant Oaks,'" which was probably a particular tune at that time.

The title also gives us the occasion of writing: "When the Philistines had seized him in Gath," an event recorded in 1 Samuel 21:10-15. Gath was a Philistine capital. David so greatly feared Saul and all his agents, who seemed to be everywhere in Israel and Judah, that he felt there was no safe place to go. So he fled to Gath—which was like getting out of the frying pan into the fire. When he realized his danger, David disguised his sanity in front of the Philistines. David must been a very convincing actor to pull this off—another of the many talents of this extremely gifted person.

"Be merciful to me, O God, for men hotly pursue me," David prays in verse 1.

"In God I trust; I will not be afraid. What can mortal man do to me?" is David's expression of confidence in verse 4 (and again in verse 11). This verse is reproduced in Hebrews 13:6.

In verse 7, David asks God to deal with the Philistines.

"Record my lament; list my tears on your scroll," says David in verse 8. David was a traveler, and in those days, travelers carried water with them in leather bottles. They very carefully preserved the water lest it leak out. So David uses that image to portray God as preserving every tear he shed, every lament he uttered. In times of distress, many people are tempted to think God has forgotten all about them. But David knew better. God is aware of us—so much so that He can be said to "list" our tears. He's kept a record of our sorrows and griefs so that, someday He can wipe away every tear (Rev. 21:4).

These are beautiful images, full of faith. David was one of the greatest poets who ever lived, as well as one of the greatest saints.

"God is for me," states verse 9, and Romans 8:31 echoes it: "If God is for us, who can be against us?"

In verses 12 and 13, David says he is under vows to God (see Num. 30:2) to present thank offerings because of God's deliverance. This tells us that David wrote this psalm after he had escaped from Gath.

PSALM 57

This psalm, which is a companion to Psalm 142, was written by David "When he had fled from Saul into the cave," says the title. We don't know which cave it was—Adullam in 1 Samuel 22:1, Engedi in 1 Samuel 24:1-3, or a cave mentioned in 1 Samuel 26. Adullam provided a temporary refuge, but not a permanent one. The prophet Gad told David to get out of it, probably because he could so easily be trapped there, sealed off by Saul and his troops.

I am inclined to think it was the cave of Adullam. In any case, David felt trapped, as the tone of this psalm indicates. A cave is a terrible place to hide. "Have mercy on me, O God, have mercy on me," David cries in verse 1. He felt he was being hotly pursued (verse 3).

What bothered David was not merely the persecution by Saul, but the company he, David, was forced to keep during his exile. In verse 4 he says, "I am in the midst of lions; I lie among . . . men whose teeth are spears and arrows, whose tongues are sharp swords." We tend to think of David's band as good people who were oppressed, but any guerrilla movement or outlaw group also attracts a criminal element.

First Samuel 24:4-7, when David's men exultingly urge him to kill Saul, shows that these men were far more murderous than appears on the surface. It would have been easy for him to rationalize their anger against Saul, but David was a godly person who refused to lift even a hand against God's anointed. The same thing happened in 1 Samuel 26:8-11.

His calling these people "lions" shows that they caused David deep anxiety. He was the sweet singer of Israel (verses 7, 8), a musician, poet, and sensitive soul, surrounded by this tough crowd. In some respects, David's experience here was like the Apostle Paul's in prison. It must have been very difficult for Paul, such an highly educated and sensitive person of gracious manners, to spend years locked up with the tough criminal class of the Roman Empire.

David's refusal to allow his men to kill Saul must have been a continual source of agitation to them. Later, when they suffered a setback at the hand of a group of raiders in Ziklag, his men turned viciously on David (1 Sam. 30:1-25). I think the only reason they did not kill him was that God prevented them. David was also an extremely wise person. He knew how to handle people, and he was able to turn away the wrath of his band of exiles on this occasion.

In the midst of this group of toughs, though, David still takes comfort in his God, his music, and his poetry (verses 9, 11).

PSALM 58

Psalm 58, the title tells us, was to be sung "to the tune of 'Do Not Destroy.'" Both the preceding and the following psalms were written during the time of David's flight from Saul; so it's possible that this one also applies to the period when David was greatly distressed because of persecution by Saul and his aides.

On the other hand, because he addresses the "rulers" and judges of the people in this psalm, it could have been written shortly after David became king in Israel. He was distressed with the quality of justice in the land when he returned from years of exile and became king. Under Saul, moral conditions had deteriorated terribly (see 2 Sam. 2 and 3).

Another possibility is that David, before he was forced to flee Saul's court, was lamenting the low, low moral tone which he saw then.

"Do you rulers indeed speak justly? Do you judge uprightly among men?" begins verse 1. These are rhetorical questions. Their answer is obvious. But to drive home his point, David gives the answer in the next verse anyway: "No, in your heart you devise injustice" (verse 2)

Verses 3-5 describe these evil people, sitting in a place of authority, yet hopelessly corrupt. Verse 3 describes them as liars. There's quite an emphasis in the Psalms on the awfulness of lies. The truth about lies and liars is fully developed in the New Testament, where we read that Satan is the father of lies, and his followers are those who do not know the truth. Everyone who follows the Lord, however, is following the truth. When people become Christians they no longer adhere to the lie of the devil, but have come to the One who is the Truth. People who go on telling lies are revealing by their behavior who is in control of their lives.

David uses a picture of lions in verse 6 to describe these fierce, devouring people—a picture he often paints. He continues his evoking of God's curse on these wicked people in more graphic language: may they be "like a slug melting away ... like a stillborn child [that does] not see the sun" (verse 8). The ultimate fate of the wicked is that they will be "swept away" (verse 9).

Verses 10 and 11 remind us again that it's God who takes vengeance, not David. "The righteous will be glad when they are avenged" (verse 10). In all the years that Saul hounded him, David never lifted up his hand against Saul.

"Surely there is a God who judges the earth" (verse 11). The lament of many today is that there is no justice—that God seems to be blind to what's happening on earth. Here the psalmist says, No, that's not true. When the wicked are judged, people will recognize that it pays to serve God. The wicked will not get away with it forever.

We can use this psalm to pray for those in authority today, that they will judge uprightly and speak righteously.

PSALM 59

This psalm is set to the same tune as the preceding two, Psalms 57 and 58, the tune of "Do Not Destroy," as the title says.

The title also notes the occasion of writing: "When Saul had sent men to watch David's house in order to kill him." Saul, in his mounting jealousy, had made up his mind to kill David, who was by then his own son-in-law. But Jonathan warned David. Jonathan also pled with Saul on David's behalf, got Saul to take an oath not to harm David, and once more brought David before Saul. But Saul went back on his word and flung his spear at David, trying to pin him to the wall. David escaped, but Saul was so enraged he posted a guard on David's house with orders to kill him. Michal, David's wife and Saul's own daughter, helped David escape, and he fled to hide with Samuel at Ramah.

"Deliver me from my enemies, O God," prays David in verse 1.

In this psalm, as in others written during the days when he was being pursued by Saul, David protests his innnocence (verse 3). We don't find this in his later psalms. During his pursuit by Absalom he knew full well his guilt.

The "wicked traitors" of verse 5 probably refers to those whom Saul employed in an attempt to get David. These people went around "snarling like dogs" (verse 6). This is a picture of a predatory, Middle Eastern dog, a creature more like our idea of a jackal or a wolf than a beagle or a poodle. David sees his would-be killers as a pack of wild dogs, sniffing and snarling around the city for something to devour. We don't know how much time elapsed from the night Michal let David down out of the window to the time he escaped to Samuel. But it sounds like he hung around long enough to see the assassins return again and again to his house, bloodhounds trying to pick up his scent.

"But I will sing of your strength, in the morning I will sing of your love," says David in verse 16. David is singing about God's love in preserving him. We can use this and verse 17 in our own prayer lives: "O my strength, I sing praise to you; you, O God, are my fortress, my loving God."

PSALM 60

Psalms 60 and 44 are closely connected. While David, as king, was gone fighting one battle, the Edomites invaded the land and the Israelites suffered a terrible military defeat. So many Israelites had been killed that David had to come back to help Joab bury the dead. Then, together, they routed the Edomite forces in what became a stunning victory, and the Edomites became subservient to David (2 Sam. 8:13; 1 Kings 11:15, 16).

"You have rejected us, O God," is verse 1's cry of military defeat, much like verse 9 of Psalm 44.

The reference in verse 3 to wine is a figure of speech. David is saying their defeat at the hands of their enemies is a bitter cup—it's "staggering."

Verses 6-8 express David's conviction that God was going to defeat the enemy, which in fact He did. David uses more figures of speech to describe the different countries. If we look at a map of Bible times, perhaps one in the back of our Bible, we can see that Canaan was divided among the twelve tribes of Israel. Gilead and Manasseh (verse 7) are what we today would call the East Bank of the Jordan, or Jordan. "Ephraim," says God, "is my helmet, Judah my scepter."

Moab, Edom, and Philistia were the ancient enemies of Israel, and they are described in very uncomplimentary images. Moab, for instance, is God's "washbasin." This is quite a comedown, considering that the people of Moab were marked by "overweening pride and conceit . . . and insolence" (Isa. 16:6).

We can focus on verse 12 for our own prayer life: "With God we will gain the victory."

162

PSALM 61

Psalm 61 is part of a little package consisting also of Psalms 3 and 4, which echoes David's experiences when he was in flight from Absalom. We know this because verse 4 refers to the sanctuary ("tent"). This psalm is unlike others in this collection of Book II, some of which were written during David's persecution at the hands of Saul.

The title tells us it was to be sung to the accompaniment of "stringed instruments" (*neginah* is the Hebrew word). Because this was set to music there's the musical pause, "selah" (verse 4).

"Hear my cry, O God; listen to my prayer," is a good way to begin a prayer (verse 1). David begins more than one of his psalms this way, as if he were appealing to God to hear him. He does this particularly in his later psalms, when his guilty conscience over the Uriah affair causes him to feel less assured than when he was younger. The sins he committed cast a long shadow over his life.

"Lead me to the rock that is higher than I," prays David in verse 2, referring to Zion. This was the fortress he had captured, and which was now held by his enemies.

"You have been my refuge," in verse 3, means that God had preserved David from death at the hands of his enemies.

David's reference to "vows" in verse 5 may mean vows such as he made in Psalm 51 or any of the penitential psalms.

In verses 6 and 7, David expresses his confidence that he as the king would be spared. He was looking beyond the immediate deliverance from Absalom to endless life. It may be that in the shadow of death he saw clearly that the God whom he loved and served would preserve him forever. These verses are also prophetic of the Messiah, the royal king, of whom David saw himself as a representative.

In verse 8, David combines the idea of eternity with the idea of daily existence: "Then will I ever sing praise to your name and fulfill my vows day after day."

The psalm contains many lovely verses for use in our own prayer life: verses 1, 2, 3, 4, and 8.

PSALM 62

This psalm was prepared to be sung, and is therefore dedicated "To Jeduthun," who was one of three choir directors mentioned in 2 Chronicles 35:15. Jeduthun, formerly called "Ethan," was more than a song leader. He was also a prophet—the "king's seer."

Although David undoubtedly wrote this during the time of his exile from Jerusalem, it expresses more composure than other psalms of that period of flight from Absalom. David's position was very shaky. His kingdom, indeed his very life was threatened because of the disarray following his own moral breakdown. Yet he writes this psalm expressing his confidence in God, using some of the most beautiful and poignant language in literature.

The psalm is structured in three parts of four verses each, marked at the end by "Selah": verses 1-4, 5-8, and 9-12. If we read this psalm in light of Psalm 39, we conclude there are internal similarities. Psalm 39 is also linked by content to Psalm 38, one of the penitential psalms.

"My soul finds rest in God alone," begins David in verse 1. In verse 2, he speaks of God as his rock, meaning God is his solid foundation. It's significant that the first psalm in which David refers to the Lord as a rock, Psalm 18, is entitled, "When the Lord delivered him from the hand of all his enemies." David's life, his "path," was a dangerous one, especially in the times of flight, whether from Saul or from Absalom. But the Lord was his security.

Verse 2 becomes a refrain which is repeated in verse 6.

In verses 3 and 4, David expresses his dismay at liars. David was a very truthful person and simply could not comprehend the deceitfulness of his enemies (Psalm 28:3; Psalm 55:20, 21).

"Find rest, O my soul, in God alone" (verse 5) is an intensely practical expression. Militarily speaking, David didn't have a chance. Absalom's army not only outnumbered his, but contained most of the really good generals. Yet in spite of these overwhelming odds, David was trusting in God. And as things worked out, David's army did defeat Absalom's.

David urges the people to trust in God, too; to "pour out [their] hearts to him" (verse 8), an expression that refers to earnest prayer such as Hannah offered before the Lord (1 Sam. 1:15).

Verse 9 is very similar to Psalm 49:2. David means the wicked are shallow, light, empty, worthless people.

"One thing . . . two things . . . " in verses 11 and 12 is a little formula (Job 33:14; 40:5). David is speaking in these verses about an inward revelation to his own conscience. He says he has learned two lessons: one, that God is strong; two, that God is loving. The God of power had lovingly preserved David's life. Not only is mercy made available because God is powerful, but retribution also is. God is just as well.

These things that David learned and the example of his relationship with the Lord are of permanent value to us.

PSALM 63

Psalm 63 is one of a class of psalms that is very similar to the preceding psalm. Like it, this psalm took place while David was running from Absalom. The term "desert of Judah" is very broad. Here, I think it refers to the wilderness David fled through on the way to his rendezvous with Absalom. David spent two days in this wilderness; then, on the third or fourth day, the battle took place that terminated Absalom's rebellion (2 Sam. 17:16, 22, 29; 18:6-9, 14).

Psalm 63 also contains ideas similar to Psalm 61. In Psalm 61, David prays that he may take refuge in the shelter of God's wings; in Psalm 63, in the shadow of God's wings he sings for joy. Similar veins run through psalms dealing with the same experience.

"O God, you are my God," begins David in verse 1. He uses the name *El* for God rather than *Jehovah*. *El* is a name signifying "Almighty God," and David used it to invoke God's power. We do the same thing today. Sometimes we may address God as "Our Father." But if we are up against a very difficult situation, we may address God as "O God, Creator of all things, Thou Almighty God" and so on. We wish to invoke the power of the God who can do for us what we cannot do for ourselves.

Verse 1 tells us that David's journey was a tough one. He left Jerusalem, went up the bridge called the Mount of Olives, and set out for Jericho. It was a "dry and weary land where there [was] no water," and David felt his own soul corresponded to the desert around him.

Verse 2's reference to "power and glory" is about the ark of the covenant (1 Sam. 4:1-11; Psalm 78:61).

In verses 3-5, David says the loving-kindness of God is better than life itself.

David learned so much in the night (verse 6). In more than one place he tells us that he often prayed and meditated at night

(Psalm 4:4; Psalm 16:7). What he meditated on was God—God's help and protection (verse 7). "I stay close to you," said David of his sheltering, upholding God (verse 8).

"Those who seek my life will be destroyed" (verse 9). David is talking about people like Absalom and Ahithophel and all those who pursued him. "The mouths of liars will be silenced," David concludes in verse 11. Lying was one of the distinctive characteristics of those out to get David.

PSALM 64

Psalm 64 seems to have been written about the same time as Psalms 62 and 63, the time of Absalom's rebellion.

We can't be completely sure of that later date, though; it's possible that the psalm dates from the earlier part of David's life when it was the aides of Saul who were devising lies against him. We have noted repeatedly that in his pursuit of David, Saul was driven to a frenzy by the lies and plots of his principal aides, his cabinet. I think this cabinet capitalized on Saul's hatred of David. They fed it to the point where Saul became a psychotic killer, obsessed with his insane desire to do David in.

On the other hand, because of its position in the collection I think Psalm 64 probably does speak of the time of Absalom's rebellion; specifically, the days immediately preceding David's flight. It seems to give the feeling of those days when David lay desperately ill and the secret council of evildoers took full advantage of the situation. They would actually come in, check up on him, and go out and report that he was a goner. This psalm gives us another angle on those days: these iniquitous people were a sore trial to David.

PSALM 65

Let's think of this psalm not only as a poem, but as a word from God.

The psalm is described in the title as having been prepared for the choir director. As we go through the psalm, we conclude that parts of it—verses 6 and 7, for instance—were chanted by a chorus in response to what was said by someone else. We have this in cantatas and other choir arrangements today. One group will stop and a chorus will be taken up by others.

This psalm was first sung in the choir at Gibeon, Gibeon being the second of the two choirs David set up. Book II of the Psalms was used by the Gibeon choir.

This is one of a series of psalms David wrote after the rebellion caused by Absalom. Psalms 62 and 63 are more intense, but this psalm also echoes some of David's experiences at that time.

In verse 1, David speaks of his silence: "Praise awaits you, O God, in Zion." This is the silence of the soul filled with thoughts that are simply too big for it to utter. David was overwhelmed, so he sat in silence, meditating. Then the silence was ended in praise and the performing of the vow. Everything that follows verse 1 is praise.

"O you who hear prayer," David addresses God in verse 2. The God who hears is a vivid contrast to idols, which don't (Psalm 115:6). Knowing that God hears can inspire us to speak.

"When we were overwhelmed by sins, you atoned for our transgressions" (verse 3). The emphasis in this sentence, because of the position of the pronoun, is on *you*. *You*, O God, atoned for our transgressions.

In verse 4, David expresses a certain amount of apprehension about whether he will ever get back to Zion.

In verse 5, David speaks of God as his savior. He's thinking

170

primarily of salvation from death at the hands of Absalom. If we collect all these references in the Psalms to salvation, we can see how they are linked with times of great peril in David's life.

The chorus comes in at verses 6 and 7. David thinks of God's power over nature and says He has the same power over people (see also Isa. 17:12-14).

David speaks in verse 8 about the morning and evening singing for joy because God quells the roaring of the sea and the turmoil of the nations. David is probably thinking here of the Red Sea. He is likening his own deliverance to the deliverance of the Israelites from Egypt.

"You care for the land and water it," begins David in a beautiful section of nature poetry from verses 9-13. David had a sense of wonder at nature. He did not consider the earth something to be plundered, but a creation of God to be marveled at and used wisely.

PSALM 66

Psalm 66 is not attributed to David in the title. But some psalms with no title at all probably were written by David anyway. For instance, we know Psalm 2 was because the Book of Acts quotes it and attributes it to him. Other unattributed psalms we can attribute to David because of internal evidence. It's quite conceivable that this psalm was written by David.

The psalm was written for public recitation in the sanctuary; so some Bible students believe it was composed by a Levite, along with Psalm 67. We don't know.

The occasion seems to be a great deliverance from enemies, following a bad battering. This leads me to believe it's one of a class of psalms including Psalms 44, 60, and 67. These celebrate the Israelites' victory over the Edomites after an initial defeat. Another reason I come to this conclusion is the presupposition I began with: that Book II of the Psalms was put together during David's reign. I see this as the second of two hymnbooks used during the early years of the monarchy.

The psalm's structure is verses 1-4, 5-7, 8-15, and 16-20. The word "Selah" is used to mark musical pauses.

"Shout with joy to God, all the earth!" begins verse 1. This reference to "all the earth" gives us a hint that this psalm is messianic—not in the technical sense that it's quoted in the New Testament, but in the sense that only the Messiah could fulfill the vision described here. In the day that's coming, all the earth will indeed worship Christ (Zech. 14:16). "All the earth bows down to you" (verse 4).

In verses 5-12, the psalmist becomes a historian, describing all God's mighty works in the past: "Come and see what God has done."

Verse 10 is a wonderful way to view tragedy in your life: "You, O God, tested us, you refined us like silver." Not that

God sent the trial, but He used it to refine us. He allows whatever evil happens to happen.

Verse 13-15 are wonderful for use in our prayer lives. Though the psalmist offered "burnt offerings" (verse 13), there are other offerings, such as "a sacrifice of praise—the fruit of lips that confess his name" (Heb. 13:15).

Verses 16-20 are the testimony of such a one, who acknowledges to all what God has done.

PSALM 67

The title of Psalm 67 doesn't tell us who the author is; but like Psalm 66, it could be attributed to David. It could also have been written by a Levite, an assistant to the priests.

Whoever wrote this psalm prepared it for liturgical use, for public singing in the congregation. It was designed to be set to the lyre or whatever other stringed instruments they had.

The psalm is obviously connected to Psalm 66. It was written in the aftermath of a victory which followed a crushing defeat at the hands of the Edomites. It also anticipates the Messiah in the sense that the hopes the psalm expresses could be fulfilled only by the manifestation of God in Christ.

The psalm's structure includes verse 1, an introductory prayer; then verses 2-4, and verses 5-7.

"May God be gracious to us and bless us and make his face shine upon us," begins verse 1. This is the high priestly prayer of Numbers 6:24-26 in which the priest invokes the blessing of God. In the Old Testament, the name of God used in reference to the special covenant relationship with Israel is *Jehovah*. The name of God used in reference to Gentiles is *Elohim*. In this psalm, which has in view the conversion of the whole world, the psalmist takes the name *Elohim* and uses it in calling for the same blessing God had promised Israel.

Verses 2 and 3 are great prayers: "May your ways be known on earth. . . . May all the peoples praise you, O God; may all the peoples praise you." We as Christian people have been sent into the world to be its salt and light. Yet in some places, the name of Christ is blasphemed among unbelievers because of some of us Christians. We need to use these verses as our own prayer.

Verse 4 is a vision of a universal kingdom of righteousness. It is going to come. God here is described as the guide of the nations.

Verse 5 echoes the prayer of verse 3: "May all the peoples praise you, O God. . . ."

The description of abundance, prosperity and peace in verses 6 and 7 is taken from Leviticus 26:4, God's blessings for obedience.

PSALM 68

Psalm 68 has the same kind of title as Psalms 66 and 67, the addition being the name of David as author. I think that supports my own conviction that Psalms 66 and 67 were written by David also.

Like the two preceding psalms, this one is liturgical—that is, written for public worship. Some Bible scholars believe it was composed to celebrate the bringing of the ark to Zion (2 Sam. 6; 1 Chron. 15, 16). The problem with that interpretation, however, is that in 1 Chronicles we're given the psalm David wrote on that occasion. It is possible David composed two psalms on that occasion; if so, this could be the second, perhaps written for the second choir.

Another alternative is that Psalm 68 was written after a military expedition—perhaps the very one celebrated in Psalm 66, the victory over the Edomites. Several images in the psalm suggest a military scene, for instance, verse 14: "When the Almighty scattered the kings in the land, it was like snow fallen on Zalmon." Zalmon was a mountain (Judg. 9:48), and here it's pictured poetically as part of a battle during wintertime. The people also looked like "the wings of my dove sheathed in silver" (verse 13)—in other words, they were covered with snow. Verse 18's reference to captives is also a military image.

"May God arise, may his enemies be scattered," begins verse 1 in a note of triumph.

During the initial defeat at the hands of the Edomites (Psalm 44), they took some prisoners. The psalmist blamed God for that, although he really had no right to do so. But as a Hebrew, he had a tremendous sense of God's sovereignty. God, however, is never directly involved in making widows and orphans. This psalm, in verse 5, provides an antidote to Psalm 44's view: God is "father to the fatherless, a defender of widows."

In verse 7, David becomes a historian as he describes the exodus from Egypt and the wilderness wanderings. Sometimes we think the only thing the Israelites ate during those long years in the desert was manna. But here we see that God turned that desert into a productive land (verses 9, 10). These verses could also refer to their arrival in the Promised Land itself.

Verses 11-19 describe the Israelites' victories over the Canaanites, and Deborah is mentioned, though not by name. The battle she directed is often alluded to here, as is her victory song from Judges 5. Women were often the ones who brought news of victory in battle—"the company of those who proclaimed it" (verse 11). Miriam led the women in a victory song in Exodus 15:20; women sang of David's victory over the Philistines in 1 Samuel 18:6, 7.

In verse 12, the writer may be heaping scorn on those who didn't go out to battle. Or perhaps he's describing those who stayed home and divided the plunder.

In verse 15 David describes the rugged mountains of Bashan. In verse 16 he addresses them directly, as though they were present. This is a figure of speech called *apostrophe*. David contrasts these big, impressive mountains with Mt. Zion. It's there, in Zion, that God has chosen to dwell.

Obviously, much of this psalm is poetry. It's worthwhile learning how to understand poetry. If we don't, we forfeit understanding a tremendous amount of the Psalms. We also run the risk of interpreting literally something that was intended to be poetry, or of making a big deal out of something which is simply part of the poem. For instance, it would be a mistake to take verse 14's reference to snowing on Zalmon as the text for a sermon. That's significant simply as part of the poem.

In verse 17, the "chariots of God" are a poetic reference to the armies of God, the invincible hosts by which David is surrounded (2 Kings 6:17). The chariot in those days was the most awesome and deadly instrument of war; so it came to be a symbol of war.

"You led captives in your train," says verse 18, echoing the language of Judges 5:12: "Take captive your captives." A victor in those days would bring back his captives in a triumphal procession. David is thinking of God as bringing His captives

177

to Zion; of God entering His temple and there dwelling with the people. Not only does He receive gifts from the captives, but He gives gifts to His people from His bounty.

In Ephesians 4:8-12, Paul takes this verse and applies it to Christ, seeing in it Christ's triumphant victory over the hosts of hell at His ascension. He also applies the line "he gave gifts" to mean Christ's giving of spiritual gifts to His people for the building up of the Church. This New Testament citation of this Old Testament reference means this is a messianic psalm.

In verse 24, the subject changes from the imagined procession of verse 17 to a visible procession. The description is quite majestic.

In verse 32, David is anticipating the day when the kingdom of the Lord will will be worldwide, and His rule will originate from Zion. It anticipates the Millennial reign, and we can use it in our prayer life as we anticipate His coming.

PSALM 69

I think David wrote this psalm immediately before he was driven from Zion by Absalom, or immediately after. He is either anticipating or experiencing the terrible ordeal of fleeing from his own son.

This psalm blends the autobiographical and the prophetic. Some things in this psalm could not apply to David, but apply to Jesus. Other things, however, could not apply to Jesus, but to David. Some verses apply to both. Verses 21-28 for instance, in which David describes his own agony at the hands of his enemies, also picture for us the sufferings of the Lord Jesus.

"Save me, O God, for the waters have come up to my neck," says David in verse 1. He is speaking poetically; he didn't just say, Lord, I'm in trouble, I'm miserable.

David was surrounded by jealous and wicked people who hated him without any reason at all (verse 4). He was trying to run the country as a godly country; that's why he endured scorn for God's sake (verse 7). It was also the reason the "insults of those who insult you fall on me" (verse 9). David was very badly mistreated by his people at this stage of his life. Verse 9 also anticipates the sorrows of the Lord Jesus, and is quoted in John 2:17 in reference to Jesus. In Romans 15:3, Paul sees Jesus as the divine scapegoat, in that all of the insults that were directed against God fell upon Christ.

Verses 13-19 again describe David's feeling of sinking in the mire. In your own life there may be times when you feel like you can't "keep your head above water." Use these verses then as your own prayer.

Verse 21 is an instance of remarkable prevision, which could not have been true in David's experience literally: "They put gall in my food and gave me vinegar for my thirst." But when we come to the Gospels, we find this passage quoted as it was

179

fulfilled: when the soldiers dipped a sponge in vinegar and handed it to Jesus as He hung on the cross.

Verses 22-28 is the imprecatory portion of this psalm. This is David speaking, a person nearly driven mad by the apparent victory of the evildoers. Although the language is not the language of the Lord Jesus, this is a prediction of the sorrows that will come upon the people who persecuted the Lord. These things have been only partially fulfilled; one day they will be fulfilled completely.

Verse 28 refers to the "book of life," a term found many places in the Bible. In the New Testament it's used of the record of those who are eternally saved (Phil. 4:3; Rev. 13:8; 20:15). In the Old Testament it seems to refer to a register of the living (Exod. 32:32, 33). So I don't look at verse 28 as a prayer that these people would be tossed into hell.

PSALM 70

Psalm 70 is the same as Psalm 40:14-17. Apparently the last few verses of that psalm were lifted out for liturgical use. It's significant that the title says "A petition"; the mood created in these verses is very similar to the one in Psalm 69.

A large portion of David's psalms, at least up through the first two books, are devoted to his two times of exile, either the earlier one when he was being chased by Saul, or the later one when he was being chased by Absalom.

If you count them up, you'll find far more are devoted to that later period. David was an older man, a better poet. He'd had years to reflect upon the great things God had been teaching him in his adversity. The whole thing began with the sins of adultery with Bathsheba and the murder of Uriah. Those terrible crimes were followed by what we generally call the penitential psalms, as David remembered the terrible time when he was being chased by Absalom. We link this psalm with Psalms 39 and 40.

PSALM 71

Psalm 71 is the prayer of an old man for deliverance. While there is no title to it, it becomes apparent it was written by David because the language is his. If we read a writer or a poet for a long time, we begin to know when we're reading the same author. Also, this psalm corresponds to Psalm 41—just as Psalm 70 corresponds to Psalm 40. Psalm 41, the prayer of a sick old man, is near the close of Book I. Now that we near the close of Book II we see a similar type of psalm: the psalm of a frightened old person.

As David neared the end of his life, he became apprehensive because he could no longer wield the sword and the spear the way he could when he was young. He was very concerned about Solomon's succession after his death, and worried about the difficulties Adonijah, Solomon's half-brother, was going to give him (1 Chron. 23, 28; 1 Kings 1). Adonijah was in many ways behaving just like Absalom had, and it could have been his shenanigans that inspired the writing of Psalm 71. (Eventually, Absalom had to have Adonijah executed, as 1 Kings 2:13-25 records.)

"In you, O Lord, I have taken refuge; let me never be put to shame," begins verse 1. Since verses 1-3 are the same as Psalm 31, we can also conclude David was the author of Psalm 71.

Mary, Queen of Scots, quoted the first few verses of this psalm at her execution. No matter what we may think of her, nevertheless she died nobly and with dignity. These first two verses were a favorite prayer of hers.

"You have been my hope, O Sovereign Lord," says the psalmist in verse 5. Many times in the Old Testament the Lord is spoken of as our source of hope (Jer. 14:8). The New Testament writers describe our hope as resting in the Lord Jesus (Rom. 15:13; Col. 1:27; 1 Tim. 1:1).

Verse 6 is very similar to Psalm 22:9.

"Do not cast me away when I am old," pleads the writer in verse 9. This is obviously the prayer of an old person. It's difficult to be old, especially these days. We are becoming like the ancient Greeks, to whom good health was a god. We are rapidly approaching that pagan value. As David got old, he had less confidence that he had lived such a holy life, that all he had to do was ring God's bell and everything would be given to him. He was apprehensive because of his past sins with Bathsheba, with Uriah, and in numbering the people; so he prays verse 9.

Maybe it was Adonijah David was considering as his enemy in verse 10.

Verse 11 shows that David was much more conscious of his old age.

Verses 12 and 13 we've also seen in Psalms 22, 25, 38, and 60.

"Since my youth, O God, you have taught me," says verse 17. The fact is that David was a godly person all his life. In a sense, the terrible sins he committed were relatively insignificant compared with the overwhelmingly Godward direction of his life over the long haul.

In verse 19, David speaks of the righteousness of God. God's righteousness is the basis of our justification and also the grounds of our trust in His fulfillment of all His promises. "Who, O God, is like you?" Indeed, no one is like God.

"You will restore my life again," says David in verse 20; "from the depths of the earth you will again bring me up." If Psalm 16 anticipates the resurrection of the Lord, here we have David anticipating his own resurrection.

PSALM 72

Psalm 72 was not originally part of the collection of Book II, but was added by a later editor. Books I and II were each used by the two choirs David set up, one in Zion, and the other in Gibeon not far away (1 Chron. 16). Each had its respective hymnbooks, and David added psalms to each as he wrote them.

Psalm 72 was written some time after the death of David, probably early in the reign of Solomon, by Solomon. It was added to Book II; then verse 20 was added to it to complete the Book: "This concludes the prayers of David son of Jesse."

Solomon composed Psalm 72 for liturgical recitation, a psalm in which the people could give expression to their devout aspirations connected with the king, the head of the theocratic kingdom of Israel.

The psalm has a strong messianic tone throughout, depicting the Millennial reign of the Lord Jesus Christ. I think that in his early rule, Solomon felt himself to be a type of the Messiah whose reign really would spread "from sea to sea and and from the River to the ends of the earth" (verse 8). I'm not sure that the Hebrew people living in the days of Solomon understood there would be a Messiah who would reign. I think they might have thought that Solomon actually would extend his kingdom as this psalm describes. But when we read the psalm, we come to the conclusion that Solomon, at least, must have known he was writing words that transcended his own experience; that he was actually being a prophet as his father David had been.

Will there be a Millennium? I think it's portrayed in type in the seven days of creation when the Lord God rested. The feasts of the people of Israel provide another type: the last feast, the Feast of Tabernacles, is a type of the Millennial reign of our Lord Jesus. Then, there are some beautiful descriptions of a Millennial reign in Isaiah (Isa. 2:2, 3; 11:6, 10; 32; 33; 35; 65; 66). A number of the Psalms describe His reign, Psalms 95—

100 particularly. These are not talking about His reigning in heaven, but about His reigning here on earth. The reason we use the word *millennium,* meaning "1000 years," is that in Revelation 20:1-7 the expression "one thousand years" is repeated many times.

This was a favorite psalm of the fourth century archbishop Athanasius, a staunch upholder of the doctrine of the Trinity against the heretical Arians. He said, "Against all assaults upon thy body, thine estate, thy soul, thy reputation; against all temptation, tribulations, plots, and slanderous reports; say this Seventy-second Psalm."

Psalm 72 is structured as follows. Verses 1-7 refer to the judgment of the king; verses 8-11 are an obvious reference to the extent of his kingdom; verses 12-14 describe the quality of justice in his kingdom; verses 15-17 are a prayer anticipating the kind of thing described in Isaiah 11 and 35, the removal of the curse from the earth; verses 18-20 seem to anticipate the fulfillment of God's promises to Abraham when He said, "In thee will all the nations of the earth be blessed."

"Endow the king with your justice, O God, the royal son with your righteousness," begins verse 1. At the beginning of his reign, Solomon did execute just judgment. The effect of his judgment was to stabilize a kingdom that had been somewhat chaotic during David's later years, as rebellions broke out in the wake of David's sin, and with his increasing age. Some of Solomon's first actions were to execute troublemakers like Adonijah, Joab, and Shimei, actions important in securing the future peace and stability of his kingdom. Christ's own reign will begin with judgments; in Revelation 19 we read about the judgments that will take place at the battle of Armageddon. Matthew 25:31-46 offers a description of the judgment of the sheep and the goats, which is analogous to this.

"He will endure as long as the sun, as long as the moon, through all generations," says verse 5. Luke 1:33 tells us that Christ "will reign over the house of Jacob forever; his kingdom will never end." Christ's kingdom has not begun except in a spiritual sense. He has never literally reigned over the house of Jacob. If there is to be this literal kingdom, then it still lies in the future. That is why we believe in the Millennial reign of Christ.

"He will be like rain falling on a mown field" (verse 6), is a beautiful figure of speech we find in various places in the Old Testament.

Verse 8 is probably talking about the extent of the kingdom as it was in the days of David and Solomon. After their deaths, it began to shrink as the enemies of Israel regathered strength and began to chip away at its borders. At the time of the captivities there were no safe borders, and the Babylonians came in and did what they wanted with the land. Verse 10 again describes the borders of this Millennial kingdom as being universal.

The messianic King will rescue the people from oppression and violence (verses 12-14). Can you imagine this utopian world which is yet to come?

Verse 15 is a reference to the visit of the Queen of Sheba (1 Kings 10).

Verse 16 anticipates the reversal of the curse, when decay will be no more, and all of creation will be redeemed (Romans 8:19-22).

Yes, one day "the whole earth [will] be filled with his glory" (verse 19).

PSALM 73

With Psalm 73 we come to the beginning of Book III of the psalms. Five books actually make up the volume which we today call the book of Psalms. These five Books were put together at different times in Israel's history. The first two were compiled for two different choirs during the time of the monarchy under David, and under Solomon, who was king for forty years after David's death.

Book III includes Psalms 73—89; of these, 73—83 are all attributed to Asaph. Asaph was originally one of David's three choirmasters. It's possible that these psalms were written by someone with the same name. Family names were passed down from generation to generation then as they are now. Psalms 84, 85, and 87 were written by or for the sons of Korah, and Psalm 86 is the only psalm in this collection that was written by David.

Book III covers the period of civil war which began after Solomon's death and resulted in the Divided Kingdom (1 Kings 12:1, 16-19). Rehoboam, Solomon's son, refused to listen to the wise advice of his older counselors to reduce taxation on the people. The result was that ten tribes seceded, named Jeroboam king, and were called "Israel." But it was a throne God never acknowedged as legitimate. The remaining two tribes, Judah and Benjamin, stayed loyal to Rehoboam. They were called "Judah."

I think Psalm 73 was written after the rebellion had occurred. The theme is the question, why do some wicked people prosper while good people suffer? Jeroboam, the rebel king, immediately set up idolatry as part of his new kingdom (1 Kings 12:25-33). He invited anyone who wanted to pay a price to become a priest. The result was that the true priests of God were driven out. They went to Judah, but could not make a living there.

187

The psalm begins with the psalmist's confession: "I envied the arrogant when I saw the prosperity of the wicked" (verse 3). The writer is trying to understand what seems to him to be a world gone out of whack, an abnormal situation, a denial of the harmony that should exist under the rule of a holy God. How, he is asking, could a good God tolerate this state of affairs?

In verses 4-12, the psalmist describes in vivid imagery these prosperous, wicked people. "Their pride is their necklace" (verse 6); "their mouths lay claim to heaven" (verse 9); "always carefree, they increase in wealth" (verse 12).

"Surely in vain I have kept my heart pure," is the psalmist's bitter conclusion in verse 13 after looking at all these things. The reason why God tolerates evil—in fact, the reason why God permitted evil in the first place—is as mysterious to us today as it was to this Old Testament writer. We do not really know.

But we can do what this psalmist does in verses 17-28. We can get God's perspective.

I would like to make a distinction between two expressions: "in control," and "controlling." When I say God is in control, I do not mean that God is controlling everything that is happening. If God were actually controlling, there would be no sin. But God is in control, meaning He allows people to do what they want; and sometimes He intervenes, sometimes He stops them.

God is in control in the sense that eventually everything is going to work out according to His plan. He is in control of the future.

God is in control of the present in the sense that nothing happens that He does not permit to happen. This does not mean that God wills evil to happen. God permits many things to happen that He does not will to happen. He does not want me to sin, but He does permit me to sin.

The writer was very troubled by all these kinds of difficult thoughts, and the seeming inconsistencies of life. Then he came into the sanctuary of God.

At once, his mind began to clear, and he saw the truth (verse 17). The way things appear is not the way they will always actually be. It's the end that's important. As he prayed in God's sanctuary, God's Temple, the psalmist saw that the wicked are actually on "slippery ground," and will be "cast ... down to ruin" (verse 18). The violent have no future, he sees, because God is going to get rid of them (verse 19).

He says the Lord is like someone dreaming right now, but when He wakes up He will take action (verse 20).

In verse 22, the writer says he didn't make the responses he should have made as a human being created in God's image. Instead, in his bitterness he was like a beast, living on the lower level, living without awareness of God.

In the conclusion of the psalm, verses 25-28, the psalmist has been into the sanctuary and gotten a new perspective. He no longer sees life as measured by present possessions or situations. He realizes the destruction of the wicked is guaranteed by the word of God.

It's useless to ask people in the outside world what they think about eternal things. There's no way they could possibly know. It's the Spirit of God who makes these eternal truths real to our hearts.

PSALM 74

Like Psalm 73, Psalm 74 refers to the destructive time when the whole nation of Israel was divided as civil war tore it apart. The sacred institutions—the priesthood, the Levites—were being systematically destroyed. Everything was in upheaval. In this time of horrible chaos, godly people expressed their dismay in psalms like these in Book III.

The specific occasion for the writing of this psalm is found in 2 Chronicles 12:1-12 and 1 Kings 14:21-28. Because of Rehoboam's apostasy, the Lord allowed Shishak, the king of Egypt, to attack and invade the land of Judah and even the capital city of Jerusalem. When Rehoboam repented because of the prophet Shemaiah's warning, God kept Shishak from totally destroying Rehoboam's kingdom.

Some interesting external details support this Scriptural record. On his return to Egypt, Shishak made inscriptions on the south wall of the temple of Karnack. He is portrayed as dragging captives by the hair to the altar of the Egyptian god Marduk, holding a battle axe threateningly above them as if he's about to bash their brains in. All the names of the cities he conquered are listed—about 133 in all, and included in these are names of some of the fortified cities of Judah. These inscriptions can still be seen today.

Second Chronicles says that Shishak attacked "with twelve hundred chariots and sixty thousand horsemen and the innumerable troops of Libyans, Sukkites, and Cushites that came with him from Egypt." Obviously, such a massive invasion would have caused tremendous and terrible suffering in the land of Judah and Israel. In the psalm, we find that not only did Shishak take captives, he wrecked the Temple.

"Why have you rejected us forever, O God? . . . Remember the people you purchased of old," begins the psalm in verses 1 and 2. The people are reminding God as if He had forgotten—

but this is what God wants us to do. He likes us to "remind" Him in our prayers of His ways in the past in order to say, "And that's what we expect You to do again in the future."

Verses 3-8 describe Shishak's violence toward the temple, giving us details we don't find in the records of Kings or Chronicles. Verse 4 describes the enemies' "roaring" in the place where God had ordained music. "They set up their standards as signs." A standard is a flag, an emblem that armies carried. No doubt these bore pagan religious symbols. From the point of view of the Jewish people, not only was their temple being destroyed, it was being desecrated. The devastation wreaked by these invaders was a terrible experience for the saintly people.

The complaint when Psalm 74 was written was that the pagans had burned down all the meeting-places of God in the land and that no prophets were left (verses 8, 9). I don't think this means that all the prophets had been killed, but rather that there was no word from the Lord as to when the oppression would end. Even at the time of the later captivities there were prophets, such as Jeremiah, who told them their captivity would last for seventy years.

Verses 10 and 11 are saying that the Lord is standing there with His hands in His pockets, not doing anything to save them.

When the people couldn't look forward to a time when this oppression would end, they looked backward. Beginning with verse 12, they look back to times of God's deliverance in the past, such as His defeat of Egypt, in the hope that He will deliver them again. Times of oppression always seem to evoke reminiscing.

Verse 14 mentions "Leviathan," a word meaning crocodile. Sea monsters and crocodiles are referred to in this psalm because they were symbols of Egypt.

Verse 15 is a reference to God dividing the rock in Exodus 17:6.

Verse 16 reminds them that God is the Creator of the sun, the moon, and the stars—but the invaders who come worship only light bearers.

"Do not hand over the life of your dove to wild beasts," pleads verse 19. The dove, or turtledove, is a term of great affection, a symbol of one's lover (Song of Songs 2:14).

191

Verse 20 urges God to remember His covenant (Gen. 17:7). It describes how "haunts of violence fill the dark places of the land," "dark places" often being used in the Old Testament for Sheol or the grave.

We can think of so many dark places in our land today; then we can be moved to pray verse 22: "Rise up, O God, and defend your cause."

PSALM 75

Psalm 75 was written during the same period of history as the two previous psalms, a time of disruption when the Levites had been driven out of their territory and sent to Judah. It was a time of great distress and upheaval; so this psalm prays that God will come as the judge.

The psalm is set to the same music as Psalms 57 and 58—a tune that is appropriate to songs about God as judge.

The structure is: verse 1 as introduction, followed by four strophes of two verses each, followed by one concluding verse.

"We give thanks to you, O God, . . . for your Name is near," proclaims verse 1. Verse 2 is messianic, but the psalmist wanted judgment now.

Verses 4 and 5 speak of the pride, arrogance, and boasting of the enemies of God. The "horn" is a symbol of power, like a great bull tossing its horn ("lifting up") in disdain.

In verse 8, the "foaming cup" is a symbol of the wrath of God. This is a poetic image. Just like a foaming cup of wine, God will pour out His wrath.

PSALM 76

Some Bible scholars have assigned this psalm to the time of Hezekiah and the threatened invasion of the land by the king of Assyria, Sennacherib, as recorded in 2 Kings 19 and Isaiah 39. I don't think this psalm belongs to that time period for several reasons. First, the psalm says the battle it is describing took place in Jerusalem ("Zion," "Salem," verse 2). But Sennacherib's army was defeated when an angel of the Lord killed 185,000 of the soldiers—long before they ever reached Jerusalem.

Secondly, in the psalm we read of horses being killed (verse 6). But the Assyrian defeat did not result in the killing of horses.

So I think that this psalm, like the preceding one, refers to the invasion of Shishak described in 1 Kings 14:21-28 and 2 Chronicles 12. But because of its timeless nature, this psalm could certainly be read with meaning by those who faced Sennacherib's invasion, or at other times of trouble.

When Rehoboam faced Shishak's invasion and was told by the prophet this was in punishment for his apostasy, he repented. We can personalize this by realizing that as we hear the Word of God, we ought to acknowledge and confess our sins. Confession to God is an essential part of our Christian experience. Only God knows how much chastening has been forestalled by our humbling ourselves.

Though Rehoboam had become apostate, the Levites, who wrote these psalms, never did. Although the Levites were forced out of their country and their jobs during the civil war, and suffered personally and professionally, they never lost their faith in God. These psalms attest to that faith.

Verses 1-3 declare God's victory in Jerusalem. It was there "he broke the flashing arrows."

Verses 4-10 shift to prayer, as the psalmist describes God's supremacy: "You alone are to be feared" (verse 7).

Verse 10 speaks of God's restraining action. The world today is as full of dictators and warmongers as it was then, and sometimes God seems to us to be so inactive. But the peace the world does have is because of His restraining hand.

PSALM 77

This psalm of great poetry was written also at the time of Shishak's invasion, a judgment of God on Rehoboam and his kingdom for their backsliding (1 Kings 14:21-28; 2 Chronicles 12).

"I cried out to God for help," begins the psalmist in verse 1. This indicates the earnestness of his prayer, as he cried out to God in deep anguish of soul.

In verse 3, though, the writer admits that he was disturbed, too, when he thought of God—God wasn't working the way he had expected.

In verses 5-9, the psalmist expresses his befuddlement over God's apparent inactivity on behalf of Israel. It was a low point in his spiritual experience.

Then, beginning in verse 10, he repents of that attitude and realizes he can trust God. It's comforting to us in our walk of faith today to realize that godly people in the past have had their times of deep doubt too, times when they felt God was far from them. When they had these doubts they took positive action, and that is what we need to do too. We need to make up our minds to think about what God has done. We can look back in history and conclude that the eternal God who did those things in the past is absolutely consistent. He's unchanging, and is as powerful now as He ever was.

This remembering is what the psalmist decided to do in verse 11: "I will remember your miracles of long ago."

In verses 15-20 he recalls God's mighty deliverance of Israel as He led them through the Red Sea. "The waters saw you and writhed; the very depths were convulsed" (verse 16). "Your path led through the sea, your way through the mighty waters" (verse 19). This psalmist would certainly agree with William Cowper's poem, "God moves in a mysterious way, His wonders to perform."

196

When you have doubts, look back and see the ways of God in history, especially at Calvary. Think of the holiness of God with reference to the judgments you see upon earth at any time. Remember, the footprints of God may not always be visible (verse 19).

PSALM 78

Psalm 78 is both a poem and a meditation. Like the previous psalm it's historical, reviewing the history of the people of Israel from the time they were led out of Egypt until the writer's time.

The background of this psalm is the national apostasy of Rehoboam's reign (2 Chron. 12). In this psalm, the writer shows how the current apostasy is part of a pattern of Israel's past. They fell repeatedly into apostasy, and God from time to time punished them in an attempt to bring them back.

"O my people, hear my teaching," begins verse 1. The introduction (verses 1-8) says that this psalm is being written to keep alive the knowledge of God's greatness for future generations. "Then they would put their trust in God and would not forget his deeds but would keep his commands" (verse 7).

Verse 9 begins the recounting of Israel's history. Even though God did wonders to show them He was their God, yet "they forgot what he had done" (verse 11), and "they continued to sin against him" (verse 17).

The psalm describes various rebellions. Verses 17 and 18 allude to the people's complaining about their hard rations, an incident described in Exodus 16 and Numbers 11. Their real problem was that they did not believe in God, though God gave them every reason to do so (verses 22, 23).

This constant unbelief characterized the Israelites during their entire wilderness wanderings. The psalmist's point in verses 56-64 is that, unfortunately, the current generation of Israelites was just like the wilderness generation. They were unbelieving also.

Verses 65 to 72 refer to the reign of "David." This picture of David shepherding the people of Israel also depicts God's shepherding rule. God is presented as the true shepherd of Israel, of whom David and Moses are just little glimpses (Psalm 77:20; 78:72; and 80:1). In the New Testament we find that God is the great shepherd not just of Israel, but of the flock of God, which includes all of us (John 10:11; Heb. 13:20; 1 Pet. 2:25).

PSALM 79

The occasion for this psalm is the same as for Psalm 74: the invasion of Shisak, the king of Egypt (2 Chron. 12; 1 Kings 14).

I think this psalm is prophetic as well as richly historical. Revelation 11 tells us Jerusalem will be captured in a time yet to come.

This psalm also gives me clues about what to do in times of national calamity.

"O God, the nations . . . have defiled your holy temple," is the psalmist's cry in verse 1 as he sees the temple being desecrated by Shishak's armies.

Verse 8 seems to imply they were suffering because of their ancestors' sins, but that is not the case.

In verse 10, it's for the sake of God and His name that they are asking for help.

Verse 11 refers to prisoners. In ancient times, conquering armies returned to their homelands with mobs of prisoners, many of whom were then publicly executed for sport and display.

"Seven times" in verse 12 is a number symbolic of perfection. The writer is asking God to reward Israel's enemies evil for evil.

The motif of Israel as the sheep and the Lord as the shepherd runs all through this psalm (note particularly verse 13).

"From generation to generation we will recount your praise," says verse 13, reiterating the desire of Psalm 78:4. All of us today have this same solemn obligation to teach our children the knowledge of God.

PSALM 80

The reference in the first verse of this psalm to the cherubim on the ark of the covenant tells us this was written before the Temple was torn down during the complete destruction of Jerusalem. The background of this psalm is the national apostasy under Rehoboam (2 Chron. 12; 1 Kings 14:21).

The psalm has four strophes which get longer by degrees. The first has three verses, the second has four verses, then there are two strophes of six verses each. Verses 3, 7, and 19 are a refrain which increases in intensity. Verse 3 says, "Restore us, O God"; verse 4, "Restore us, O God Almighty"; and verse 19 combines the two, "Jehovah" and "Elohim," and prays, "Restore us, O Lord God Almighty."

"Hear us, O Shepherd of Israel," pleads the writer in verse 1.

Benjamin is mentioned in verse 2 because he was the only full brother of Joseph.

In verse 3, the prayer of these refrains to "restore us" is because of the people's apostasy and the resulting destructive invasion. The people need spiritual and physical restoration.

In verse 8, Israel is pictured as a vine, which is a lovely figure of speech first used of Joseph in Genesis 49:22. A vine is a beautiful, living, leafy plant, which sends out its "boughs" and its "shoots" (sons and daughters).

But because of the invasion of Shishak, the vine's wall is broken down, so that "all who pass by pick its grapes" (verse 12) and "boars from the forest ravage it" (verse 13). Isaiah 5:1, 2, 4-6 describes in similar imagery God's punishment of His "vine," Israel.

"The son you have raised up for yourself" in verse 15 refers primarily to the nation of Israel, but we can also see in it the Messiah, since Psalm 80 is a messianic psalm anticipating the "true vine" (John 15:1).

201

PSALM 81

Psalm 81 is a poem written for music, probably for the Feast of Tabernacles (verse 3). It was written sometime between the rebellion of Rehoboam and the captivity.

"Sing aloud unto God our strength," exults the writer in verse 1 (KJV). "Make a joyful noise unto the God of Jacob." "Make a joyful noise" is an allusion to the custom of blowing trumpets at every joyful festival (Lev. 23:24). This psalm is telling the people to sound the trumpets at every new moon, and especially at the Feast of Tabernacles (verse 3).

The Old Testament says quite a bit about the value of music in our corporate worship, as does the New Testament. Paul talks about music and singing in Colossians and Ephesians. In a well-ordered church quite a bit of attention is given to the singing of songs and hymns, and there's no reason why they should not be accompanied by musical instruments. Certainly in the Old Testament they were.

From verse 6 to the end of the psalm the speaker is not Asaph but God. God testifies to the people's wickedness in their refusal to listen to Him.

Verse 6 is talking about God's rescuing the Israelites from Egypt. "The burden" refers to the burden of brick-making which the Israelites had in Egypt; "the basket" probably to the baskets in which they carried clay to make the bricks. The Israelites were spending their lives laboring for the Egyptians— some even think these slaves built the pyramids. But God delivered them and brought them to the Promised Land (Exod. 2:24).

"I answered you out of a thundercloud," says God in verse 7. During the Exodus, God led the people in a pillar of cloud by day (Exod. 13:21; 14:19, 20). "I tested you at the waters of Meribah" (see Exod. 17). The same kind of unbelief and backsliding that characterized this wilderness time also characterized the time between the Divided Kingdom and the eventual captivity.

In verses 12 and 13, God refers to a time when He "gave them over." Stephen makes reference to this same time in his speech of Acts 7.

Yet God still makes them the offer of His generosity: "Open wide your mouth and I will fill it" (verse 10); "With honey from the rock I would satisfy you" (verse 16). This is God's offer to us today. He offers us Christ, and Christ offers us everything: "I have come that they may have life, and have it to the full" (John 10:10).

PSALM 82

In this poem the writer, Asaph, is denouncing the crooked judges of Israel. He represents God as sitting in judgment upon the judges.

Injustice was one of the results of the apostasy of Rehoboam's reign. Injustice is always one of the consequences when people forsake God and begin to deny that their fellow human beings are made in the image of God. The minor prophets also describe such a situation. During these terrible times of apostasy, terrible things were being done. The judges who should have rebuked the wrongdoers were instead collaborating with them.

"God presides in the great assembly; he gives judgment among the 'gods,'" says verse 1. "Gods" here refers to the rulers, or judges.

In verses 2-4, God addresses the crooked judges, accusing them of wrongdoing (verse 2), and telling them what they ought to be doing instead (verses 3, 4). Instead of defending the unjust, they should "defend the cause of the weak and fatherless" and "maintain the rights of the poor and oppressed."

Verse 6 points out that these judges are good judges, reflecting God ("sons of the Most High"), to the extent that they acknowledge the Most High God.

Jesus quotes this verse, "I said, 'You are "gods,"'" in His claim to deity in John 10:34.

PSALM 83

Psalm 83 was written when the Moabites and Ammonites came to make war on Jehoshaphat, but God delivered Israel. Second Chronicles 20:1-30 tells the story. The list of the enemies given there is strikingly similar to the list in this psalm, as is the action.

In fact, there was very little action—of a military kind! Second Chronicles and this psalm tell how the army of the Lord marched out, not to do battle, but to witness the battle. As they went out, they were preceded by those who sang to the Lord and those who praised Him—a vast choir both of lay singers and professional singers.

What happened was this: Israel's enemies turned on each other and completely destroyed each other, leaving Israel untouched. After looting their enemies, the Israelites returned joyfully to Jerusalem, singing and praising.

What seems to be an imprecatory psalm is really seeking the honor of the Lord.

PSALM 84

This psalm was written shortly after the civil war started. When the rebel Jeroboam set up his kingdom, he instituted idol worship. The godly people said they would not serve these gods, so they left for Judah (2 Chron. 11:14-16).

To the descendants of Korah, who wrote this psalm, that situation of idol-worship and setting up false places of worship reminded them too strongly of their own ancestors' sin of setting up tents of worship other than the one of Moses (Num. 16). These were called the "tents of wickedness," and Moses urged all the people to get away from them. Those who didn't were destroyed; those who did were saved. Obviously, some of Korah's relatives did choose the Lord's side and were spared; this psalm is written by their descendants.

"How lovely is your dwelling place, O Lord Almighty," says verse 1. The authors are saying in effect, "We don't want those dwelling-places of the gods of Jeroboam any more than our ancestors wanted the tents of wickedness of Korah."

"My heart and my flesh cry out for the living God," says verse 2. The psalmist is indicating that his body and his soul are in tune, and he is praising God.

"Even the sparrow has found a home," says verse 3. Even the birds were better off than people living in the territory under Jeroboam.

"Blessed are those who dwell in your house," says verse 4— *your* house, not those places set up by Jeroboam.

The descendants of Korah say in verse 10, "I would rather be a doorkeeper in the house of my God than dwell in the tents of the wicked." They'd rather stand in the doorway of God's true house than dwell in those "tents of wickedness" like their ancestors.

Paul repeats the lesson of Korah in 2 Timothy 2:19: "The Lord knows those who are his." With that background we can enjoy this psalm. God doesn't cheat us, but gives us everything we can use.

PSALM 85

This psalm was written by the sons of Korah. There's a main theme running through the psalms of Asaph and the psalms of Korah. These psalms were written during times of terrible anxiety because the land had been invaded, either by the Egyptians, or by the enemies listed in Psalm 83.

The psalm's structure is two parts of six verses each, with verse 7 forming a petition between them.

"You restored the fortunes of Jacob," says verse 1. Or, "thou hast brought back the captivity of Jacob," as the *King James Version* has it. "Captivity" in that version does not refer to the Israelites' captivity, but is an idiomatic expression.

The changes in thought are so abrupt, it's possible this psalm was composed for recitation in the Temple service. Verse 4 would be spoken; then verse 5 would be the response.

"Show us your unfailing love, O Lord, and grant us your salvation," says verse 7. This is a prayer each of us can pray.

"I will listen to what God the Lord will say," writes the psalmist in verse 8. We can all take this to heart, too. Instead of talking so much, we often need just to listen to God.

PSALM 86

This is the only psalm of David's in Book Three of the Psalms. As the title tells us, it's a prayer.

The five books of the Psalms correspond to five periods in Israel's history. The first two books were put together by David, one for his main choir in Zion, and the other for an auxiliary choir in Gibeon. Book Three corresponds to the period immediately after the death of David. So why is this psalm of David's found in Book Three?

I believe the answer is that the theme of verses 8 and 9 complements the theme found in Psalm 87 and in other psalms of this Book: the goodness of God, and the promise of blessing coming to many nations through the Messiah. All the other themes of Psalm 86 are found repeatedly in Books One and Two except this theme of verses 8 and 9. That seems more to echo Psalm 87. So apparently the people who compiled these psalms into books felt this psalm fit better in Book Three than in Book Two.

I think David was an old man when he wrote this psalm. It is similar to Psalm 25, so I think it comes from a similar phase in David's life. He was no longer the exuberant youth; he was no longer free from the dark shadow cast over his life by his sin. Verses 16 and 17 sound a note of desperation, because as David got older, he wasn't so sure anymore that God was hearing his prayer. I think the memory of his sin against Uriah and Bathsheba troubled him all his life. Even though God had forgiven him, as David himself makes clear in Psalm 32, "Blessed is he whose transgressions are forgiven," David apparently had a hard time forgiving himself.

As I said, this psalm is quite similar to Psalm 25, and contains numerous allusions to it. For example, compare verse 4 with Psalm 25:1; verse 11 with 25:4; and verse 15 with 25:6.

"Hear, O Lord, and answer me, for I am poor and needy,"

209

cries David in verse 1. He means he is poor in the sense of afflicted; needy in that he is defenseless against his enemies.

"Guard my life, for I am devoted to you," says David in verse 2, or as the *King James* has it, "I am holy." David is simply saying that he is one of the godly, in contrast to those he describes in verse 14.

Verses 3 and 4 imply that he is depressed and dejected; but then he says he is going to lift up his soul and talk to God.

Verse 5 is his expression of pure worship, that is, of ascribing worth to God. David says, "You are kind and forgiving, O Lord, abounding in love to all who call to you." This is a wonderful way to begin our own prayers, as we remind ourselves of God's loving character.

Verses 8-10 are purely messianic. "Among the gods there is none like you, O Lord" (verse 8). The "gods" David saw around him were the gods of the Philistines and the Moabites. David knew these "gods" were not like his God. "All the nations you have made will come and worship before you, O Lord" (verse 9). Here David looks forward to the time when all the nations will worship God. This is partially fulfilled in the Church and the preaching of the gospel, and will be completely fulfilled in a coming day, as we read in Revelation 5.

"Teach me your way, O Lord, and I will walk in your truth" (verse 11). Note David's prayer, and his affirmation. These often go together in the Bible. Certainly the spirit of affirmation is necessary if prayer is going to be answered. James tells us about the double-minded person, who reserves the option of refusing what God wants him to do. Unless we are willing to act according to what God tells us, God will not reveal His mysteries to us. Here, David says he will walk in truth. He asks for an "undivided heart," one that will have no other object of its love and obedience than God Himself. David didn't want to entertain mixed opinions. He didn't want to vacillate between fear of the Lord and indifference toward Him. He wanted singleness of love and purpose.

In verse 12 David again affirms his intention to "praise you, O Lord my God, with all my heart." He will do everything he can to enhance God's reputation, to "glorify" Him, so that others too will praise Him.

"For great is your love toward me," says David again in verse

13. David knew what he was talking about, having experienced God's great love many times.

In verse 14, David says "the arrogant are attacking me." I link this not with the court of Saul, but with David's own court in the later days of his reign.

Again in verse 15 David speaks of God's great love: "You, O Lord, are a compassionate and gracious God, slow to anger, abounding in love and faithfulness." This is the fundamental characteristic of God we find described in the Old Testament: God's love and faithfulness. The source of this verse is Exodus 34:6, and it's repeated here and in Psalm 103:8; Psalm 145:8; Nahum 1:3; Jonah 4:2; and Joel 2:13.

"Save the son of your maidservant," says David in verse 16, referring to his mother. This and Psalm 116:16 are the only two references David makes to his mother using this phrase. He never refers to his father as far as we can tell. Apparently it was David's mother who influenced him to be a spiritually-minded person, as can so often happen. A godly Christian mother or father are a great gift, as are parents who are both Christians. David here says that his mother was God's servant, and so he appeals for mercy on the grounds that he is the son of a servant of the Lord.

PSALM 87

In this very short psalm, the descendants of Korah are acting as the spokespeople of God. These descendants of Korah were Levites in the Temple of God. They loved Zion, because that was the place where the Lord's name was. In this psalm, they describe Zion and what will happen to it because of the Messiah.

"I will record Rahab and Babylon among those who acknowledge me," says God (verse 4). "Rahab" is a code word used in the Old Testament for Egypt. "Babylon" was a fierce enemy, much feared by the Israelites even before they were carried away into captivity there. Yet these are the ones God says will acknowledge Him.

We don't yet see this fulfilled today. Egypt and the peoples of the Middle East are terribly hostile to the nation of Israel. They detest Israel, and they detest Jerusalem. Yet one day we will see this fulfilled, and also verse 3: "Glorious things are said of you, O city of God."

The psalm goes on to say that "Philistia too, and Tyre, along with Cush" will all be converted to the God of Israel. The remarkable part of the passage is that God said that they would be admitted to all of the privileges of citizenship in Zion. Again, this is messianic in the sense that it is predicting what will be done through the Messiah.

This idea of the conversion of the nations during the messianic rule is echoed many places in Isaiah, such as 2:2-4; 11:10-12; 18; 20; 23; and 56:1, 3, 6-8. At that time, the nations will acknowledge that Zion is the source of everything that gives joy.

PSALM 88

Psalm 88 is the saddest of all the psalms in this collection—or even in all 150. The structure, poetically speaking, is of very slow, unbroken laments—the monotony of misery.

What would cause someone to write a dirge like this? I think that the author was one of the captives taken by Shishak, king of Egypt, when he invaded Israel (2 Chron. 12). Captives such as these were dragged back to the conqueror's homeland to be executed. I believe this was written as the author languished in prison, awaiting transport to his fate. Perhaps eventually the psalm made its way back into the land of Israel.

The title tells us the author was "Heman." First Chronicles 6:33 tells us that Heman was a Kohathite, a Levite. That must have made his imprisonment all the more torturous to him: he had served God all his life, yet now it seemed that God had forsaken him.

"O Lord, the God who saves me," cries the psalmist in verse 1, "my life draws near the grave" (verse 3). In verse 4, he sees himself being as good as dead already. Anyone taken captive knew what his fate was. He would be taken off to Egypt and put to death. It was simply delayed execution, and the conquerors did it for its psychological impact on the conquered. King Shishak was graphically showing how any enemies of his had no fate other than death.

The various figures of speech indicate that this writer was in prison. Darkness was his only companion. A dungeon in those days could have appeared to be a grave.

"Your wrath lies heavily upon me" (verse 7). When God judges a nation, the good and the bad suffer alike. God's wrath fell upon this innocent person, as well as upon those who deserved it.

Verse 8 means that the writer felt he was all alone and forgotten. It doesn't mean his friends thought he was contemptible,

213

but that when someone has been put in prison, very few people visit, especially if it's a political imprisonment as this one was. People don't want to be identified with the political prisoner. That's a terrible affliction, because the prisoner needs the affection of friends.

"Do those who are dead rise up and praise you?" says the psalmist in verse 10. He's asking, what good is my death to you, God? He was someone who, in his life, had led the praises of God. He would not be able to do that, he says, after he dies. This is the Old Testament view of death: going to a land of forgetfulness where they could not praise God. We who have the light of the New Testament know that view is incomplete.

"I cry to you for help, O Lord," says verse 13. The psalmist didn't get any comfort. He prayed continually and nothing happened. But I like the fact that he never gave up praying even though he felt God was not answering. God was not angry at him, but at the nation; yet he suffered as a kind of scapegoat. How glad we are for the light of the New Testament.

PSALM 89

This psalm is by Ethan the Ezrahite, as the title tells us. Psalm 88 was written by Heman the Ezrahite. We aren't quite sure what this term "Ezrahite" means, but I think it may refer to a group of Levites who were singers in the Temple service. We find reference to them in various places, beginning with the reign of David.

It's quite possible that these two, Heman and Ethan, lived in the days of David when he brought the ark to Zion and there established the Temple service. They survived David; they survived Solomon, whose reign lasted forty years. Then very shortly after the death of Solomon, the disasters happened which brought tragedy into the lives of these old, old men: Heman was taken captive by Shishak; Ethan watched these terrible circumstances he found hard to understand.

In the first part of the psalm, the writer celebrates the promises God had made to David. "I will sing of the love of the Lord forever; with my mouth I will make your faithfulness known through all generations," he declares in verse 1. The writer is thinking of Psalm 101, the covenant David made with the people when David was being anointed as king over the entire nation. At that time, God renewed the covenant He had made with Abraham and added certain other features (2 Sam. 7).

David's kingdom was just a type or symbol of a kingdom that would last forever, the everlasting kingdom of the Messiah (verses 27-29). It will be fulfilled in the person of David's descendant, the one described in Revelation as the root and offspring of David, the Lord Jesus Christ. There is no throne of David now, but there is that throne of David's greater son, the Lord Jesus Christ, and that throne will last forever.

God's faithfulness is a theme in the psalm (note especially verse 49). The psalmist is saying that even though everything seems to have fallen apart with the Egyptians invading the land,

215

yet God has promised and God is faithful. God had promised to give the land not only to David, the descendant of Abraham, but to David's descendants forever.

The emphasis in this psalm is on the faithfulness of God. The psalmist could lift his eyes above the present disaster and see the ultimate fulfillment of all that God had promised to His people.

PSALM 90

Psalm 90 is the first psalm in Book Four, a collection put together during the time of the exile (2 Kings 17:13-23; 2 Kings 25; 2 Chron. 36:16-23). This exile, or captivity, was God's punishment on the people of Israel for their constant refusal to heed His warnings via the prophets about the Israelites' disobedience.

The demolition of Israel took place in stages. First the nation called Israel was taken into exile by Assyria in 722 B.C. The territory formerly occupied by these ten tribes was denuded of people except for the Samaritans, Jews who intermarried with foreigners.

In 586 B.C., about a hundred and fifty years later, the remaining two tribes, the nation called Judah, was taken into exile by the Babylonians. The Babylonians tore down the wall of Jerusalem and sacked the city. They completely destroyed the Temple, and carried off everything of value. The Babylonian captivity was to last for seventy years, a fact predicted by Jeremiah (Jer. 25:11). To some of the captives, this meant certain death in a foreign land because of their age. To others, like Daniel, it meant hope: they began to look forward to and pray for their return.

The duration of the captivity—seventy years—provides an ironic twist. Every seven years the Israelites were to have let the land lie fallow—a Sabbath rest for the land. But they never did it. They could never quite believe that God would meet their needs for a whole year if they didn't plow their fields (Jer. 25:11; 2 Chron. 36:21). Now the land would lie fallow for seventy years—seventy Sabbath years of rest.

This is the background of Book Four. The godly people among those in captivity had some of the Scriptures: probably the Pentateuch, some of the historical books up to the time of their exile, and the first three books of the Psalms. In the captivity, they began to compile and write more psalms, those of Book Four.

The constant theme of Book Four is that God reigns. Taken captive in a foreign land, surrounded by thousands of foreign deities, the Israelites wanted to make clear their captivity was not due to the foreign deities' supremacy. God still ruled supreme; and it was He who had allowed the Israelites' captivity as punishment for their disobedience.

Having said all this, we come to the first psalm in this collection, Psalm 90, written by Moses. What is a psalm by Moses doing as the first in this collection? Verse 1 explains it. The people were being uprooted from the land given to their ancestor Abraham and to them in perpetuity, carried off to live in a strange land. Yet they still had a "dwelling place"—a home, a place of refuge: the Lord. They were just like Moses, who had never had a real geographical home, but lived in a basket in the Nile, then in Pharoah's court, then fled to the wilderness for forty years, then wandered the desert for another forty. He never did live in the Promised Land. Yet Moses could say as he wrote this psalm near the end of his life, "the Lord is my home."

"You turn men back to dust," says verse 3. These verses contain many allusions to ancient Scriptures, including Deuteronomy 32 and 33, and Genesis 3:19, all of which were written by Moses. I think Moses had in mind here the conversation God had with Adam after the Fall.

Verse 4 speaks of God's attitude toward time. Since God is timeless, chronological time to Him is relative: "a thousand years in your sight are like a day that has just gone by."

From verse 5 on we see several literary images: death is likened to a flood, to sleep, and to the withering of grass. This psalm is only partly mournful because it's filled with hope in verses 14-17.

"We are consumed by your anger," says verse 7. Here Moses is referring to the deaths of the rebellious generation of Israelites in the wilderness. Every one of the Israelites who was twenty years and older when he left Egypt died in the wilderness. This means that Moses saw every one of his peers, except Joshua and Caleb, put into their graves. Small wonder he wrote verse 7.

This is another reason this psalm is so appropriate to this

collection. Very few survivors actually went to Babylon. King Nebuchadnezzar killed off thousands, and took captive only those who could be useful to him. Lamentations tells us of the appalling slaughter. Those taken into captivity could certainly identify with Moses' poem. It was as if the history of the people in the wilderness had repeated itself.

"Teach us to number our days aright, that we may gain a heart of wisdom," is the prayer of verse 12. Though time is relative to God, the human being has only a short life on earth. Teach us, Moses prays, to learn how temporal our earthly life is, so that we may become wise.

PSALM 91

Although this psalm has no title attributing authorship, I believe it must be the work of Moses. It has many connections to Psalm 90, and also reflects other works of Moses such as Deuteronomy (32 and 33).

Some scholars believe this is a pilgrim psalm. I think Moses wrote this long before; then the people sang it when they were en route to their captivity in Babylon. Included in that motley crowd of prisoners were quite a few believers, who would encourage each other as they traveled with this psalm.

One voice speaks in verse 1; a second voice replies in verse 2. The first voice responds to the second voice in verses 3-8. The second voice responds in verse 9a. The first voice replies in verses 9b-13. Then God responds in verses 14-16.

"He who dwells in the shelter of the Most High will rest in the shadow of the Almighty," says verse 1. This verse stresses the same idea as Psalm 90:1 did: the shelter is God, not the Temple. The focus of these exiles is shifted from the Temple to the person of God.

Zion was the place where they had put their hopes (verse 2), but now that fortified city was destroyed. Now the Lord is their refuge and their fortress.

In verse 3, the people in captivity certainly must have felt like they were in a hunter's trap. Yet Psalm 124:7 makes it clear that they will escape.

"He will cover you with his feathers, and under his wings you will find refuge," says verse 4. This is the figure of God as if He had His own outstretched wings to bear them up on one hand and cover them on the other (Deut. 32:11).

"The terror by night" (verse 5) refers to all kinds of unknown terrors, even surprise attacks. Those who walk with the Lord and make Him their refuge will not be afraid of the terror by night.

Verse 9 divides the psalm into two parts, the theme of verse 1 being repeated in verse 9.

This psalm contains many words the captives would have found so very encouraging as they trekked on to their unknown servitude. "A thousand may fall at your side . . , but it will not come near you" (verse 7). "No harm will befall you, no disaster will come near your tent" (verse 10). And verses 11 and 12: "For he will command his angels concerning you to guard you in all your ways; they will lift you up in their hands, so that you will not strike your foot against a stone."

These latter are the very verses Satan misquoted to try to persuade Jesus to throw Himself down from the Temple, because, said Satan, then the angels will bear you up (Matt. 4:6). As Jesus pointed out, the psalm does not say we are to put God to the test by throwing ourselves in harm's way.

But how are we to interpret these verses? Do they promise inevitable protection of God's people from disaster? During World War II, for instance, verse 7 was a favorite of believing soldiers. We need to realize that in this psalm, God is expressing the principle of His preservation of the rightous. This principle does not apply in every particular case. The reasons for that are locked up in the mystery of God's ways. Hebrews 11:35 describes this paradox: some received their dead brought back to life; others were tortured and killed. We need to keep passages such as Hebrews 11 in mind when we interpret other passages such as Psalm 91.

PSALM 92

This psalm, which the title tells us was prepared to be sung publicly, was probably written by David after Absalom's rebellion. I think David was the author because verses 10-12 sound very much like his writing. I would also link this psalm with Psalm 71, also the prayer of David as a very old man.

This psalm was appropriate for Book Four and the period of the captivity because of its title: "For the Sabbath Day." The captivity was the time when the land finally enjoyed its Sabbath rest (2 Chron. 36:21).

"It is good to praise the Lord and make music to your name, O Most High," says verse 1. God's title, "Most High," would have been very important to the people during the captivity, surrounded as they were by so many little "gods."

"Though . . . evildoers flourish, they will be forever destroyed," states verse 7. Many of God's suffering people have been sustained through the years by the knowledge that ultimately the wicked have no future because the Lord is supreme forever.

"You have exalted my horn like that of a wild ox; fine oils have been poured upon me" (verse 10). This sounds so very much like David. He is saying, You have made me king, anointing me with oil to establish my authority. David's authority had been challenged by Absalom, but God had defeated Absalom and "exalted" David's "horn like that of a wild ox." A wild ox was a symbol of tremendous power; nobody tangled with the wild ox. Though this was not particularly appropriate imagery to the time of the Israelites' captivity, they took the psalm as a whole and could use it in anticipation of what they longed for.

"The rightous will flourish like a palm tree, they will grow like a cedar of Lebanon. . . . They will still bear fruit in old age, they will stay fresh and green" (verses 12, 14). The cedar is a symbol of permanence. Righteous people are like these trees. They will abide, while the wicked perish. This shows the justice and righteousness of God. He is upright, unlike the false gods of the foreigners.

PSALM 93

I suspect this psalm was also written by David. Its poetic description compares with Psalm 29. It is included here because of the theme stated in verse 1: "The Lord reigns." The people were exiled, living in Babylon, putting together a book that spoke to their specific needs. It was important to them to assert the sovereignty of the God whom they knew and worshiped when surrounded by idols and idol worshipers.

So they used this psalm to remind themselves continually that the Lord reigns and His throne is established. Nothing can shake this fact.

PSALM 94

God sees and God avenges evil. If it weren't for that asurance given us in the Bible, we wouldn't be able to think as much of our God as we do. We would feel there was a fatal flaw in His character. A God who simply created the heavens and the earth and then backed off is the God of the deist, a God who is not actively involved in the world. The God the Bible presents is actively involved. He is sovereign. This is the God we see in this psalm.

"O Lord, the God who avenges . . . , shine forth," says the psalm. This is not simply a call for vengeance for evil done to the writer personally, but a call for the vindication of the righteousness of God. The writer is asking God to show He cares about justice, that He is deeply offended by the cruelties of the wicked. Seen in this light, this psalm and others like it not only make sense, but are an essential part of the picture God wants to give us of Himself. We don't need to be offended when we look at psalms like this, thinking these are just the expressions of an angry person. Think of them rather as an appeal for God to act according to His holiness.

We don't know who the writer of this psalm was. But it echoes the anguish of someone who saw the city of Jerusalem destroyed by Nebuchadnezzar.

The first verse refers to God as "the God who avenges." There are references like this in the Old Testament—Nahum 1:2, for example. God is going to demand accountability. Isaiah and all the prophets talk about this aspect of God's character. God is the One who someday will come and settle accounts (Isa. 35:4).

We may feel like praying verse 2 after watching the news on T.V. "The proud" this writer was talking about were the Chaldean soldiers.

Verse 3 expresses the psalmist's eagerness for the Lord to act

225

quickly. The psalmist was a human being like you and me and was very anxious for God's justice to be effected immediately.

Verses 4-7 remind us of Isaiah 37:10—the boasting of the wicked oppressors.

In verse 8, the psalmist is talking about how their tormentors called them "senseless ones."

Verse 10 means that Hitler and others of his ilk don't get away with it. In Isaiah 47 and Daniel 5 and 6:28 we read of God's judgment on Babylon. God even calls Cyrus, a Persian, His "servant," because Cyrus would be the instrument of doing to the Babylonians exactly what they had done to the Israelites.

"For the Lord will not reject his people," says verse 14. Daniel and Ezekiel and others like them are evidence that God did not abandon His people.

PSALM 95

This very important psalm was written and added to this collection during the time of the captivity in Babylon. The composer was a genuine believer, and despite his circumstances was so filled with real joy that he wanted to express that joy with his fellow worshipers. No one can be down all the time. Even people in prison have moments of joy. Even some of the people condemned to death by the Nazis did express in their last letters some moments of deep, deep joy.

The theme here is singing for joy to the Lord because He's not like the little gods in Babylon. Surrounded by a foreign culture with all its artifacts of idolatry, the Israelites became so sick of idolatry that they never again became idolaters.

We don't know who the author of this psalm was, but we assume it was a priest, a Levite, someone familiar with poetry.

"Come, let us sing for joy to the Lord; let us shout aloud to the Rock of our salvation," begins verse 1. The psalmist was anxious to have others who knew the Lord join him for mutual comfort and worship. As they came together, they were filled with a sense of joy. "Rock of our salvation" is one of David's expressions. This writer was familiar with it and so used it. In spite of these people's transportation as exiles, they did not lose sight of the God of their salvation. He didn't lose sight of them, either.

"The Lord is the great God . . . above all gods" (verse 3). The expression "gods" refers to the spiritual powers behind the idols. All these pagan gods were expressions of some characteristic of Satan. The fertility gods demanded sexual excesses and temple prostitutes. The gods of war demanded human sacrifice. All were deceitful and destructive.

There was also the notion among the pagan people in Babylon and Assyria that gods were local deities—that is, there was a god of the mountains, and a god of the plains, and so forth.

227

We can see why the theme that God is the God of all creation runs through these psalms.

"Come, let us bow down in worship," urges verse 6. It's important to realize that we are body, soul, and spirit. What the body does should correspond to a certain extent to what the soul feels. Why not have a little exuberance in a church service, as we express with our bodies what our souls feel—the greatness of our Creator God (see also verse 1).

Verse 8 refers to Meribah and Massah, which is one and the same place. Meribah is the geographical name, and Massah the designation given to it, meaning "the temptation." This refers to the Israelites' wilderness wanderings. As they wandered, they felt repeatedly that God was not there. They knew they were on the way to the Promised Land, but they griped and complained until things came to a head at Meribah. There, they found out that God's patience did have limits, and He would not put up with their constant unbelief (Num. 19). The psalmist remembers that the same thing happened among his people's immediate forebears, and it led straight to this captivity. So he's appealing to the survivors, saying, don't make the same mistake. Don't harden your hearts, lest you suffer more than you are suffering now.

Hebrews 3:15, 17 refers to this sin of unbelief which characterized the Meribah Israelites. It was unbelief the Hebrew Christians were being tempted to, and against which the writer of Hebrews warns. It wasn't just ordinary sin, but this specific sin of unbelief.

Some people have the idea that God feels exactly the same about everybody. Verses 10 and 11 remove that illusion. Some people, such as Daniel, Job, or David, for example, were more responsive to God. Human response to God is very important. People like this were very precious in God's eyes because they responded. To the extent that a person becomes indistinguishable from his sin, then that person is rejected by God.

The writer of this psalm was urging his people not to repeat the mistakes of the previous generations of Israelites. He was urging them to behave in such a way that they would have the hope of going back to the Promised Land when the seventy years were up. Don't forfeit your entrance into God's "rest," the Promised Land.

In Hebrews 4, God's "rest" refers to Heaven. The writer to the Hebrews is saying that we can forfeit Heaven. He is not saying that we can be saved and then lost. He's telling these people that having drawn near to Christ, it was important that they complete the journey and become genuine believers lest they forfeit Heaven.

PSALM 96

"Sing to the Lord a new song," declares verse 1 of Psalm 96. It was important that the captives sing. It was one thing for them to refuse to sing the songs of Zion for the benefit of their drunken captors (Psalm 137); it was another for them to sing spontaneously a new song to God.

"Proclaim his salvation day after day" (verse 2). Many of the captives felt God could not do anything. But here the psalmist declares God's greatness—in contrast to the insignificance of the stone and clay gods.

I think the reference in verse 6 to the sanctuary is not to the Temple but to the universe. The writer is looking at the heavens and saying they reveal the glory of God.

In verse 7 the writer calls upon the Babylonians and all the various ethnic groups to "ascribe to the Lord the glory due his name." The ancient Israelites knew, as do Christians today, that God alone is the Sovereign One.

The theme that the Lord reigns (verse 10) was very important to these captives. Nebuchadnezzar and his sucessors said *they* were the ones who were reigning. Not only does the Lord reign, but He will judge the people in equity, in contrast to the kind of judgment given by someone like Nebuchadnezzar.

"He will judge the world in righteousness" (verse 13). This idea of just judgment is repeated again. In Babylon, the people began to think of these themes which they'd forgotten during the backsliding which preceded their captivity. These were the things they should have remembered before God judged them as a nation.

PSALM 97

The call to sing to the Lord and the idea of the Lord reigning are repeated continually in these psalms.

"The Lord reigns, let the earth be glad," says verse 1. There's a link between the Lord reigning and the earth rejoicing. The earth mourns when it is under the control of evil people. The world now is a wretched place to the extent that it lies in the arms of the evil one—that is, Satan. But prophets like Isaiah predict the world that will be, when the Lord, the Messiah— that is, Christ—reigns on earth. Then the earth will rejoice.

A more immediate meaning of this verse was that finally the land of Canaan was resting. It was slowly recovering its vitality, exhausted by the Israelites' refusal to observe the Sabbath rest. In that era when there were no fertilizers to restore the earth, the Israelites had been commanded to let it lie fallow one year in seven. They refused to do it. When they went into exile, the Lord through Jeremiah said they would stay there seventy years, until the land had enjoyed its Sabbath.

Verses 2-6 describe the appearance of the Lord at Sinai. The writer is remembering the righteousness and justice of the Lord as lawgiver. I think the Israelite captives in Babylon were getting the shock of their lives when they saw how unjust and terrible a pagan kingdom could be. Daniel, in his dream interpretation to the king, told him to show mercy to the poor. The contrast between the pagan king and the just God was uppermost in the minds of those who were writing and singing this psalm.

So they remember the giving of the law, the Ten Commandments—which they did not keep. But here in captivity they develop a love for the law, and a love for the Lord as the lawgiver, the One who rules in righteousness.

"Light is shed upon the righteous and joy on the upright in heart" (verse 11). Light and joy are wonderfully attractive.

231

There's a notion abroad today that the only way to have fun is to ignore the Church, the preachers, the Bible, and especially the God of the Bible. But if we had the experience these Israelites had of living in a land of darkness, we would quickly conclude what they did: wherever God reigns, there is light and joy.

PSALM 98

We don't know when Psalms 98 and 99 were written. They could have been composed by David or Solomon or Asaph, but whenever they were written, they became very appropriate to the survivors taken into captivity in Babylon. It was very important to them to "sing to the Lord a new song" (verse 1); to call upon "all the earth" to "shout for joy to the Lord" (verse 4); and to acknowledge the Lordship of God in a land filled with idols (verse 9).

"Let them sing before the Lord, for he comes to judge the earth. He will judge the world in righteousness and the peoples with equity" (verse 9). This verse is the same as Psalm 96:13; so it's possible these psalms may have been written about the same time. The writer was very conscious of the sovereignty of the Lord and the futility of idolatry. People make idols, but God, Jehovah, made the universe.

The writer was also conscious of the Lord's just judgment, in contrast to the evil and injustice of the ruler under whom the captives lived, Nebuchadnezzar.

This psalm contains some striking poetry. "Let the rivers clap their hands, let the mountains sing together for joy" (verse 8). Looking, perhaps, at a turbulent river with white caps on it, the psalmist sees that as the river "clapping" its "hands." This is a poetic expression.

PSALM 99

"The Lord reigns," begins verse 1. We have the same themes tirelessly repeated in these psalms: Psalm 95, "Sing for joy to the Lord"; Psalm 96, "Sing to the Lord a new song"; Psalm 97, "The Lord reigns"; Psalm 98, "Sing to the Lord a new song"; Psalm 99, "The Lord reigns." The writers were almost harping on the idea that because of God's sovereignty, the people can rejoice.

"Great is the Lord in Zion," says verse 2. Because of this reference to Zion, I presume this was written before Zion was destroyed by the Babylonians. Yet because of its content, the captives found it perfectly apropos to their situation.

Verse 6 speaks about the giving of the Word of God and the response to it. The people realized that they were in captivity because they had sinned against God (verse 8). They knew they deserved to be there, but they took heart in the fact that God is "a forgiving God." They remembered that He hearkened to those who paid attention to His statutes, people like Moses, Aaron, and Samuel. So the psalm was an appeal to the people living in captivity to be like Moses and Aaron, who were priests to the Lord, and like Samuel, who called upon the Lord.

"Exalt the Lord our God . . . for the Lord our God is holy" (verse 9). This is an appeal for the people to give God sincere worship, not the mixed kind of allegiance they had had before when they also bowed to idols.

PSALM 100

This psalm is part of the liturgy in many churches; in some, people move into the church singing this psalm set to music. Verse 4 makes this particularly appropriate: "Enter his gates with thanksgiving and his courts with praise."

"Shout for joy to the Lord, all the earth," begins verse 1. Although this is a poetic expression, it may also refer to the physical earth. The earth throughout this section of the psalms is called upon to sing and to shout joyfully to the Lord. One reason for this may be that the land was finally getting its Sabbath rest, and so was able to rejoice. Another is that the prophets often speak of the Millennial reign of Christ as a time when the earth would be renewed. These psalms also link the reign of the Lord and the renewal of the physical earth.

"Know that the Lord is God. It is he who made us, and we are his" (verse 3). This would have been a powerful affirmation for the captives. They belonged to God, not Nebuchadnezzar.

Because of verse 4's reference to entering God's "courts," I doubt that this psalm was written at the time of the captivity, but rather was composed when the people had access to the Temple or the Tabernacle. This verse does introduce that familiar theme: to shout joyfully to the Lord because His greatness contrasts so sharply with the insignificance of the idols around them.

Even though the people couldn't fulfill the invitation of verse 4 at the time, the theme of verse 5 was very important to them: "The Lord is good and his love endures forever; his faithfulness continues through all generations."

No matter how wretched the world may be in which you are now living, no matter how dark the clouds that loom on the horizon, the Lord is faithful in every generation. There was never a worse time to be born than when Moses was born, for instance. As a male slave child, he was born condemned to death. But his parents saw he was a beautiful child, and they were not afraid of the king's edict calling for the death of a baby. With God's help, they shielded him, and Moses grew up to be one of the greatest leaders his people ever had. He was also called the friend of God (Exod. 33:11).

PSALM 101

This and Psalm 103 are the two psalms written by David in Book Four. The only authors we can identify in this collection are David and Moses; Moses wrote Psalms 90 and 91. Why are David's psalms in this collection, compiled so long after his death? Because what he said was significant to the people at this particular time of their captivity.

I think this psalm gives us the text of the covenant David made with the people of Israel when they crowned him king (2 Sam. 5). Psalm 15 also refers to that occasion and gives part of that covenant. In this psalm, David describes what kind of king he is going to be—his goals and his ethical standards—in contrast to Saul, who had been rejected.

David started out with lofty standards (verses 3 and 4), which was good. It is sad that he personally failed to keep them in one major sin that, for him, darkened the rest of his life. God does set high standards for us, and he expects us to keep shooting for them. That is the essence of holiness: not that we achieve it in this life, but that we never give up aiming for it.

Why did the captives sing this song in Babylon? First of all, because singing had become so vital to them. But more importantly, because they saw in this psalm the sincere vow of a godly person to live a godly life. They were making the same vow. They were saying that they would not succumb to the idolatry of their captors, nor become like their brothers and sisters who did give way and become as corrupt as the pagans.

"I will be careful to lead a blameless life," says David in verse 2. "I will walk in my house with blameless heart." Here David is saying that he is going to be a different kind of person than his predecessor, Saul, and his cohorts. We find the corruption of these people described in psalms like 11, 12, and 13. David says he will live a "blameless life," have a "blameless heart," and look at no "vile thing." He will be a person of character—

237

quite a contrast to those who were "faithless" and "of perverse heart."

The eleven particulars that describe the godly character David vows to maintain make up the covenant found in Psalms 15 and 101. David vowed this not only to the people, but to God.

This is rather a sad psalm, since David could not have known at the time how badly he would fail. For a time, he did even take on some of the characteristics he loathes in this psalm—he became deceitful and false (verse 7) after his sin with Bathsheba and Uriah. But then, when Nathan the prophet confronted him, he admitted the truth and repented.

This psalm gives us the ambition of a young person setting out to be the Lord's servant. It and Psalm 15 describe the kind of character to which we all can aspire.

PSALM 102

Our lives have been too easy for most of us to use this entire psalm as our own prayer. It is the deeply anguished prayer of an afflicted person, as the title tells us.

This psalm was likely written during the actual captivity in Babylon. A strong reason for believing this is found in verses 13 and 14, where the psalmist is telling God it's time to be gracious to Zion. There's no other period in the history of Israel when this would apply exactly as it did then. The prophet Jeremiah had predicted the captivity would last seventy years (Jer. 25:11). Those in exile knew this; they knew "the appointed time has come" (verse 13).

The title does not indicate who the author is. But many commentators for the last two hundred to three hundred years suggest that Daniel wrote it. He was one of the people in Babylon during all the time of the captivity. He was very much aware of the timetable Jeremiah had indicated; in fact, Daniel 9, in which Daniel weeps, fasts, confesses, and pleads with God for Israel's return, mentioning specifically the seventy years, sounds very much like this psalm.

Daniel was a most remarkable person. Not only was he trained in the university in Babylon, but he was given incredible wisdom and spiritual insight by God. He was called the beloved of God. Scripture records of him no wrongdoing—Daniel seems to be someone who was absolutely flawless. I have a feeling that if I were to meet Daniel, I'd feel awestruck and wouldn't quite know what to say. I'd be looking all the time for a little halo of light over his head. I'd feel much more at home talking with someone like King David or even Jeremiah.

But if it's true that Daniel did write this psalm, then we have in it a record of his human side. He was like the rest of us in some respects—someone who had chinks in his armor. He could weep and be so distressed that he could actually forget to eat (verse 4).

But maybe we can see a little of that in Daniel 9 anyway. When Daniel confesses on behalf of his entire nation, he uses the plural pronoun *we*. He doesn't say, *they* did all those terrible things. No, he says, *we* did them.

"Hear my prayer, O Lord; let my cry for help come to you," begins verse 1. The first eleven verses describe the writer's tormented and weakened physical condition: he can't eat; he is "reduced to skin and bones" (verse 5).

The writer suffers emotionally, too. Daniel was a "big shot," and such people are always targets. Daniel was no exception; everyone knows the story of the lions' den. "All day long my enemies taunt me," says verse 8. I think Daniel probably got tremendous criticism from his own fellow Jews, too, because he refused to worship the foreign gods as they did. He refused to be assimilated into the pagan culture.

In verses 18-20, Daniel, the exile, sees the whole nation of Israel and knows that God heard them. Daniel could have been likening the captivity in Babylon to the captivity of the people of Israel in the land of Pharaoh.

"So the name of the Lord will be declared in Zion," says verse 21, looking ahead to the future, when God will gather the people of Israel from the U.S., from Canada, from Germany, and from wherever they are, and will take them back to their land.

Verses 23-28 is a messianic passage, referring doubly to the writer and to the Messiah. The writer again is lamenting his weakened physical condition—in fact, he's afraid he's going to die. But then his faith comes back in a great surge in verses 25 and 26: "In the beginning you laid the foundations of the earth. . . ." Our Lord Jesus, the second person of the Godhead, is the One to whom the creation of all things is attributed in the Bible (Col. 1:16). "The heavens . . . will perish, but you remain." The writer might not survive, but God will survive. The future of humanity is made secure by the eternity of God.

"The children of your servants will live in your presence" (verse 28). The eternity of our Lord Jesus Christ is the guarantee of the faithful succession of those who trust in Him (Col. 1:17-20).

PSALM 103

We seldom feel the need to put this beautiful and familiar psalm in its historical context. But we know it was written in the time of David, though not included in his collections of Books One and Two. Not until the time of the captivities did the people feel the need for this psalm.

When they did, it was again because of familiar themes we've discussed in the preceding psalms. One such theme was that God was in charge. We can understand how that would be important to them, living as they were in captivity. Many people living in places dominated by dictatorship today remind themselves frequently that God reigns. God is in heaven, and the mystery of His will is unknown to us. We can't understand why God tolerates dictators who contend with Him for rule over people's hearts and minds. But we do know that God rules, and that ultimately He will assert that rule and put down such dictatorships.

Other themes were thanksgiving, and the eternity of God.

"Praise the Lord, O my soul, and forget not all his benefits," opens the psalm (verse 2).

In verse 7, David remembers Moses. The captives felt themselves to be in a second Egypt—Babylon, a place of bondage. They knew they were there because of their national sins. God had not dealt with the survivors on the basis of their personal sins: "he does not treat us as our sins deserve" (verse 10). When David wrote this, he was probably thinking of some of the dark events in his own life, or possibly in the life of the nation. When the captives read it, they let it remind them of the compassion and graciousness of God: "The Lord is compassionate and gracious."

This verse, verse 8, is repeated many times in the Old Testament (Exod. 34:6; Jonah 4:2). It's important for us to know this verse, because it completely blows the foolish notion that

241

the God of the Old Testament is a God of "fire and brim-tone." No, the God of the Old Testament is the same as the God of the New. He is "the same yesterday and today and forever" (Heb. 13:8): He "pardons sin and forgives . . . transgression." He "[delights] to show mercy" (Mic. 7:18).

Verse 13 is the tender expression of one of God's aspects, His fatherliness.

Verse 14's reference to "dust" reminds us of Genesis 2.

Verse 15 gives the image of human beings as "grass," an image Isaiah and Peter both borrow from David.

But despite human frailty, "from everlasting to everlasting the Lord's love is with those who fear him" (verse 17).

PSALM 104

This psalm doesn't have a title to identify its author. Perhaps David wrote it; certainly he *could* have written it. A "nature poem," the 104th Psalm is not unlike other psalms attributed to David.

As a nature poem, the psalm is very different from pagan nature poems. God is the Creator of the universe, and He is active in all its parts. Everything lives by and through Him. Conceivably, when Paul wrote that "by him (i.e., God the Son) all things were created . . . and in him all things hold together," he had this poem in mind. (Cf. Colossians 1:15, 17.) The psalmist, on the other hand, was recalling Genesis 1.

It could be said that the psalmist reworks Genesis 1. But he is a poet, not a prose writer. Hence, instead of saying, "And God said, 'Let there be light,'" he "sees" God as wrapping Himself in light as with a garment. God stretches out the heavens as a tent. The poetry is magnificent. Who but a great poet could think of God as making the clouds His chariot and riding on the wings of the wind?

To enjoy the psalm, read it as poetry. See how it takes the prose of Genesis 1 and turns it into graphic images.

The structure of the psalm is irregular. Someone has said that you might as well try to analyze a sunset as a poem like this. Nevertheless, it is possible to mark off a few stanzas. Scholars tell us the poem is divided concentrically. The main body of the poem has nine verses, and on each side of the main section there are two stanzas of three and five verses each. But that leaves two additional stanzas, including a three-version conclusion.

The conclusion acquires great significance if the psalm is read as part of the hymnbook of the exiles. Whether David was its author or not is of no importance. What matters is its affirmation of the creative greatness of the Lord. Truly godly people among the exiles began to understand the significance of

Genesis 1. If their God was indeed the Creator of the universe, He was present with them in their exile. He would care for them even as He cared for the beasts of the field. Even the lions sought their food from God. Why should a man not trust Him and sing praises to Him as long as life endured?

The last line or two of Psalm 103 are similar to Psalm 104. In Psalm 103 we have a description of benefits of the Lord in reference to human beings, and in this psalm you have the kindness of God in reference to the whole of creation. It's as if the psalm writer was thinking of Genesis 2 and 3 when he wrote Psalm 103 and now goes back to Genesis 1, when God made the heavens and the earth.

The first fifteen verses were extracted from an earlier collection (1 Chron. 16:1-15). Either David wrote these words and gave them to Asaph, or Asaph and his friends wrote the words and sang them on the occasion of the bringing of the ark of God to Mt. Zion.

Verse 4 is quoted in the New Testament in reference to angels. I'm not sure it's the primary meaning here. It could be that he means spirits, but I think it more likely that he uses the things which God has created in order to serve mankind. Beneath the surface we find the meaning in Hebrews 1:7.

After he talks about creation (v. 5), he talks about the way God makes provision for His creatures.

Verse 27 suggests beasts are conscious of a great Creator and sustainer of the universe.

The Spirit of God was present in Genesis 1 and is mentioned in verse 30.

Have you ever thought that God looks down upon the earth and He's glad? In verse 31, the psalmist is referring to Genesis 1, where God liked what He saw. In spite of the sin which marred God's creation, the psalmist prayed this beautiful verse.

Verse 32 refers to such things as earthquakes or the effect of lightning—God's hand upon the earth.

Verse 34 is reminiscent of Psalm 19.

PSALM 105

I think David wrote this psalm, though it doesn't have a title. David was the kind of poet who could have and would have written a nature poem of this length and majesty. Psalm 29 is also a nature poem.

The psalmist starts off as if he were talking to himself and then starts talking to God. He switches to the third person in verse 4. That's merely an idiom, a linguistic thing. In some languages and cultures it's considered quite proper when speaking directly to an eminent personage to use the third person.

You can use this prayer addressed to God in your time of worship. You are praising Him, you are worshiping Him, you are declaring to Him the wonderful things He has done.

The psalm was wonderfully comforting to the people, who felt themselves to be forsaken, captives forever in Babylon, far from Jerusalem, the home of their hearts. This is reproduced in part in the New Testament.

The occasion is the bringing of the ark of God to Mount Zion. The theme: God intervenes in history and is a God of miracles. He will do miracles in order to fulfill the promise He made to Abraham. In fact, without miracles the whole story of the ancient people of Israel is meaningless. It would have no significance or credibility.

Psalm 105 is similar to Psalm 78 (which was a historical psalm when the country was reeling under Shishak) and identical to part 1 of Chronicles 16 (note verses 18-22 in Chronicles).

Verse 8 is a wonderful word of encouragement.

In verse 12, the people remember that God gave promises to Abraham, Isaac, and Jacob when they were only a few in number and strangers in the land.

Verse 13 is probably a reference to the Pharaoh of Egypt,

245

who was reproved by God when Abraham went down to Egypt. Or it could have been Abimlech. The significance of putting it here is that the spiritually minded people in Babylon thought they were a very small group of people. Most of their peers had been killed before they went to Babylon. They remembered the promise that God had made to Abraham, and they felt that if God could bring Abraham into the land and sustain him there while surrounded by danger and could reprove kings for his sake and the sake of the others, then He could do the same thing for them in Babylon.

Verses 16-18 give details not found in Genesis. Some translations render the last part as "iron came into his soul."

Commentators have been divided on verse 19—whether it meant the word that Joseph gave to the butler and baker, or whether it was the word he had given to his own family saying they were going to bow down to him. The Hebrew here is ambiguous, but it doesn't make any difference. Joseph said to Potiphar's wife, "How can I sin against God?" It was God who had said, "Thou shalt not commit adultery," and that word was testing Joseph. He came through with flying colors.

Concerning verse 22, I doubt that Joseph rounded up Potiphar and protested being thrown into prison when he was innocent. You can hardly expect a man like Potiphar to take the word of a slave over the word of his wife. Yet if Potiphar really believed his wife, he would have had Joseph put to death. In putting him in prison, he showed a certain amount of confidence in Joseph and at the same time a desire to preserve him. What we read in this verse is that Joseph was given a lot of power.

Verses 23 and 24 parallel Exodus 1, which says there were 600,000 men of Israel in the exodus though only seventy had gone into the land. God had indeed caused them to be very fruitful.

Verse 25 to the end is reflected in Exodus 1—12. As the people remembered history, they were greatly encourged.

For verse 36ff., see Exodus 12. Verse 39 mentions the pillar of cloud and fire by night.

Verse 42 takes us back to verse 8. The writer is anticipating a second exodus—this time not out of Egypt, but out of Babylon. Ezra and Nehemiah tell us they did leave with joy.

We find in this psalm all the good things that God did, and in Psalm 106 we'll find the bad things His people did. There is a connection between the two.

PSALM 106

This psalm was probably written toward the end of the captivity. Again, I think Daniel was the author. Verse 6 of this psalm is very similar to Daniel 9:5—"We have sinned, even as our fathers did; we have done wrong and acted wickedly." A confession like this was needed before the people went back to the land. God was going to take them back, but there had to be first this cleansing by confession. When they got back to the land, Nehemiah used this psalm as part of the confession the people made then, too.

This psalm recounts the history of rebellions. Verse 7 mentions the first of ten rebellions. Each time we see God saving the people—and the people promptly forgetting what God has done.

Verse 12 takes us back to Exodus 15, when the people sang after they came out of the land of Egypt (Exod. 15:1-21). They sang to God—but "they soon forgot what he had done" (verse 13).

Verses 16-18 allude to Korah's rebellion, described in Numbers 16.

Verse 19 refers to the time when God was giving them the Ten Commandments (Exod. 32).

"They forgot the God who saved them, who had done great things in Egypt" (verse 21). We, too, forget the things God has done, and we live as if we were not much better than the idolatrous world around us.

Moses interceded for the people (verse 23), and we find this wonderful truth: God relents on behalf of His people. In this psalm, the writer is doing what Moses did. He is speaking up for the people.

PSALM 107

Psalm 107 is the first in Book Five. There is no title, and the author is not indicated. However, because of the similarities between this and the preceding psalms, particularly 106, the author may be the same. In that case, the author of Psalm 107 was Daniel, and he returned to Jerusalm according to the prayer he had made in Psalm 106:4, 5. If I am correct in saying Daniel wrote Psalm 107, we could add a P.S. to the book of Daniel and imagine him saying, "I had to sign off here—I'm on my way to Jerusalem. I'll tell you all about it when I get there." After he got there, Psalm 107 was what he wrote—and who knows—maybe a few more in Book Five also.

If we agree that the Books are put together during successive periods of the nation Israel's history, then we can see the connection between Psalm 107 and the preceding psalms of Book Four. Book Four was compiled during the time of exile, when Israel was a nation of prisoners of war in Babylon. That was a terrible experience. By no means did all the captives have as sheltered a life as Daniel did, who was taken into the king's palace. Some of the Israelites were slaves. As we read this psalm, we hear Daniel describing problems, perils, and dangers common to those who came out of Babylon.

Book Five was compiled by the godly people during the postexilic times. Many of the people who came back to the land were no longer spiritually believers—they were simply racially Jewish. Then there were others who were sincere believers. It was these godly people who put together this collection of psalms, often called "the song of the redeemed." These postexilic Israelites were ministered to by prophets like Haggai, Zechariah, and Malachi.

"Give thanks to the Lord, for he is good" (verse 1). The first note the captives strike is one of thanksgiving—thanksgiving for their release from bondage. Jeremiah had prophesied the

249

exile would last seventy years. Daniel knew this; he knew when the time was to be up, and that was why he prayed the intercessory prayer of Daniel 9 and Psalm 106. In fact, this first verse of Psalm 107 is taken from Jeremiah, whom Daniel quoted in Daniel 9—another reason I think Daniel wrote this psalm.

It was the king of Persia, Cyrus, who issued the edict saying the Israelites could go back to Jerusalem (Ezra 1:1-3). Daniel had a high position in that government, and I believe it was Daniel that the Lord used to help move Cyrus to make this edict. The Spirit of God would have been working in the heart of Cyrus so that he heard what was brought through the Lord's messenger, Daniel. This is the way the Lord usually speaks, through a combination of two or three agents: the Spirit of God, the Word of God, and the messenger whom the Spirit uses.

I believe verse 1 speaks not only of the Israelites' immediate return to their land, but also anticipates the Millennium.

Verse 2 is an exhortation. The redeemed of the Lord are those He has redeemed from the hands of the adversary—from the Assyrians and the Babylonians and anyone who had held them in bondage.

From verse 4 on, the psalm describes people who wandered. I think this refers to their wandering as they tried to get back to the land. It wasn't easy for them to do. Apparently, instead of taking the long northern route Abraham had used many centuries earlier, they tried to cut across the desert to get to Zion. So they were hungry and thirsty. This is kind of like people who try to make their way back to God after years of spiritual absence. Sometimes the way back is not easy.

"Then they cried out to the Lord in their trouble, and he delivered them from their distress," says verse 6. He led them straight to Zion (verse 7).

Verses 8, 15, 21, and 31 give us the theme of this beautiful psalm: those who have been helped by the Lord should give thanks to Him.

Verses 10-15 describe people in prison. Whether they were in prison in Babylon and were released in order to go back to the land isn't clear; but we do know that the prison is described as darknesss and the deepest gloom. They were locked up as if they were animals. But in verse 16 God leads them out of prison.

Verses 17-22 describe "fools," those who rebelled and "suffered affliction because of their iniquities." But, verse 20, "he sent forth his word and healed them." The word of God is described here as if it were God's messenger, running very swiftly to do God's commands. This personification of the word of God is designed to prepare people to receive an even more impressive and powerful enfleshing of God's word: the Word Himself, Jesus (John 1:14).

Verses 23-32 are a marvelous poetic description of those who went to sea. Verse 29 reminds us of the Lord Jesus stilling the storm in the New Testament. On the surface of our lives storms often blow, but God speaks to us sometimes through a word, a message, a passage we read, and in this way He causes storms to be still.

In verses 33-36, the people are saying that their land lay desolate for seventy years because of the wickedness of their ancestors. But God can change that dry land into springs of water.

PSALM 108

When the people got back to Jerusalem, the first thing they did was begin to rebuild the city—its walls and the Temple. But some of the inhabitants, such as Sanballat and Tobiah, objected to their coming and raised tremendous opposition to their rebuilding projects (Ezra 6; Neh.). The rebuilding of the wall was done by the workers with a trowel in one hand and a sword in the other.

These people were too busy to write the kind of psalm that would express their anxiety or faith, nor were they talented enough. So they dipped into their archives, lifted some paragraphs from earlier psalms, and added them to this collection to express their feelings. Verses 1-5 of this psalm are lifted from Psalm 57; verses 6-13 from Psalm 60. I think it was Nehemiah who did this compilation.

Both Psalms 57 and 60 were written by David, to express his faith in God at a time when he was being terribly oppressed. Psalm 57 is David's affirmation of faith when he fled from Saul in the cave, and yet felt his soul was among lions—his own companions. Now Sanballat and Tobiah are the equivalent of those "lions."

Psalm 60 was written when David had to come back from the military campaign he was on to rescue the people (1 Kings 11:14-16). God gave David victory over the Edomite enemies. David uses insulting terms for his enemies: "Moab is my washbowl" (verse 9).

"With God we will gain the victory, and he will trample down our enemies" (verse 13) was the returning captives' exultant hope.

PSALM 109

Psalm 109 is a prime example of an imprecatory psalm. Many feel this is below a Biblical standard of morality; yet I think we'll conclude the sentiment expresssed here is natural in light of the concepts that prevailed among the ancient people of Israel.

The psalm was written by David, but was compiled into this book during the postexilic period. The verses apply to David and his experience of betrayal; they also are prophetic of something that happened in the life of Christ. The psalm is quoted in Acts 1:20 as having its partial fulfillment in the case of Judas.

Verses 1-5 are a description of the evil of David's enemies: they have attacked him (verse 3). This is similar to Psalm 55, which describes David's betrayal by Ahithophel, a person he loved. David suffered grievously because of this betrayal.

Verses 6-20 is the imprecatory part, a calling down of a curse. Some scholars believe these were the curses David's enemies called down on him. I don't think so. I think these are divine imprecations on the evildoers and their families. David is praying that God would pronounce these curses against his enemies. The evil person being cursed here is the prototype of Judas (Acts 1:8, 9).

In regard to verses 9 and 10, we should remind ourselves that the ancient Israelites viewed calamity or blessing as punishment or reward, extending from parent to child. It didn't work out that way, but that was the idea they had. It's true that in some places the mistaken notions of the people are recorded. Inspiration in such a case has to do with the recording of it. These imprecatory psalms are really a plea that God's divine principles of rewarding the good and punishing the evil be seen in life. What these imprecatory psalms express is the desire that God be vindicated.

The strong language of verses 14 and 15 is in anticipation of

253

Judas. At the time, it was a very normal expression of David's anger against Ahithophel.

Verses 21-25 are a description of David's inner distress. The historical record in 2 Samuel 15 simply says he ascended the Mount of Olives, weeping; and as he went, he prayed, "O Lord, turn Ahithophel's counsel into foolishness" (2 Sam. 15:31). In this psalm, we have a much fuller record of the extent of David's feelings.

"My knees give way from fasting," David says in verse 24. There was a long, long period in David's life when he simply wasted away and his health was destroyed. David died relatively young at seventy years of age. His fasting under the terrible pressure of accusations from his enemies (verse 25) was likely part of the cause.

Verses 26 and 27 express glory to God for saving him.

Verse 30 is an assertion to give thanks continually to the Lord.

This psalm was probably put here by Nehemiah to express his feelings when he was being opposed by Sanballat. Nehemiah's enemies were planning to harm him; and in order to do so, they hired a Jew (Neh. 6:10-14). This act of treason caused Nehemiah to feel many of the same things David had felt earlier when he was betrayed.

PSALM 110

David was the author of this psalm. I say that on the basis of our Lord's statement in Matthew 22:41-44. We find more New Testament references to Psalm 110 than to any other passage in the Old Testament.

Psalm 110 contains many references to the priesthood. The background, then, is probably David's bringing of the ark to Zion (2 Sam. 6:11-14). David wore the ephod as he brought the ark, the ephod signifying he was a priest. David was the only king of Israel in whom these dual offices of king and priest were combined.

In fact, the only person who had previously combined royalty with the priestly role was Melchizedek, mentioned in Genesis 14 as bringing out bread and wine and blessing Abraham. As David the king performed similar priestly duties, blessing the people and giving them bread and raisins (dried grapes), his mind went back to Melchizedek.

And something wonderful happened. He began to speak in the power of the Holy Spirit, and to say things he would not normally think of (2 Sam. 23:2). In this psalm, he rose above his own experiences and tells of a much mightier king and priest than either himself or Melchizedek. He looks forward to the anointing of this One as "a priest forever in the order of Melchizedek," and he describes this One as his Lord. Terms like these can refer to none other than the Messiah.

This psalm is included in Book Five because when the people of Israel came back from Babylon, they had to repeat what David did earlier. David brought the ark back to Zion. Now, they were bringing back the holy vessels of the Temple, returned to them by Cyrus; they were going to rebuild the Temple and the city.

The opening line in the Hebrew really means "an oracle of Jehovah." The word for Lord is *Adonai*. It means God, but it was also used to mean sir. When using it, the speaker recognized the superiority of rank of the person addressed. When we read here, "The Lord says to my Lord," we have an acknowledgment by the one writing the psalm, by David. He says that Jehovah says to my superior, the one who is greater than I, "sit at my right hand. . . ."

In verse 2, David is speaking to his Lord, that is, the one to whom Jehovah has addressed an oracle. He's telling him that he will overcome his enemies by the help of Jehovah and the willing devotion of the people (verse 3).

"Womb of the dawn" is a very poetic expression that speaks of the eternal youthfulness of this king-priest. The king goes forth to war as one who is strengthened by his God. He is accompanied by this host of people all dressed in beautiful clothing, and they are inspired by the Spirit of God to offer themselves as freewill offerings.

If this is a prophetic psalm, as I believe it is, it predicts first of all the ultimate victory of the Messiah; and secondly, the nature of his priesthood as Messiah. His priesthood is one in the order of Melchizedek—it lasts forever (verse 4).

This priesthood "in the order of Melchizedek" is very important, because it's in contrast to the priesthood patterned after Aaron. Those priests had to be replaced continually, because they died. Those priests also had to offer sacrifices for their own sins, as well as for those of the people. But Christ is a priest after a different pattern. Christ is perfectly sinless; Christ is eternal.

Many people wonder who Melchizedek was. He was a real, historical person, as described in Genesis 14. The reference to him in Hebrews 7:3, "like the Son of God," is simply a case of the Spirit of God suppressing information about him in order that he may appear as a type of Christ. Obviously, Melchizedek did have a father and mother because no one can exist without father and mother except the Lord. The point was simply to suppress information about his genealogy and origins, so that it appears he had no beginning or end. This is meant to be a picture of Christ, our great High Priest, who really is eternal.

Psalm 2 is very closely related to this psalm, and also looks forward to the future triumphs of the Messiah.

PSALM 111

This psalm begins with the word "hallelujah" in the Hebrew. Modern translations have "Praise the Lord," and note "hallelujah" in the margin. This is one of ten psalms that begin this way. Some others are Psalms 106, 111, 112, 113, 135, 146, and 150. Six of these psalms had special titles and were used at the great festival of the Passover. Psalms 113 and 114 were sung in families on the night of the Passover before they drank the second cup. Psalms 115—118 were used after the celebration and the fourth cup.

Some scholars believe Psalms 111 and 112 were used as a preface to the very solemn psalms, 113, 114, 116, 117, 139, and 146.

Psalms 111 and 112 are very similar in construction and tone. They both start off with the Hebrew alphabet.

My guess is that the writer was Ezra, Nehemiah, or Zechariah. It was someone living during the postexilic time.

Psalm 111:4 and Psalm 112:4 are connected. It's as if the psalmist is saying that now that they have come back from Babylon to their own land, they are aware of God's compassion and graciousness. No longer will they despise Him, but they will be like Him.

Verse 9 alludes to God's bringing them back from Babylon. I believe the land of Canaan will eventually belong to the people of Israel. I am not saying the present government is a fulfillment of any prophetic Scriptures. I am saying that eventually all Israel will be regathered, and the land will no longer be disputed. It will belong to the Jews because God will remember His covenant forever.

PSALM 112

This is a companion psalm to the preceding one. Psalm 111 ended with "the fear of the Lord is the beginning of wisdom"; Psalm 112 is immediately linked to that in verse 2: "Blessed is the man who fears the Lord."

Furthermore, verse 3 is the same as Psalm 111:3; verse 4 is similar to Psalm 111:4; and verse 6 is similar to Psalm 111:5.

Verses 7-9 are an attempt to describe the Lord, and then the kind of person who wants to be like the Lord.

Verse 10 of both psalms describes the permanence of the righteous, here in contrast to the impermanence of the wicked.

PSALM 113

Psalm 113 is a great psalm. You and I are so accustomed to singing a psalm of praise like this about God that we seldom stop to think that the gods of the heathen are not praised. They are dreaded. They seldom do much of anything for the benefit of their worshipers.

We don't know who wrote this psalm. But it seems fitting that it's part of this collection, because from verse 5 on, we read of what God had done for the people. They would never have said this while they were still in Babylon.

This psalm is structured in three parts: verses 1-3, an exhortation to praise; 4-6, a description of God's glory; 7-9, His willingness to show us miracles of mercy.

This psalm is part of the Easter service in the Anglican church; verse 3 makes that appropriate: "From the rising of the sun to the place where it sets the name of the Lord is to be praised."

Verses 7 and 8 describe how the Lord "raises the poor from the dust" and "seats them with princes." I get the impression from reading Ezra and Nehemiah that once they returned from captivity, the Israelites were no longer so class-conscious. The high- and lowborn alike labored side by side to rebuild the wall in a most democratic fashion.

The phrase "in her home," according to scholars, implies a house with children (verse 9). Without that, some feel, there's nothing but four walls.

PSALM 114

This psalm recounts the miracle of God's leading His people out of Egypt. It could have been written at any time in Israel's history, but it's part of this collection because the returned captives felt like they'd been freed from a second Egypt, Babylon. They felt that their return under Cyrus' edict was a second exodus. They weren't led back by Moses, of course; but they did have leaders like Ezra, Nehemiah, and Zerubbabel. In the deepest sense, it was God who brought them back.

"When Israel came out of Egypt . . . , Judah became God's sanctuary" begins the psalm (verses 1, 2). The psalm is celebrating the fact that God is all-powerful, able to deliver His people.

"The sea looked and fled" (verse 3). This is a poetic way of describing the parting of the Red Sea, one of the miracles of the exodus. "The Jordan turned back," also verse 3, describes their crossing of the Jordan River. These were the two chronological borders of their journey out of Egypt. As soon as they left Egypt, they crossed the Red Sea. Then, after forty years of wandering in the wilderness, they crossed the Jordan River to enter the Promised Land.

Verse 4's allusion to an earthquake refers, I assume, to Mount Sinai.

"The God of Jacob . . . turned . . . the hard rock into springs of water," says verse 8. This refers to a time when water flowed from a rock because God caused it to when Moses struck it.

We can see how these spiritually-minded Israelites of old were historians. We are also told to be historians, in the sense that we are to remember the great salvation events in Scripture and in our lives (2 Pet. 3:2-5).

PSALM 115

This psalm contains many allusions to or quotations of Isaiah. Although no author is given, some scholars believe it may have been written by Hezekiah. I don't think so. I think it was written by someone who came back from Babylon, because of the extensive description of heathen idols in verses 4-8. Whoever wrote this had personal familiarity with the idols of Babylon—and great contempt for them.

The psalm is structured antiphonally for use in public worship. We can imagine a vast crowd of people being led in the recitation of this psalm, beginning with verse 1: "Not to us, O Lord, not to us, but to your name be the glory," and responding, "Because of your love and faithfulness."

Many pastors or preachers whose work has been crowned with success have often reminded themselves publicly that whatever they've accomplished has been because of the Lord, just as this psalmist does in verse 1. We are only God's tools.

Though the nations taunted them (verse 2), the people's reply was firm: "Our God is in heaven" (verse 3).

Verses 4-8 describe the idols: unseeing, uncommunicative, unfeeling. It is a divine principle that we become like the God—or gods—we worship. Those who worship idols will become like the objects of their worship: senseless and missing dimension. In the case of the idols the missing dimension is life; in the case of the worshipers the missing dimension is spiritual life.

Verses 9-11 addresses Israel in general, then the priests, then all true believers; the benediction is given to them all in verses 14 and 15: "May the Lord make you increase, both you and your children. . . ."

261

PSALM 116

We don't know who wrote this psalm, but Jewish tradition says it was Hezekiah. There are many similarities to Isaiah 37 and 38, which records both messages written to and messages written by Hezekiah.

But the psalm also bears similarities to Psalm 18, a psalm of David, which may give us some evidence for thinking he was the author. The reference in verse 16 to the writer's being "the son of your maidservant" is similar to what David said about his mother in Psalm 86:16—she was God's servant. I'm inclined to think this was written by David.

The psalm expresses thanksgiving from one who has survived great danger and now wishes to "sacrifice a thank offering" to God. "I love the Lord, for he heard my voice," says the writer in verse 1.

Verse 2 is similar to our expression, "lend me your ear."

Verse 3 is autobiographical. The writer is referring to some terribly dangerous, life-threatening situation. The captives who compiled this psalm into this collection saw it as descriptive of their captivity in Babylon.

From verse 8 on, the writer directs his words to the Lord.

Verse 11 is rather obscure. It could have been Hezekiah's response when he got the message from the prophet that he was going to die. Hezekiah might have called him a liar—in other words, denied the prophet's words. Often a person's first response to tragic news is denial. Or it could have been the writer's cynical response to living in Babylon to say, "no one can be trusted." Either way, it's an expression of the writer's personal feelings, and is not meant to be taken as a statement of universal truth.

"Precious in the sight of the Lord is the death of his saints" (verse 15). Many martyrs being led off to their deaths have recited this verse. They wanted to remind themselves that their lives and deaths counted for something. We know this is true of all of God's people: our lives and our deaths do have meaning to God.

PSALM 117

This short little psalm of only three verses has a great message: it is messianic—it looks forward to the time of the Messiah.

The psalm says, "Praise the Lord, all you nations" (verse 1). Moses said the same thing in Deuteronomy 32:43: "Rejoice, O nations, with his people." So the psalm looks back to that. Then, in Romans 15:11, Paul quotes the psalm, showing he believed it to be messianic. The prospect of the nations praising the Lord anticipates the time of the Messiah, when the Gentiles will bring praise to the God of Israel.

It's this missionary zeal for the nations round about that in part characterized this fifth Book. The Israelites did not express that kind of concern for the other nations in the preceding Books.

The psalm is so short, it may have been used as a benediction at the end of a service, or as a preface to another psalm, for example, Psalm 118.

PSALM 118

This is the last psalm of what was called the "hallel," hallel of course being connected to "hallelujah." Sometimes these are called "hallelujah psalms," because they all begin or end with a call to "praise the Lord."

Psalms 115—118 were sung at the Passover after the celebration and after the taking of the fourth cup.

The Paschal, or Passover, supper began with the head of the company or family pronouncing a benediction over the first cup of wine, which had been filled for each person. It was then drunk. A basin of water and a towel were handed around, or the guests got up to wash their hands. Afterwards the blessing was pronounced. These were preliminaries.

Then the table bearing the Paschal meal was brought in. The person presiding over the feast took some herbs, dipped them in the sauce, ate, and gave them to the others (Matt. 26:23). After this, all the dishes were taken from the table and the second cup of wine was filled. The son asked his father, "Wherefore is this night distinguished from all other nights?" The head of the house replied by relating the national history, beginning with Terah, Abraham's father, and especially explaining the Passover.

The supper dishes were then put back on the table, and the person presiding took up in succession the dish with the Passover lamb, the dish with the bitter herbs, and the dish with the unleavened bread, explaining the meaning of each one. Then the first part of the Hallel was sung—Psalms 113 and 114.

After the singing they said these words: "Blessed art thou, Jehovah our God, King of the Universe who has redeemed us and redeemed our fathers from Egypt." Then the second cup of wine was drunk and hands were washed the second time, with the same prayer as before, "Blessed art thou. . ."

One of the two unleavened cakes was broken, and thanks

was given. Pieces of that broken cake, with bitter herbs between them, were dipped and then handed to each person. In all probability, this was the "sop" by which Jesus identified Judas as His betrayer in answer to Peter's question (John 13:26, KJV).

Then hands were again washed, the third cup was filled, and they drank it.

The service ended with the fourth cup. After they took the fourth cup, they sang the second portion of the Hallel, Psalms 115—118. The whole ceremony ended with a blessing.

The significance of Psalm 118 is this: it is the psalm sung by the twelve apostles and the Lord on the very night He was betrayed. He met with His disciples for the Passover. They ate it, and sang the appropriate psalms. The last words they sang are the last words of Psalm 118: "Give thanks to the Lord, for he is good; his love endures forever" (verse 29).

We don't know who wrote the psalm. Some think it was David, in which case it was probably when he brought the ark to Zion. I think, however, that the psalm was written after the exile, and that the author is unknown. It may have been written to celebrate either the Feast of Tabernacles (Ezra 3) or the laying of the foundation stone of the Temple (Ezra 6:15-18). I think the latter is most likely.

"Give thanks to the Lord, for he is good," begins verse 1. This opening part was sung in the Temple in a responsive fashion.

Verse 5 can be interpreted as one person recounting his experiences and speaking for the nation, or as the nation expressing itself in the first person singular. In either case, whatever happened to the first person stands for the whole nation, which is why the psalm was used in the Temple service.

Verse 6 of this psalm is taken out of its context in the Hebrews 13:6 quote in order to comfort people who were struggling with covetousness.

"It is better to take refuge in the Lord than to trust in man" (verse 8). The nation of Israel had learned that. Earlier they had turned to other nations, but they had learned that no one could help them but God.

Verses 12 and 18 seem to support that the writer was Hezekiah. His enemies swarmed around him (Isa. 39); he was given a reprieve on his death sentence (Isa. 38).

"The stone the builders rejected has become the capstone" (verse 22). This verse is mentioned in Matthew, Mark, Luke, Acts 4, Ephesians 2:20, and 1 Peter 2:7 as referring to Jesus. The term "builders" refers to the people of Israel. Jesus became the "capstone" at His resurrection, and only the Lord could have done this—raised someone from the dead (verse 23).

Because Jesus rose from the dead on the first day of the week, Christians celebrate Sunday. Verse 24 is the Old Testament anticipation of this day which "the Lord has made."

"Blessed is he who comes in the name of the Lord" (verse 26) is a verse we can link with Jesus' entering Jerusalem, and then the Upper Room.

Verse 27 is remarkable in light of Jesus' great desire to eat the Passover feast with His disciples. He alone knew its ultimate meaning; He alone knew He was soon to be the Passover Lamb. Yet He could eagerly join with His disciples in celebrating this feast, and sing with them the words of this verse: "Bind the festal sacrifice with ropes and take it to the horns of the altar" (verse 27, marginal note).

I think the disciples probably chimed in with verse 29, and then they all went out and made their way to Gethsemane.

Psalm 118 is a beautiful psalm, anticipating so many things that were fulfilled in Christ's death. We think of this psalm and remember that festal sacrifice every time we take the bread and cup of Communion. We do it in memory of the Lord until He comes. This is an eternal ordinance. It never stops, until the day we eat a new feast in the kingdom of God.

PSALM 119

This magnificent acrostic psalm contains twenty-two para-graphs, each corresponding to the twenty-two letters of the Hebrew alphabet: *aleph, beth, gimel, daleth,* and so on. Each paragraph contains eight verses, the first letter of which is the appropriate letter. So, for example, verses 1 through 8 all begin with the letter *aleph* in Hebrew; verses 9-16 with the letter *beth;* and so on. There are other acrostic psalms, but they all skip some letters. This one, however, is perfectly complete in that it uses all twenty-two letters, and it uses them the same number of times each. Whoever wrote this spent an incredible amount of effort in working out the details of this acrostic.

The psalm contains 176 verses, and with the exception of only three or four, each verse refers in some way to the Word of God. Many synonymous expressions are used throughout the psalm for the Word of God: *law, statutes, ways, precepts, de-crees, commands, word, promise.* Though each carries a slight-ly different emphasis to convey to us the fullness of divine revelation, they are basically used interchangeably throughout the psalm. The expressions are varied predominantly for poetic effect.

Another feature of the psalm is the use of the first person singular. *I, me, myself, your servant,* and the like permeate the psalm. Obviously, it wasn't written for the Temple service. It's a very individualistic psalm, and as such is particularly suited for use in our own prayer lives.

Whoever the "I" of the psalm was, the writer was someone suffering persecution. About sixty-five verses mention the writ-er's suffering—his affliction, his trouble and distress, the streams of tears flowing from his eyes. I believe the writer was Ezra, though others have suggested Hezekiah, David, or some unknown young man who describes himself in verse 9. I think the author was Ezra because of the psalm's placement in this collection, compiled after the people returned to the land under the leadership of Ezra and Nehemiah. Ezra was a great leader and a scribe, who read the law of the Lord to the people. I think he used his talents to write this psalm. We also know he suffered persecution (Ezra 4).

The Israelites' captivity was a result of their ignoring the Word of God given to them by the prophets. They would not listen to the prophets, they rejected the statutes of God, they refused to obey His Word, and they forsook all the commands of the Lord (2 Kings 17). In captivity, however, they learned a new respect for God's Word. This psalm is a celebration of that newfound, or recovered, respect. The people who survived to come back to the land were godly people who could make good use of the verses of this psalm, as we can today.

Many of the verses of Psalm 119 make lovely memory verses. Verses 9 and 10 are a prayer I often make, as is verse 11: "I have hidden your word in my heart that I might not sin against you." Or verse 18: "Open my eyes that I may see wonderful things in your law."

Throughout the psalm we find key words like *love, understanding, delight, heart, obey,* and *meditate.* The psalm is filled with expressions of satisfaction, love, and delight in the Word of God, by which a person can keep his or her ways pure. This psalm records one person's spiritual journey toward a life of victory.

PSALM 120

The first thing you see is the title, "A Song of Ascents." Older versions of the Bible have "degrees" instead of "ascents." Fifteen psalms bear this title, and because they follow each other in sequence (Psalms 120—134), they are generally taken to belong together.

Four of these psalms are attributed to David, and one to Solomon. The ten remaining psalms are not associated with anybody's name. It isn't necessary to identify the authors to understand and appreciate these psalms. But two other questions require answers: what does the title mean? And, when and where were the psalms used?

Some scholars render the title, "a song of the goings up," citing Exodus 34:24 and 1 Kings 12:27 in support. If "goings up" or "ascents" is correct, any of several theories about the use of the group is possible.

Many Bible students believe these psalms were used during annual pilgrimages to Jerusalem. In support, they cite passages such as Exodus 23:14-17, Psalm 84:5-7, and Luke 2:41-51. In our imagination, we can see the pilgrims moving along dusty roads, singing as they went.

We don't know what they sang in the early years of their history. We know that they didn't sing the complete set of Psalms of Ascents. David wrote four, Solomon one, and perhaps Hezekiah the rest. Thus, the set of fifteen was collected over many years.

A strong case can be made for the theory that the psalms belong to the time of Hezekiah, and that he himself is the author of the anonymous ten. To his own psalms were added four by David and one by Solomon, making a total of fifteen. The number corresponds to the years given to him after his serious illness, and to the ten steps the sun went back on the stairway of Ahaz.

To appreciate the strength of that explanation, you'll have to read Isaiah 38, preferably in a modern translation such as the *New International Version*. Some scholars also point out that the contents of the Psalms of Ascents reflect the history of Hezekiah's reign. Isaiah 36—39 provides details, as do the separate accounts in 2 Kings 18—20 and 2 Chronicles 29—32.

Authorship of the set is not important. David could have written Psalm 120, reflecting his experiences at the hand of Doeg (cf. 1 Sam. 21:7; 22:9). But the psalm was used by others in similar predicaments. It would have been appropriate for returnees struggling with opposition from enemies such as Sanballat, Tobiah, and Geshem (cf. Neh. 2:19). Those men had "lying lips" and "deceitful tongues."

The writer's complaint that he lived in Meshech or Kedar is not to be taken literally. Both places were extremely remote, and stood for the ends of the earth. It was the writer's way of saying that he felt as far from home as he could get.

PSALM 121

These psalms are titled, "song[s] of ascents." I think they were probably sung by pilgrims going to Jerusalem on one of their periodic trips to one of the festivals indicated by the Lord.

It might have been that as they caught the first sight of the hills of Judea they began to sing the first verse of Psalm 121: "I lift up my eyes to the hills."

On the other hand, this could be a question: Shall I lift up my eyes to the hills? The hills were the places where their pagan ancestors had built shrines for worshiping idols. If we interpret it this way, the writer of Psalm 121 is saying, Is that where my help comes from? Immediately he answers in the negative: No! Those idols don't help me at all. And he gives this affirmation: "My help comes from the Lord, the Maker of heaven and earth" (verse 2).

I think the people who came back from Babylon had these psalms as part of their literature. As they approached the land of their ancestors on their return, they may have sung them. It would certainly have been a fitting affirmation, whichever interpretation we take of verses 1 and 2 of Psalm 121, of their newfound faith in God.

"He will not let your foot slip," says Psalm 121:3. The people might have felt as if Isaiah 35:3-10 was coming true in their lives. "Steady the knees that give way; say to those with fearful hearts, 'Be strong, do not fear; your God will come.' . . . The ransomed of the Lord will return. They will enter Zion with singing" (Isaiah 35:3, 4, 10).

"The sun will not harm you by day" (verse 6) is certainly appropriate for a journey across the desert. The Israelites were moving closer and closer to Jerusalem as they returned from Babylon, and they used psalms like these to express their great faith in the Lord's willingness to protect them from evil.

Psalm 121 contains some of the most powerful and beautiful expressions of faith in God's protection in all of Scripture. "The Lord will keep you from all harm—he will watch over your life; the Lord will watch over your coming and going both now and forevermore" (verses 7, 8). We must not misread this as a blanket promise that nothing bad will ever happen to us. We know for a fact that bad things happen to faithful Christians all the time. But we can see this as the beautiful statement it is: that God is our keeper, the one who guards us day by day as we live our daily lives. Whatever does happen to us happens with the knowledge and permission of the God who watches over us.

Some might think that is not too comforting. But there's comfort to me in the certainty that nothing can happen to me apart from God's knowledge. Nothing can happen to me apart from God's tacit permission. It may not be according to His will, but it's according to His permission. Eventually the God who controls the future will show us that whatever evil may have happened to us, He has in some way turned to good use. He is the sovereign God.

PSALM 122

David was the author of this psalm, as the title tells us; it was added to this collection because the people were very conscious of the first few words.

"I rejoiced with those who said to me, 'Let us go to the house of the Lord'" (verse 1). It was difficult for the Israelites to leave Babylon after seventy years there. Many of the older people had died; to the younger ones, born and raised in Babylon, far-off Israel must have seemed almost a mythical place. Yet, those who had the faith and courage were able to echo the words of this psalm with a new twist: Yes, let's leave this pagan land and go see Jerusalem!

The ancient Israelites thought of Jerusalem not just as a city, but as the place were God had put His name (verse 2). It was the place where the ark of the covenant was in David's day, the ark signifying the presence of God. It was the place where the Lord had ordered Solomon to build the Temple. It was the place from which the law went forth. It was the place to which the tribes "went up."

So important was its spiritual significance, so powerful its pull, that when Jeroboam split the kingdom in two he knew he'd have to do something about this matter of Jerusalem. So he set up two shrines of idolatry: one in Dan, about as far away from Jerusalem as you could get, and one in Bethel, just close enough to Jerusalem to satisfy those who hankered after Judea.

"Pray for the peace of Jerusalem," is the prayer of verses 6 and 7. Unfortunately, the beautiful alliteration of this prayer in Hebrew doesn't come across in English.

Verses 8 and 9 mean the psalmist had no ulterior motives in seeking the peace of Jerusalem. Not for his own prosperity, but "For the sake of my brothers and friends . . . , for the sake of the house of the Lord our God, I will seek your prosperity" (verses 8, 9). All of us as Christians today might say this.

PSALM 123

Psalm 123 was composed by someone suffering affliction, someone who was fed up with the contempt with which others were treating him. When the Israelites got back to the land after their captivity, they found it wasn't completely empty. People who'd been planted there by their Babylonian captors still lived there, and they were quite hostile to the returning Israelites (Neh. 2:19; 4:1-9).

So the psalmist prays for help. He says he looks to God for mercy as attentively as a servant or employee watches a master or boss to see what the next task is (verse 2). "Have mercy on us, O Lord, have mercy on us, for . . . we have endured much ridicule from the proud, much contempt from the arrogant" (verses 3, 4).

PSALM 124

The title attributes the psalm to David. If so, the occasion may have been any of a number of experiences in David's life. More than once he and his friends escaped traps that Saul had set for them. Or the occasion could have been an invasion by Edomites. References to David's war with Edom are highly condensed. For example, 2 Samuel 8:13 says only that David killed 18,000 men in the Valley of Salt. His own army probably suffered a lot of casualties.

Because David's name is not included in some manuscripts (e.g., Septuagint, Vulgate, Syriac), some interpreters think that Hezekiah wrote the psalm. If so, the psalm expresses his great relief at finding the Assyrian army destroyed. The psalm should be read with 2 Kings 19 in mind.

Men and women returning from Babylon would have no difficulty adapting the psalm to their own uses. For them personally, it was a song of deliverance from captivity in a foreign land. If the Lord had not been on their side, their captors would have swallowed them up. Nobody would have survived to return to Zion.

We Christians can use this psalm to praise God for delivering us from a foe more grim than any of ancient Israel's enemies.

The psalm is powerful poetry. Devices such as reiteration of words and phrases create great intensity of feeling.

PSALM 125

Psalms 123, 124, and 125, no matter who may have written them, were all put into this collection because the feelings they expressed were appropriate to the Israelites' return from captivity and their attempts to rebuild Jerusalem in the face of hostile opposition.

Ezra and Nehemiah give the background for the times when these psalms were used. See in particular Nehemiah 6:1-9, 11-14. When we understand the feelings of these returning captives, we can see how a verse like Psalm 125:3 would have helped them strengthen their resolve to see God's Temple and city rebuilt: "The scepter of the wicked will not remain over the land allotted to the righteous."

PSALM 126

In this psalm we have the deep emotion of the people who came back to Zion. The psalm tells us something that the more prosaic accounts of Ezra and Nehemiah only hint at (Ezra 3:10-13): the people were uninhibited in their joy. When they returned to the city and actually saw it with their own eyes, they weren't quiet about it! "Our mouths were filled with laughter, our tongues with songs of joy" (verse 2). This is something to remember as we come to our own times of worship.

Verse 2b says the nations acknowledged, "The Lord has done great things for them." That was true; but there were others of the foreigners who stringently opposed the Israelites' rebuilding project.

"Those who sow in tears will reap with songs of joy" (verse 5). I think this and verse 6 mean that what the people prayed for will indeed happen. I think the psalmist is talking about the sorrow of those weeping in the land of captivity. Now they are having the joy of seeing those dreams coming to fruition, just as the harvester has joy on harvest day.

PSALM 127

The title of this psalm is another "song of ascents." In my judgment these songs of ascents, some of which were written during the days of David and others after the exile, were used as the pilgrims went to the city of Jerusalem or Zion for one of the Temple services, one of the annual feasts. Eventually all these songs of ascents were collected here in Book Five.

This psalm is titled "Of Solomon," as though Solomon were the author. But this title is not in all of the ancient manuscripts. In one, in fact, it's ascribed to David, not Solomon. It may have been composed by David when he was thinking about building the Temple. However, I'm inclined to think it was composed by someone after the return to Zion from the exile. Possibly Nehemiah was the author.

"Unless the Lord builds the house, its builders labor in vain," begins verse 1. All the efforts we may put into our local church are in vain unless the Lord works through us. This is a great principle.

Verses 3 and 4 mean that just as a warrior who has arrows is well-equipped for battle, so people who have children are well-equipped with a source of help and protection in their old age. This was especially true in an agrarian society like the Israelites'. When children come to a married couple today who are prepared and eager to receive that child, it is a wonderful gift. The psalm means to say that the ability to procreate is one of God's great gifts to humanity.

I think this psalm's referring to doing battle is one reason it was included here. In Nehemiah 4:16, 20-23, we read how the people were prepared to do battle. But they were also very conscious that it was God who would fight for them. If they hadn't had that assurance, they would have been completely

279

demoralized. This psalm expresses the great assertion that God would fight the battle for them and allow them to rebuild the city. The Lord is willing to build the house if we will allow Him to use us.

PSALM 128

According to one ancient version, called the Syriac Version, Psalm 128 was written by Zerubbabel. Zerubbabel was the leader of the first party of Israelites to return to the land after the captivity (Ezra 2). In all probability, Zerubbabel wrote this psalm after the early days of antagonism to the Israelites' resettling the land had passed, when everything was much happier and more tranquil.

"Blessed are all who fear the Lord, who walk in his ways," says verse 1, expressing a thought found often in Scripture. It is the wise person who is truly blessed.

The Hebrew poets thought in agricultural images (verse 3). I've never thought of my children as olive shoots, but in those days olives were a symbol of prosperity and rich blessing.

The similarity between Psalms 127 and 128 is fairly obvious. Things are much more peaceful now. The wall has been built and all the gaps closed; the fighting is over. The Temple has been rebuilt and the service reestablished. Consequently, instead of thinking of children as arrows, the psalmist now describes them as olive plants around the table.

Verses 5 and 6 are a beautiful benediction. Zion, the capital, was thought of as the place from whence God always sent His blessings. The allusion to prosperity in verse 5 takes me back to the prayer of Psalm 122:6, 7 for the peace and prosperity of Jerusalem.

PSALM 129

Here is another "song of ascents." This one was probably composed during the early days of the return from exile as the people reminisced about the terrible experiences they had had in the land of Babylon: "They have greatly oppressed me from my youth" (verse 1).

"But they have not gained the victory over me" (verse 2). Neither in Egypt nor in Babylon did their captors succeed in overcoming them. In fact, wherever the Jewish race has gone, even since the Dispersion of 70 A.D., they have prospered and have not been absorbed into the nations. Even a slight knowledge of history tells us how unusual this is. Many, many tribes and ethnic groups have been assimilated by larger, more powerful nations; but Israel never.

"Plowmen have plowed my back and made their furrows long" (verse 3). This could be applied to the Lord Jesus, as could Isaiah 51:23. Historically, as applied to Israel, this verse gives us some of the tragic detail of their Babylonian captivity not mentioned in books such as Daniel or Esther.

"He has cut me free from the cords of the wicked" (verse 4) is an image that could refer either to the ropes being cut that bound a steer to a plow, or to the thongs of a whip being cut. In either case, it means that God has freed them from slavery.

The imprecation of verses 6 and 7 made sense to people living in an agrarian society; it meant, let them be like weeds or worthless stuff.

Ruth 2:4 contains a beautiful benediction to which verse 8 seems to allude. "The blessing of the Lord be upon you." The custom in a limited area of Portugal was to greet each other similarly: "May the Lord bless you richly." To which the reply was, "May the Lord bless you indeed." There were variations of that. One was, "Blessed be the name of our Lord and Savior,

282

Jesus Christ"; and the reply, "Yea, verily, let it be blessed forever." Though I suppose these greetings had become perfunctory to the average person on the streets in Portugal, yet I thought it was an extremely beautiful way of greeting.

PSALM 130

I'm inclined to think the author of this "song of ascent" was Ezra. The psalm sounds like the kind of confession we find in the book of Ezra, where he deals with the return from Babylon and the various things they had to do when they got there (Ezra 9:4-7; 10:1). I don't think this psalm was a public confession, but it may echo the prayer that Ezra made privately, which in turn is echoed in the public prayer recorded in Ezra 9.

It is possible that David wrote this psalm. It has certain similarities to Psalm 86, which bears a title of his authorship. But I favor Ezra being the author.

"Out of the depths I cry to you, O Lord" (verse 1) means "out of my terrible trouble." God's name is mentioned eight times in this psalm.

"But with you there is forgiveness" (verse 4). The particular word translated "forgiveness" here is found in only three places: here, and in Nehemiah 9:17 and Daniel 9:9. This helps us assign the writing of this psalm to the days of Nehemiah. The sin that troubled Nehemiah and Ezra was the Israelites' failure to continue to build the Temple. The Israelites also formed mixed marriages with the people in the land, and this was an appalling sin in the eyes of both Ezra and Nehemiah.

Verse 4 says that it's because of God's forgiveness that He is to be feared. We might tend to think it was the other way around—that He would be feared if He didn't forgive. But, no; it's God's goodness that leads us to repentance (Rom. 2:4). It's this possibility of forgiveness that causes us to repent.

The "hope" the psalmist refers to in verse 5 is this hope of forgiveness.

Verse 6 could be read as, My soul is wholly given over to the Lord.

"With the Lord is unfailing love and with him is full redemption" (verse 7). This is another of the Old Testament expressions of the loving character of God.

PSALM 131

I think the occasion for David's writing of this psalm was when he spared Saul's life (1 Sam. 24:5, 6). There we have the essence of humility—a willingness on David's part to do only what God permits, to acknowledge God's hand in events. We find a very similar attitude in 1 Samuel 26:9, when David could have killed Saul for the second time but didn't. He describes himself as a flea or a partridge.

On another occasion, David set out to kill Nabal but was restrained by Abigail (1 Sam. 25:34). David acknowledged this as the hand of God in his life.

All of these were occasions when David was truly humble, when he had quieted himself, when the storms of ambition were stilled. He describes these times beautifully in this psalm. He says he is quiet like a child who has been weaned (verse 2). When a child is being weaned, it is petulant as it continues to fight for the mother's breast. But once the child has been weaned, it can rest against the mother quietly. Just so could David rest in the Lord.

PSALM 132

It's possible that this psalm was written by someone in the days of the return from captivity. The writer goes back in his mind to the days of David and writes this psalm with reference to the bringing of the ark to Zion. The returned captives had rebuilt the Temple and were going to reestablish the service of the Temple, even as David had first done.

"O Lord, remember David and all the hardships he endured" (verse 1) refers to David's suffering as Saul pursued him.

Verses 2-5 refer to things that happened later in David's reign: he made an oath to see that the ark of God had a proper home. He "prepared a place for the ark of God and pitched a tent for it" (1 Chron. 15:1). As he brought the ark to Zion, David acted as a priest, and he was clothed with fine linen, a symbol of righteousness (verse 9).

If I were to title the psalm, I would say verses 1-9 are giving God His place—giving first place to God. David wanted a proper sense of priorities and values. And I would ask myself, Is there anything in my life that has the primary place at the expense of the Lord?

From verse 10 on, the subject is the promise the Lord had sworn to David. The "horn" in verse 17 is a symbol of power. The power will be held by the descendant of David, that descendant being the Messiah. The "lamp" is a sign of prosperity and glory. Of the Messiah, this fine messianic psalm says, "the crown on his head will be resplendent" (verse 18).

PSALM 133

We know that David was the author of this psalm; the occasion is found in 2 Samuel 5, when David finally became king over all Israel. During the first seven-and-a-half years of David's reign, the country was divided into two factions: those who followed David, and those who followed Ish-Bosheth, the son of Saul. After the deaths of Ish-Bosheth and Abner, all Israel was united under David.

Similarly, when the captives returned from their captivity they were no longer divided into a northern and southern kingdom. They were united as one nation.

"How good and pleasant it is when brothers live together in unity!" proclaims verse 1 of the psalm.

Such unity was as precious as anointing oil (verse 2). Today we lay hands on people; in those days, people such as the high priest were anointed with precious oil. The oil is a symbol of the Holy Spirit of God. David is saying that when people dwell together in unity, there is an abundant blessing of the Holy Spirit. We can certainly think of this psalm in regard to church life.

PSALM 134

Psalm 134 is the last of the "songs of ascent." This was also written when David brought the ark up to Zion; in 2 Samuel 6 and 1 Chronicles 15 and 16 we find what is summarized in this psalm.

In Deuteronomy 10 and 18 we find reference to the people who served the Lord in the night watches in the Tabernacle. Tasks had to be performed there by night as well as by day. Verse 1 of this psalm refers to that. The writer is saying that these menial nighttime chores should also be turned into an occasion of blessing and praise to God. That's something for all of us to think about in reference to our own service to God.

PSALM 135

Psalm 135 is one of the "Hallelujah" psalms. There are a total of ten of these "Praise the Lord" psalms. We can see the connection between this psalm and the preceding one.

This psalm was probably written by someone who came back from Babylon, although it's possible it was written earlier for the Temple worship David set up. In either case it's appropriate for this postexilic time, when the people once again set up this worship and served the Lord in music.

Verses 1-7 extol God in contrast to the gods of Babylon. He is great, above the pagan idols. This was a lesson the people had learned in their captivity in Babylon.

From verse 8 on, the psalm takes us back to Egypt. The people leaving Babylon felt as if they were leaving a second Egypt.

This psalm is a wonderful prayer that we can use when we look back over the things God has done. When we meet for the Lord's Supper and reminisce about the life of our Lord Jesus, His incarnation, His perfect life of love, His sacrifice for us, and His resurrection, we are doing exactly what this psalm did.

The psalm begins and ends with praising the Lord. We need to recover a sense of God as the One who can and does do as He pleases, and who is to be praised for it.

PSALM 136

Psalm 136 is an antiphonal psalm obviously designed for use in the Temple worship. Someone would chant the first line, then the congregation would respond with "His love endures forever."

I think Ezra was the author. Ezra 3:10, 11 describes the laying of the foundation of the new Temple. At that time the people sang to the Lord, and what they sang is the same as the refrain in this psalm: "He is good; his love to Israel endures forever" (Ezra 3:11).

We might think that reading this psalm is a bit tedious because of the constant refrain. But if omitted, the psalm would lose much of its power.

Verses 1-9 of the psalm speak of the Lord as Creator of heaven and earth, as the Redeemer in verses 10-22, and as the Protector in verses 23, 24.

From verse 10 on, this psalm is very similar to the preceding one. Verse 10, for instance, is very similar to Psalm 135:8.

In verse 23, the writer is thinking about the Babylonian captivity. He's already talked about the bondage in Egypt in verse 11.

When we look into the past and see the things God has done, we too can be filled with praise and with confidence for the future. We can say with the Israelites of old, "His love endures forever."

PSALM 137

"By the rivers of Babylon we sat and wept when we remembered Zion" (verse 1). This is a mournful yet beautiful psalm, written by someone who endured the captivity. This writer saw the things spoken of in Lamentations: the murder of babies as the Babylonian soldiers dashed them against the rocks, for example. This psalm tells of the desolation experienced by the captives.

Their depression was so deep it was as if they had no songs left (verse 2). They certainly could not bring themselves to sing "the songs of the Lord while in a foreign land" (verse 4).

Yet they swore in their pain that they would never forget Jerusalem, the place where God had put His name, their highest joy (verses 5, 6).

Verse 7 gives us a detail we don't get in the historical accounts of the destruction of Jerusalem. Apparently the Edomites egged Nebuchadnezzar on to do what he might not have otherwise done: tear down Jerusalem "to its foundations."

The Edomites, a fiercely cruel people, were actually related to the Israelites. The Israelites were the descendants of Jacob, son of Isaac, son of Abraham; while the Edomites were the descendants of Jacob's twin brother, Esau. It was through Jacob, not Esau, that God chose to bring the Messiah. The Edomites burned in their hatred toward the descendants of Jacob just as Esau had burned in his hatred toward his own brother Jacob, even vowing to kill him.

The entire book of Obadiah describes the Edomites' hostility toward the Israelites. Among other things, they entered Jerusalem and cast lots for the captives, thus buying their own brothers and sisters. They looted the city, and stood at the fork of the road to cut down any survivors.

These ancient hatreds still prevail in the Middle East today, and will be quelled only when Christ returns and puts an end to them.

The psalm has harsh words for Babylon in verses 8 and 9. A verse like 2 Kings 8:12 gives us insight into Babylonian war customs of the time and helps to explain the harsh imprecations of this psalm. We also need to understand that Babylon had become a symbol of organized opposition to God, and its doom was predicted in Isaiah 13.

PSALM 138

This is a psalm of David, and I see in it the echoes of many of David's earlier psalms. Verse 7, for instance, so strongly reminds us of Psalm 23.

David probably wrote this at the time of his troubles with Absalom, although it's also possible he wrote it at the time of his coronation (see verse 3). But when we read it in this collection, we can think of it more as being appropriate to the captives' return from Babylon.

Verse 1 again refers to the heathen gods surrounding the nation of Israel, which the people had seen firsthand during their captivity. In this psalm, David is expressing thanksgiving with all his heart to the true God, and the returned captives use his words to give their own thanks.

Verse 4 expresses the prayer that "all the kings of the earth" praise God. Perhaps this is an allusion to Cyrus, who viewed himself as a servant of Jehovah.

PSALM 139

This lovely psalm was written by David. Verses 1-6 describe God's omniscience, verses 7-12 His omnipresence, and verses 13-16 His omnipotence—particularly His power to create human life.

Verses 1-6 describe God's wonderful knowledge of us. He knows us thoroughly. Although this can be disturbing as we think of our sinfulness, yet it is also so comforting. We don't have to put on any masks with God. He already knows everything there is to know about us—and He loves us as thoroughly as He knows us (John 3:16, 17).

Verses 7-12 tell us that no matter where we may wander, even there, God is with us. "Even there your hand will guide me, your right hand will hold me fast" (verse 10). God not only knows me, He cares for me. He is not going to lose me or let me go. You see how beautifully David personalizes each of these important theological concepts.

"For you created my inmost being; you knit me together in my mother's womb" (verse 13). There is no point between the moment of conception and birth when the essential nature of that which is conceived changes from nonhuman to human. We talk much about the moment of conception in biological terms, but we are a long way from really understanding the mystery of it. I believe that the soul itself is passed along in the very act of conception, not added at some later point. How this happens we do not know. The moment of conception is very mysterious.

Verses 15 and 16 mean that I was a person from the moment of conception, and that God knew all about me. "You created my inmost being; you knit me together in my mother's womb." These verses are not telling us that God creates each human being, but that He has created the whole process, and He is the One from whom all life originates. They are also telling us that from the very first moment, the fetus is in fact a human being, one whom God already knows.

In verses 17 and 18 David is saying that God's wonderful love is displayed in His unceasing awareness of each one of us.

Verses 19-22 express quite a shift of thought, seemingly. These imprecations are not found in the New Testament. But here, they are an expression of David's hatred of all that is opposed to God, the enemies of God.

Verse 23 relates to verse 1. David is asking God again to search him. He's contrasting the way of God's leading him, the way of health and life, with the hurtful way, the path that he would pursue if it were not for God.

PSALM 140

This is a psalm of David, written either when he was in Saul's court and was being persecuted by jealous people, or else when David was king and was smarting under the conspiracy raised by Absalom. I tend to think it dates from the earlier period, because there is no hint of the confession and repentance that marks David's later psalms.

The psalm was appropriate for use by the returned captives because just as David had faced persecution and great danger from Saul, so too the Israelites who returned to Jerusalem faced danger and persecution by enemies there. Ezra, Nehemiah, and others who led the people back to Israel had their enemies, who viciously opposed their rebuilding project. These enemies tried to intimidate the leaders and the people by ridicule, lies, schemes, and threats (Neh. 4—6).

"Rescue me, O Lord, from evil men; protect me from men of violence," prays David in verse 1, and the returned captives could surely echo his prayer.

We can take verses 2 and 3 as descriptive of Saul and his cohorts—and by application, of the enemies who plotted against Nehemiah and others.

The psalm ends with a statement of assurance: "I know that the Lord secures justice for the poor. . . . Surely the righteous will praise your name" (verses 12, 13).

PSALM 141

This psalm was also written by David in either of the two main times of persecution in his life. I favor, but cannot defend entirely, the later time of persecution by Absalom. Otherwise I don't know how to account for verses 5-7.

However, there is a very close link between this psalm and the preceding one. Hebrew scholars tell us that nearly every verse of this psalm contains words that appear also in Psalm 140. For example, compare verse 1 with Psalm 140:6; verse 3 with Psalm 140:11. From a literary standpoint, this similarity of vocabulary establishes a link between the two psalms.

"O Lord, I call to you" (verse 1). David was in earnest about praying, so much so that he wrote out his prayers after he had made them. Many of David's psalms are in the first person singular, which makes them ideally suited for use in our own prayer life. Most of our prayer life is very personal.

Verse 2 is an essential clue as to the time when David wrote the psalm. He's saying he's on the run in the wilderness, not in a place where he can offer incense or the evening sacrifice. Exodus 30:7, 8 mentions incense; Exodus 29:40, 41 speaks of the burnt offering. Smoke seems to have been a symbol of the ascent to heaven of the saints' prayers. David can't offer these physical sacrifices, but he could offer the sacrifice of prayer (Acts 10:4).

"Set a guard over my lips," prays David in verse 3. When we are under stress, it's all too easy to speak rashly.

In verse 4, David prays that he not become like the evildoers around him. In Psalm 57 when he prayed this, David was referring to his own men.

Verse 5 is difficult. I don't know of any situation this could refer to except perhaps Nathan's rebuke of David for the sin with Bathsheba and Uriah (2 Sam. 12). I think David is expressing his willingness to accept Nathan's rebuke, as well as his horror lest he become like the evildoers who seemed to swarm over his kingdom as a result of David's sin and his loss of nerve.

Verses 6 and 7 are also difficult; they seem again to be an imprecation against the evildoers.

As it happened, the wicked did fall into their own nets (verse 10), as those who followed David achieved a great victory.

PSALM 142

This psalm was written by David either in the cave of Adullam (1 Sam. 22) or the cave of Engedi (1 Sam. 24). Psalm 57 also describes David's emotions at the time.

The psalm is structured in two parts: verses 1-4, and verses 5-7.

"I cry aloud to the Lord," says David in verse 1. He didn't pray silently the way we sometimes do, but cried out loud to God, as did Jesus (Heb. 5:7).

In verses 3 and 4 David describes his feelings of depression. He felt faint and trapped, and thought no one cared for him.

I believe the tendency to depression can be a serious problem among committed Christians, striving as we do to please God. When these times of darkness come upon us, we need neither fear them nor give way to them. God is still with us, and we can remind ourselves of His unfailing love and cry out to Him to help us feel it. Often, we can be helped to again feel His love through the love of other Christians, an important reason for having caring Christian friends (Eph. 5:19). David actually did have such a caring friend—Jonathan. But in his depression, he allowed himself to forget that fact.

David refers to God's "goodness" as he closes the psalm with an intimation of the triumph of good over evil. That did in fact happen in David's life, and that is what will happen in the world when Christ returns.

PSALM 143

This is the last of the penitential psalms. It is a psalm of David's old age, and again he speaks of his sin with Bathsheba and Uriah. This psalm was suitable for this collection because the returned captives did not want to forget it was their sins that had landed them in captivity. They didn't want to repeat their errors.

David begins this prayer by crying out for mercy, because "no one living is righteous before you" (verses 1, 2). God is merciful and loving. If He were to judge us on our own righteousness, we would not have a chance. But He deals with us mercifully, in that He has laid down a righteous basis for our forgiveness, the death of our Lord Jesus Christ.

The enemy David refers to in verse 3 is Absalom. The darkness he felt was emotional—he felt overwhelmed by not knowing what was going to happen to him. He felt faint and dismayed (verse 4).

When David remembers the past in verse 5, I don't think it's so much his personal past as the nation's past. We perform a similar memorial when we partake of the Lord's Supper and remember what God has done for us in Christ. That helps take away our own darkness—that is, our inability to comprehend what is happening. We see with spiritual sight.

David longed for God like a parched land thirsts for water (verse 6).

David asks God to show him kindness (verses 7, 8).

In verse 10, David asks God to lead him on "level ground," that is, in God's ways of righteousness.

Verse 12 gives us a little insight into the meaning of the vindictive element in these psalms. David felt that in persecuting him, his enemies were also persecuting God. He's anxious to see God vindicated, to see God deal with these people so they might know God is the Lord.

301

PSALM 144

This psalm of David was written during one of the wars he fought when he was king—perhaps after the Edomites entered the land (1 Kings 11), or when he was fighting the Ammonites (2 Sam. 10). It could have been put into this collection because the returned captives identified with the prayer for military success of verse 10.

The psalm begins with a barrage of military images in verses 1 and 2: "fortress," "stronghold," and "shield."

Verse 3 is taken from Psalm 8.

Verse 4 echoes psalms written earlier by David. Even though he got older, his vocabulary remained the same. The idea that human beings are a mere breath was an important idea to David.

David's prayer in verses 5-8 for a storm is a request that God do on his behalf what He did in the days of Joshua.

The reference in verse 8 to the "right hands" of the enemy being deceitful means they strike false deals. Then as now, people shook hands to seal a reconciliation or a business deal. In the Middle East, they always shook right hands.

Verses 12-15 are a prayer for God's blessing.

PSALM 145

This psalm introduces the last five psalms, all of which are called "praise" or "hallelujah" psalms, because they all begin with an expression of praise to God. Psalm 145 bridges the psalms that precede it and the last five, because it is both supplication and praise.

David probably wrote this in his later years; there's a reference in verse 14 to his fall. I think he wrote this in a reflective time, possibly very near the end of his life. He talks about proclaiming the goodness of God as long as he lives.

This psalm was put into this collection because the returned captives could say with David, "The Lord is gracious" (verse 8). They had seen the collapse of the Babylonian empire; they knew that only God's kingdom was an everlasting one (verse 13). God had fulfilled their desires, and brought them back to the land (verse 19). Therefore, they offered the praise of verse 21: "My mouth will speak in praise of the Lord."

PSALM 146

The first and last line of this psalm is "Praise the Lord." Each of these last five psalms, Psalms 146—150, begin and end with that phrase.

These praise psalms are a fitting conclusion to this fifth Book, as the people rebuild the walls, rebuild the Temple, and reestablish the Temple worship. Praise was the keynote in the Temple worship; so Book Five concludes with praise. These psalms were likely written during the actual time of rebuilding.

Verse 3 expresses a lesson the returned captives had learned well: "Do not put your trust in princes." The people before the captivity had done just that, and it had all come to naught. All human beings die. God is the only One worthy of ultimate trust: "Blessed is he . . . whose hope is in the Lord his God" (verse 5).

The reference to God as the Maker of all things was very important to them (verse 6). God is the One who keeps His promises (verse 7).

Verses 8 and 9 are a wonderful statement about the character and activity of the Lord. No wonder the psalmist ends with "Praise the Lord."

PSALM 147

Although we don't know who wrote this psalm, according to some editions of the Septuagint (the Hebrew Old Testament translated by seventy scholars into Greek), the authors of Psalms 146—148 were Haggai and Zechariah. These prophets worked among the people of Israel after they came back from the captivity.

However, I think Nehemiah was the author of this psalm, and I think the occasion was the dedication of the walls of Jerusalem. This psalm describes the people singing to the Lord (verse 7), and God granting peace to their borders (verse 14). I think this fits with what is depicted in Nehemiah 12:27, 43 of the day of dedication of the walls.

"The Lord builds up Jerusalem," says verse 2. This at least is certainly an indication that the psalm was written after the captivity.

Verses 3-6 describe God's care for the people during their captivity. Even there, they had some joy.

Verse 6 is an allusion to the collapse of the Babylonian empire described in Daniel 5.

Verse 10 means that the Lord has no pleasure in cavalry or infantry—in other words, in military might.

Verse 18 is considered to be a prophetic allusion to the Word incarnate, an anticipation of the coming of the Lord Jesus. Although I think that interpretation is somewhat strained, I do believe the psalm is an anticipation of the Millennial reign of Christ.

PSALM 148

Each of these last five psalms not only begins and ends with "Praise the Lord," but each seems to anticipate the final summing up of all things in Christ, when nature itself will be brought back into harmony with the mind of God, just as the captives had been brought back to the land of Israel.

This psalm is pure praise; it has no petitions. Verse 6 is an allusion to some of the promises of God.

Verse 14, "He has raised up for his people a horn," means that God had brought them back to the land and given them a certain amount of power.

PSALM 149

"Sing to the Lord a new song," proclaims verse 1. The immediate application is the people's new song after their return from captivity. They couldn't sing while in the land of captivity (Psalm 137). Now they've come back and they can. The new song is also an allusion to the time when the people of God will enter the Millennial reign.

The people's backsliding had forced God's hand, so to speak, into sending them into captivity. But now they've come back to the land and are filled with satisfaction (verse 5).

PSALM 150

Every line in this last psalm begins with or includes "Praise the Lord" or "Praise him." It's a praise psalm of praise psalms. Each of the five Books of the Psalms ends with a doxology of some kind; here, both Book Five and the entire Book of the Psalms ends with this paean of praise. Every verse is a summons to praise the Lord; "everything that has breath" is called upon to praise Him.

Make the Book of Psalms real to yourself. Use it every day, to help you in your prayer life. May God bless you richly as you use these time-honored prayers, which the Spirit of God helped the authors write for our benefit.